Copyright © 1985 by

University Press of America,® Inc.

4720 Boston Way
Lanham, MD 20706

3 Henrietta Street
London WC2E 8LU England

Library of Congress Cataloging in Publication Data

Glazier, Jack.
    Land and the uses of tradition among the Mbeere of
Kenya.

    Bibliography: p.
    Includes index.
    1. Mbere (African people)—Social conditions.
2. Mbere (African people)—Land tenure.   3. Land
reform—Kenya—Case studies.   I. Title.
DT433.545.M34G57   1985   306'.089963   85-17891
ISBN 0-8191-4949-7 (alk. paper)
ISBN 0-8191-4950-0 (pbk. : alk. paper)

LAND AND THE USES OF TRADITION AMONG THE MBEERE OF KENYA

Jack Glazier

Oberlin College

UNIVERSITY
PRESS OF
AMERICA

LANHAM • NEW YORK • LONDON

In memory of my parents

David Glazier

and

Rea Rosen Glazier

Acknowledgments

In the course of three periods of fieldwork, I have enjoyed generous support from several sources, and I gratefully acknowledge that assistance. I conducted my first fieldwork in Mbeere from May, 1969 to September, 1970 while holding an N.I.H. Training Grant (No. GM 1224) awarded to me by the Department of Anthropology, University of California, Berkeley. Thanks are especially due George Foster, who so ably administered that program. I also wish to thank the Wenner-Gren Foundation for Anthropological Research which awarded me a research grant making possible my fieldwork in 1973. Oberlin College also provided assistance at that time and in 1979, and I wish to express my appreciation for that support, as well as for the College's assistance in the preparation of this manuscript.

From my initial research to the present, I have incurred numerous scholarly debts to many colleagues, friends, and informants, who have contributed much to this work. When I first arrived in Kenya as an eager but anxious first-time fieldworker, I enjoyed the support and collegiality of the Research Associates at the Institute for Development Studies, Cultural Division (now the Institute of African Studies). I thank Alan Jacobs, especially, for his encouragement and for first suggesting Mbeere as a research site. Shortly before leaving the field in 1970, I met David Brokensha, who was just arriving to evaluate the Special Rural Development Program in Mbeere. Since that time, we have jointly published on the Mbeere and kept in close contact over our common concerns. I have benefited greatly from his keen observations of Mbeere life and his critical reading of an early version of this study. I also appreciate the very useful comments of E.H.N. Njeru. Thanks are also due Elizabeth Colson and Aidan Southall for their helpful remarks. My Berkeley age-mate Woody Watson also provided invaluable criticism of many of the ideas developed in this study. At various times, I also had very useful discussions with Harold Schneider, Ivan Karp, David Parkin, Rubie Watson, Richard Lowenthal, and David Rheubottom. In

England, I received warm collegial hospitality at the School of Oriental and African studies and acknowledge it with thanks. At Oberlin, I have gained much from various discussions with colleagues including especially Ron Casson, Linda Grimm, Milt Yinger, and Phyllis Gorfain. Since coming to Oberlin in 1971, I have also benefited greatly from the pointed comments of some of the best students any anthropologist could hope to teach.

I have also profited from the resources of several libraries and archives containing documents on the colonial history of Embu District. I wish to thank the staffs of the Kenya National Archives, the microfilm section of the Syracuse University Library, Rhodes House, Oxford, and in London, the Public Record Office and the archives of the Church Missionary Society.

Lastly, I wish to thank the people of Mbeere, especially those of Nguthi Sublocation, for their patience and generosity. At first anxious about the appearance of a European stranger in their midst, they accepted with forbearance both my unremitting questions, especially about the highly sensitive issue of land tenure, and my ubiquitous presence at elders' councils, rituals, work parties, and other events. I wish to thank David Kariuki Karura, Dunstan Mūgo Maganjo, Steven Mwake, Jonathan Mwanīki, Gerald Njiru, Jaconiah Ireri, Catherine Ngungi, Caramelina Ciaina, and Ethan Ndwiga, who were research assistants at verious times. I have used pseudonyms for the names of informants (except well-known chiefs) and lineages owing to the delicate nature of the matters discussed. I offer this collective acknowledgment for the assistance I received and for the many kindnesses shown me. I have been greatly enriched by my experience in Mbeere and have built from it a permanent store of wealth, for, according to a popular Mbeere riddle, "Wealth which is never exhausted is the thought in the heart of a person."

J. G.

Oberlin, Ohio

July, 1984

CONTENTS

Acknowledgments   v

Maps   viii

Figures   viii

Tables   viii

Note on Kimbeere/Kikuyu Orthography and
Pronunciation   ix

  1. Introduction   1

  2. The Land and People in Historical
      Perspective   39

  3. Domestic Groups   105

  4. Clanship, Descent, and Descent Groups   151

  5. Land Tenure and Government Policy   193

  6. Law and Litigation   227

  7. Conclusion   265

Appendix: The Contemporary Council of Elders   285

Bibliography   315

Index   331

Maps

1. Mbeere Country and Neighboring Areas in Kenya xii

2. Mbeere Division Showing Locations and Sublocations xiii

Figures

1. Terms of Address for Full, Half, and Classificatory Siblings 112

2. Fictive Marriage of Women 116

3. Mūkera Clan History 165

4. Kigamba Coalition of Nditi Clan 187

5. Kinsmen of Sarah and Jacob 286

Tables

1. Rainfall and Altitude 51

2. Comparison of Rainfall in Peak Months of Famine Year, 1971, With Averages for Peak Months 52

3. Mbeere Famines and Shortages 55

4. Stock Holdings in Kanyuambora and Kavengero 117

5. Incidence of Polygyny 122

6. Profile of Domestic Groups in Nguthi 139

7. Mbeere Clans Arranged By Phratry and Moiety 157

The transcription of Kimbeere words and texts follows the standard orthography of Kikuyu as it appears in Benson's *Kikuyu-English Dictionary* (1964). Kimbeere and Kikuyu are very closely related, separated for the most part by phonological and minor lexical and grammatical differences. A high degree of mutual intelligibility exists between Kimbeere and Kikuyu.

A seven vowel system characterizes both Kimbeere and Kikuyu: *a, e, i, o,* and *u* appear and, in addition, two other forms, *ī* and *ū,* occur. These vowels are pronounced approximately as follows:

a	father
e	rent
i	greet
o	ought
u	boot
ī	bay
ū	boat

Kimbeere/Kikuyu consonants, *c, th,* and *ng'* require special mention. *C* is normally pronounced in Kimbeere as English *sh,* although one may hear a *ch* version in parts of Kikuyuland. *Th* is usually voiced as in *that,* but again, voiceless *th* may occur. Finally, *ng',* the velar nasal, is pronounced as the *ng* in *singer,* and it should be distinguished from initial *ng* in Kimbeere pronounced virtually as one sound, the hard *g* of *get.*

Phonetic differences within Kimbeere exist between administrative locations. To the north, in Evurore, for example, *v* is more prevalent than *b,* although the situation is reversed as one moves southward through Nthawa and into Mavuria (official spelling). In the latter area, people are more apt to say *kabiū* (knife), *mūbīrīga* (clan), etc. People in Evurore, on the other hand, tend to say *kaviū, mūvīrīga,* etc. My fieldwork was carried out in both Mavuria and Evurore Locations, with greater time spent in the latter area. For that reason, Kimbeere terms which appear in this work will be as they are used in Evurore.

Finally, official spelling of the people and territory is Mbere, but the people themselves pronounce the word by drawing out the middle vowel, as in "Mbeere". I have selected the latter spelling. In *Facing Mt. Kenya*, Kenyatta's one brief reference to Mbeere used that form. I am using the word Mbeere to refer to the territory and to the people, either in the singular or plural. The Bantu prefixes, $m\bar{u}$- and a-, referring to one Mbeere or two or more, respectively, have been dropped in accordance with long-established practice among researchers on Bantu peoples. I do, however, use the term Kimbeere in reference to the language of Mbeere.

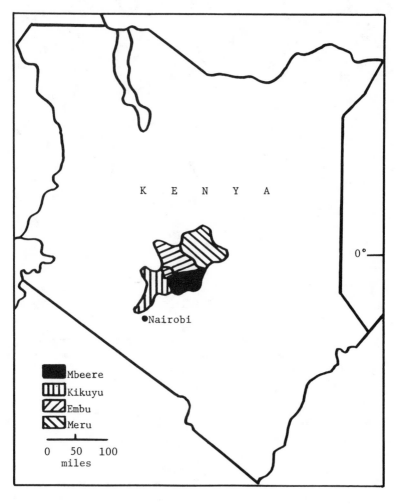

Map 1

Mbeere Country and Neighboring Areas in Kenya

Map 2

Mbeere Division Showing Locations and Sublocations

xiii

Chapter One

Introduction

This study examines land tenure and social change in a rural African community. The investigation traces the external sources of land tenure transformation and how its consequences have unfolded in Central Kenya. These issues among the Mbeere, with whom I lived as an anthropologist, are immediately germane to questions of development and the stream of changes flowing through many rural societies. This work springs from locally-oriented research and concentrates on a small, agriculturally productive area. At the same time, it examines the relationship of the Mbeere to their neighbors and to the authority of colonial rule and the succeeding independent government. As the product of recent investigation, this study provides a current view, at the local level, of extremely important events taking place in Central Kenya. Although some details of land tenure change are distinct in the way they were carried forth in Mbeere, the pivotal problems of legal conflict, malversation, land loss, and local maneuvering in the wake of individualizing tenure are very similar to the repercussions of land reform carried out earlier in Kikuyuland and in other parts of Kenya and the developing world. The findings of this study thus have a general significance beyond the immediate particulars of the Mbeere case.

The program of land reform begun during the latter years of colonial administration and extending into the post-independence period differs significantly from agrarian reforms carried out in the stratified societies of Latin America, Europe, and Asia where the impetus for land tenure change has usually come in the wake of revolution or conquest (Tuma 1965). In these areas, land reform in ideology, if not in practical outcome, has been informed by a need to redistribute land on a more egalitarian basis. Traditional societies of Africa, on the other hand, experienced no land shortages, and consequently patterns of political domination were not predicated on a ruling stratum's

1

control over access to land (Goody 1971). Land to
population ratios were consistently high in traditional
Africa, and land ownership provided no basis for
economic differentiation. Land reform in Africa and in
Kenya more specifically (except for the resettlement of
Africans on former European lands) thus does not entail
the redistribution of land from large estates or the
award of land to landless peasants or tenants; the
latter were not elements of the social landscape of
most of traditional Africa. Instead, land reform in
Kenya springs from national development policies which
regard customary systems of land tenure as inimical to
the goals of increasing agricultural output and rural
incomes. Through a process of individualizing land
tenure and creating independent farmsteads registered
to single persons, the government seeks to eliminate
customary kinship constraints on land use, sale, and
development.

Land holding and land use in relation to rural
development represent central interests for many
anthropologists, economists, political scientists, and
other professionals concerned with modernization. In
the last quarter century, extensive decolonization has
directed attention to those peoples whose way of life
is rigorously constrained by poverty, unproductive
economies, overpopulation, and other highly limiting
factors narrowing the choices they can exercise.
Accordingly, the newly independent countries of Africa
and Asia as well as older nation-states (such as those
of Latin America) conventionally regarded as part of
the Third World devote considerable effort to the
articulation of policies concerning the predominantly
rural sectors of their economies. It is believed that
these economies must be transformed if processes of
modernization are to go forward. Governments and the
experts they consult about these momentous changes
differ in the policies they set forth to reshape rural
socio-economic orders, but all are agreed that the
particular strategy they adopt will ultimately improve
the quality of life of a land-based peasantry. Most
governments, at least in officially promulgated
development policy, are committed to this goal,
although the relative success of particular policies
varies, as comparative surveys of such development

2

indices as agricultural output and rural income reveal.

Investigating rural social change, especially as it relates to development and national policy, cuts across several disciplines. Simply and perhaps crudely put, one can study modernization from the top down or from the bottom up. From the top down, the level of analysis is likely to be the nation, district, or some other macro unit. There the implications of policy are followed through the analysis of aggregate statistics and trends. The advantages of this perspective lie in its theoretical scope and range as the many monographs and articles in development journals by economists and political scientists will attest. But anthropologists sometimes express frustration with macro perspectives because they tend to ignore precisely what has traditionally been the basic subject matter of anthropology--the small scale community. It is thus the second approach to change--studying from the bottom up--which is methodologically closer to the intellectual predilections of the anthropologist. In this micro perspective, processes of change are observed in the context of a particular community and in the lives of informants and other individuals well-known to the resident anthropologist. Of course, anthropologists are keenly aware that the communities in which they conduct their research are embedded in larger political systems and that an exclusive concern with a single community as if it were isolated is at best naive. Anthropologists therefore devote much time to the examination of social linkages between a community or village and other social forms of varying scale. But the reference point for analysis remains the local community.

Land tenure change in Mbeere, and indeed in Kenya generally, can be taken as an exemplar of one of the two major models of land reform characterizing rural development strategies in post-independence Africa. These opposing models may be termed collective and individual; representing ideal types, these models may co-occur in a society which makes some provision for mixed development patterns. In Mbeere, for example, individual holdings will be the norm following land reform, but in those areas where cultivation has always

3

been a marginal endeavor, group ranches have been created. Nonetheless, one or the other model dominates development strategies, and in Kenya the individual model is central.

A collective approach to rural development, which in Africa is well-illustrated by the Tanzanian example, attempts to build on what is arguably asserted to be a traditional bedrock of cooperation and communal tenure. Regarded as modern counterparts of pre-colonial African economies, modern *ujamaa* (literally familyhood) villages vest ownership of the land in the community, and all decisions concerning land use and development are motivated by a singular concern for the commonweal as opposed to the interests of particular individuals. Individual initiative is valued in so far as it serves the common good rather than any personal gain or private advancement. Explicitly linked to the modern political concept of African socialism, the philosophy underlying the collectivist model has been eloquently articulated by President Nyerere (e.g., 1967). Indeed collectivism has become so central to state ideology that the Tanzanian government, in 1963, less than two years after independence, enacted a law proclaiming the state as trustee of the land in order to undercut an emergent class of rural capitalists and to halt the processes leading to its creation (Ingle 1972:8). But the performance of *ujamaa* villages nonetheless lags far behind their ideological promise. In terms of development, Migot-Adholla emphasizes that the *ujamaa* policy "has not led to any significant increases in agricultural productivity comparable to those found among small holders in Kenya but, on the contrary, has led to its decline." Yet this assessment is offered with the cautionary note that insufficient time has elapsed to render a definitive judgment about the *ujamaa* experiment (1979: 171, 174). Still, there is little reason to be sanguine about this version of socialist development.

In stark contrast to Tanzanian collectivism, Kenyan development programs throughout the agricultural sector represent an individualist model predicated on the value of rural capitalism. The sources for this model lie in the colonial period when the European

4

authority sought effective means, both military and political, to defeat the Mau Mau insurgency, which brought about the declaration of a state of Emergency in 1952. Land alienation in Central Kenya resulting in the displacement of Kikuyu farmers by European settlers became the flashpoint of the Mau Mau movement. But as Sorrenson has convincingly demonstrated in his admirable study of Kikuyu land reform (1967), the Mau Mau movement spearheaded by the Kikuyu must be understood as something more than an anti-colonial insurrection by displaced farmers. In addition, Mau Mau also pitted landless Kikuyu against a Kikuyu minority of chiefs and other beneficiaries of colonial rule whose loyalty had been rewarded by grants of land. Recognizing the central role of land in precipitating Mau Mau activity, the colonial government concluded that security of tenure would render small holders immune from the influence of radical politicians attempting to mobilize the disenchanted. From this perception arose the initial reforms aimed at the Kikuyu. In the late 1950s the government instituted a series of programs which would award registered titles to individual farmers. Each farmer would hold a consolidated piece of land representing the total acreage of his previously cultivated, dispersed segments, thus ending the traditional pattern of fragmentation. Aside from the various agricultural and economic rationales put forth for this reform, its major impetus was political in attempting to create a stable class of small holders, with security of tenure, whose likely conservatism would effectively put them beyond the reach of political insurgents. Seeking political stability, the colonial administration also foresaw economic benefits, including increased output and efficiency of single, consolidated farms. In both political and economic terms, the individual farmer lay at the cornerstone of the new land policies.

By 1960, the government had effectively blunted the military goals of Mau Mau while accepting the necessity of withdrawing in favor of an independent Kenya, which was proclaimed at the end of 1963. Ironically, contemporary Kenya, born in the aftermath of a violent uprising emboldened by the motto "land and freedom," has witnessed a clear continuity between the essentially conservative colonial land policies of the 1950s and those of the independence period. The irony is double edged, for Tanzania experienced a generally peaceful transition into independence yet has pursued a land policy more radical than anyone could have predicted during the colonial period. In Kenya, the economic rationale for land tenure changes of the colonial years continues to be echoed in each five year plan issued by the government. In the official view, title deeds will definitively mark land ownership, thus reducing litigation and its costs in both time and money. If land is consolidated into a single unit and farmers no longer claim widely separated fragments, farming will become more efficient as time will no longer be expended in the long treks between gardens. Moreover, farmers can use their titles as collateral for agricultural loans thereby facilitating improvements and generally accelerating the rate of agricultural development (Development Plan 1969:210).

In 1968, the land reform program was extended to Mbeere when it was formally declared a land adjudication area. This declaration introduced the first and most difficult stage of land reform during which time all land disputes were subject to legal hearings before a body of local elders supervised by a land officer. Utilizing customary law, a body of unwritten rules regulating civil matters, local elders assumed responsibility at the behest of the government for determining customary "ownership" of all disputed territory; by the time the land adjudication process was underway, very little land was not under litigation. Only after all disputes were settled could the land reform continue through its various stages culminating in the registration of titled land to individual owners. I entered Mbeere toward the middle of 1969 and found a unique opportunity to examine the consequences of the recent declaration including the course of land litigation. The outcome of litigation determined if members of various agnatic groups would gain registered title or would face the fearful prospect of landlessness.

The possibility that one might lose land as a result of land reform is particularly appalling to the

Mbeere, for landlessness growing out of scarcity or overpopulation was historically unknown. Up to the beginning of the land reform program, people enjoyed ready access to pasture and to garden lands. Although much of the land within Mbeere was desiccated and suitable only for stockkeeping or cultivating the most drought-resistant grain crops, it was nonetheless abundant. But even the areas of highest agricultural potential, which have become the major target of land reform, were not the site of overcrowding or of conflicting land claims. It is only with the land reform program that landlessness threatens to become a reality.

The prospects of gaining registered individual titles have stimulated considerable local maneuvering to enhance the possibility not only that one will be certain to gain access to good land but also that one might gain extensive acreages far in excess of what a single individual would have ordinarily cultivated or claimed. Now the cash value of land and the certainty of ownership a title will guarantee present irresistible inducements to enter the legal fray. To do so, one needs the close cooperation of lineage mates. According to the reform procedures, determination of "ownership" under customary law is the essential first step. Since the principles of customary law emphasize collective control by lineages of land rights, including usufruct and transfer, these social units have become the main litigating antagonists. To the extent that a lineage is successful at law, its individual members might be assured of gaining titles, and the size of a lineage's claims determines the amount of titled land each member will receive. Thus lineage organization and size, the capacity of the group to solicit contributions from members for court costs, and the skills and resources of lineage leadership in influencing legal decisions and land reform officers have counted heavily in shaping outcomes. The Mbeere particularly emphasize the intangible factors of political influence and nepotism in the legal success of some lineages, which are gaining inordinate acreages at the expense of their neighbors. One agnatic group, for example, enjoyed a nearly perfect record of success in land cases at court

7

at a time when one of its members was a chief and his classificatory brother and son were court administrators. Other people speak of widespread bribery and similar abuses. What is most likely, however, given the local trends of the 1970s, is that land distribution under the reform program will create a minority of large holders, a vast majority who will secure title to less than ten acres, and others who will be left without titled land.

Fieldwork in Mbeere

From July, 1969 until September, 1970, I lived in Kanyuambora, a community in Nguthi Sublocation in the northwest corner of Mbeere lying close to the border with the people of Embu. At the very outset of fieldwork and again during a three-month follow-up period of fieldwork in 1973 and a return visit in January, 1979, it was clear that the land reform program, including particularly land disputes, consumed the interest and energy of the people. Although land reform represents an effort at rural development and modernization, its short-term social costs include unprecedented litigation and a high level of suspicion among people who fear, with justification, that unscrupulous neighbors or kin may deprive them of what land they hold under the customary rules. Sizeable expenditures of time and money in preparation for the inevitable suits over land are a further consequence.

The heightened concern of recent years surrounding matters pertaining to land impressed itself on me after only a few days in the field. I had been invited by the local chief to take part in a *baraza*, a Swahili term for a large public meeting. Such meetings, scheduled periodically in the larger markets of rural Kenya, serve a vital function in disseminating information in a society with low rates of literacy and limited access to radio or other forms of mass communication. During a *baraza*, then, various officials address assembled local people on topics of immediate interest such as inoculation programs, new cattle dips, the agricultural consequences of burning as a means of clearing land prior to cultivation, and other concerns of local people and the government. I

8

accepted the invitation to address people at the Kanyuambora market in order to introduce myself and to explain my presence in their community. It seemed to me an excellent opportunity to accomplish these tasks efficiently and to make my research widely known at its outset. I did not foresee the obvious--that my participation in the government-sponsored *baraza* with the chief, subchief, agricultural and veterinary officers, would closely identify me with the government. Instead, I maintained a naive faith in my ability to convince people of the innocence of my intentions. This error was to have serious consequences for my research in its initial stages. In anticipation of my "speech" to the local people, I wrote out in Swahili a brief summary of my interest and purpose in the community. At that time, I did not intend to focus on the Mbeere land issue, which was little-known to me at the time. Rather, I wanted to begin conducting a general ethnographic survey of Mbeere since it had never been the focus of social anthropological investigation. Following an initial survey, I planned to concentrate on a more limited set of problems as they emerged. Seated in the market with various local officials, I was called on to explain my interests in local custom, language and history, and my intention to live in the community in order to study these topics. Initially, my words were met with polite nods and the rhetorical "īī," signifying "yes, I follow." Soon we heard widespread grumbling about the need for a translation of my Swahili into the vernacular, Kimbeere. Although I had studied Swahili, I had not yet had the opportunity to study any of the Central Bantu languages prior to fieldwork. Within Mbeere, Swahili was known, with widely varying competence, by men who had worked in towns or on European farms. Few women knew the language, and many men comprehended only a few words. A young Form IV graduate, whom I had retained as a research assistant, complied with the demands for translation, and my newly rendered words were quietly received until I myself said in Kimbeere that I hoped to learn about Mbeere clans. As a fundamental feature of Mbeere social organization, clans had to be investigated; from my point of view it was simply a matter of doing good social anthropology. But in communicating this

9

interest to my audience, I witnessed a sudden outbreak of shouting and near-pandemonium as a polite assembly of local people became an angry crowd. Since people think about their rights to land in relationship to their membership in lineage segments, usually designated by the broader term "clan," I had unwittingly implied that land tenure and the impending land adjudication were to be my concerns. I had no such intention at that time. Further, and unknown to me, the people had been expecting the arrival of a government land adjudication officer to begin hearing land cases, and they decided at this point that I was that official. All of this was embedded in that single, highly charged word, *mīvīrīga* (clans). They demanded to know which clans I was interested in and what I intended to do. But most of their anger was directed within, as various lineage leaders, who had been pressing land suits against each other on behalf of their agnates, seized the opportunity for recrimination and accusations. My uninformed remarks had pulled back a thin veil of amicability to reveal serious social divisions. The tension dissipated only through the efforts of the chief and a thoroughly irrelevant, almost surreal question from a somewhat intoxicated elder who wanted to know if it were dark in America, as he had heard, when it was mid-day in Kenya. Baffled by the previous outbursts, I was grateful for the quiet following this extraordinary *non-sequitur*. A common astronomical interest was perhaps stimulated by the widely-doubted reports, a few days before, that the first men had landed on the moon. Picking up three wild pomegranate-like fruits, known as *mage*, to represent sun, moon, and earth, and feeling completely absurd, I explained to an utterly incredulous audience in bright Kenya sunlight, why indeed it was dark in America. All the while I pondered my earlier *faux pas*. Concerned about its effects on my research, I wondered if rapport with these anxious people would lie beyond my reach.

It was many weeks before my efforts to dispel the erroneous impression that I was a government official were successful. During this period, a number of people, whom I later learned had only tenuous claims to land they cultivated, felt constrained to escort me around their land while explaining at length the basis for their claims and the efforts of their neighbors to seize the land. Some people insisted on pressing gifts on me including maize, plantains, chickens, and ducks. I felt considerable ambivalence about accepting these goods. On the one hand, I did not wish to offend any members of the community by refusing a gift, but on the other hand I feared that acceptance might be a tacit admission that I was an official with whom one could curry favor. I decided to accept the proferred items but to reciprocate with local beer or sugar for Christians who spurned alcohol. Thinking about Mauss, I hoped that these gift exchanges might mark the beginning of the social relationships vital to good fieldwork. Further, I resolved to avoid all inquiries about land, although I remained intrigued by these very matters, for they lay at the center of community interest. I hoped to pursue the land question subsequently when public suspicion of me had abated. Indeed, if *cherchez la vache* is the key to understanding the Nuer (Evans-Pritchard 1940:16) its Mbeere counterpart must surely be *cherchez la terre*.

In order to understand the rules of customary land tenure, the land reform program which has altered Mbeere society, and the form and variation of Mbeere attitudes and behavior concerning their land, it is essential to establish the broad ethnographic framework within which the people see themselves and the changes which are reshaping their lives. This study will therefore detail the ideology and social organization of land holding, which thus requires an examination both of attitudes and behavior concerning elderhood, patrilineal kinship, and dispute settlement. Land reform represents one of several sources of change transforming Mbeere into a segment of a larger nation from its traditionally acephalous character in which people played out their lives within highly localized kin groups, age-sets, and generation-sets. From the establishment of European rule in Embu District in 1906 and the ensuing years of Christian proselytizing, formal education, and wage-labor up to the land reform legislation of the 1960s, Mbeere has increasingly been affected by decisions made beyond its borders. This study, then, will consider alterations in land tenure

11

as the pivot of a broader movement of change which has impinged on Mbeere over the past eighty years. Yet these changes are not unique, for they are emblematic of the ways in which indigenous agricultural peoples of Kenya have been caught up in national policies oriented toward capitalist development among small land owners. Results include profound alterations in the texture of rural life such as the emergence of economic stratification in traditionally egalitarian societies.

The present work also represents a contribution to the ethnography and history of the Bantu-speaking peoples of Central Kenya. Unlike their neighbors, the Kikuyu, on whom a vast although highly uneven ethnographic literature exists, the Mbeere are little-known. It is my belief that one of the social anthropologist's major activities is ethnographic reporting in order to set down an enduring record of the people among whom he has lived. But however important this endeavor, it is not an end in itself since the task of interpretation is also essential. I find it regrettable nonetheless when ethnography is subordinated to theoretical analysis rather than bound to it. For this reason, I believe that an investigation of land tenure and the changes it has undergone must be set within a specific ethnographic framework, if the interpretation of these phenomena is to proceed effectively. At the same time, it is important to understand specific rural locales over time, since strategies of development are inevitably part of the larger flow of change engulfing these communities. The effects of macro processes related to modernization and social change can thus be analyzed in the particularly salient context of local history and culture.

Administrative Framework and Research Site

Since the first years of the colonial regime, Mbeere has been part of a hierarchical civil administration made up of officers with no counterparts in local pre-colonial history. The creation of an overarching political organization composed of specialized offices radically departed from Mbeere

12

experience, which grew out of a more fluid, flexible political system lacking chiefs; authority was diffuse rather than centralized. The centralization begun in the colonial era has been further strengthened by the independent government with the addition of more civil service staff and the expansion of their prerogatives.

Administratively, Mbeere is designated a Division, roughly coterminous with territory inhabited by the Mbeere people.[1] Internal migration between divisions and administrative alterations of division boundaries work against the congruence between the ethnic unit and territory. Thus a substantial number of Mbeere live beyond the Division across the Thuchi River in Meru District. Together with Embu Division, Mbeere Division forms Embu District headed by the District Commissioner (DC). Embu District in turn lies within the Eastern Province, whose chief administrative officer is the Provincial Commissioner (PC), coordinating the administration of numerous, ethnically diverse districts.

A division is led by the Divisional Officer (DO). In Mbeere, his office is located at the Divisional headquarters in the "town" of Siakago, which lies near the center of the Division. The DO supervises tax collection and oversees a variety of other activities from famine relief to self-help projects; working closely with other officers from such Ministries as Agriculture and Lands and Settlement, the DO is responsible for the local implementation of policy articulated at the national level. His mode of contact with local people is primarily through the periodic *baraza*, and through subordinate chiefs and subchiefs.

These latter individuals represent locations and sublocations, respectively. Both chiefs and subchiefs gain office through nomination by the District Commissioner. Unlike the various Divisional Officers, who in recent years have not been from Mbeere, chiefs and subchiefs are local people especially familiar with the problems and conditions of their home areas. They are thus especially important sources of information for the DO. Chiefs and subchiefs collect taxes, maintain order with police at their disposal, and supervise and assist informal settlement of civil disputes in their areas.

Five administrative locations now comprise Mbeere. The three oldest--Evurore, Nthawa, and Mavuria--were established early in the colonial period. The population of those locations, according to the 1979 Kenya census is 62,428 within a total area of 545 square miles. Since independence, two new locations-- Mbeti and Mwea--have been added to Mbeere Division. Mwea is separated from the rest of Mbeere by the Thiba River, and Mbeti includes some areas formerly part of Embu Division. In some parts of Mwea and Mbeti Locations, Mbeere people constitute a minority. Embu town, for example, now part of Mbeere Division, is populated mostly by Embu. Similarly, many Kamba inhabit Mwea Location. In this study general remarks about Mbeere Division or its people will apply to the three old locations, unless otherwise qualified.

Except for brief periods in Mavuria Location, I conducted the major, non-documentary part of the research for this study in Nguthi Sublocation and secondarily, in contiguous portions of Kathera and Evurore Sublocations. These three sublocations lie in Evurore Location in the northern portion of Mbeere Division. Nguthi, with more than 6,000 inhabitants in an area of 56 sq. mi., is the most populous of the Mbeere sublocations. Although ecologically varied, the Sublocation at its northern and western reaches adjacent to the Kanyuambora market contains some of the best farm land in Mbeere. Yet only in the last fifty years have large numbers of people settled in this rich area. Competition for agriculturally high potential land has culminated in the spate of land disputes beginning on the eve of land reform in the 1960s and continuing through the period of land adjudication before the final registration of titled land.

The effort to alter the system of land holding during the 1970s represents only the most recent, albeit far-reaching example of capitalist penetration into Mbeere. Like many other areas of East Africa, Mbeere was subject to colonial policies which insured that men would engage in wage labor. Working

14

predominantly in Nairobi or on European farms, labor migrants secured off-farm income for tax payment, for purchase of consumer goods which are gradually supplanting local craft production, and for payment of school fees on behalf of their children or other kin. Early on, education came to represent the best channel through which one might secure steady employment as a clerk or teacher, which were posts offering higher salaries and prestige than unskilled farm laborers or urban migrants could achieve. The ranks of the current subchiefs include a number of former primary teachers, and indeed teaching has enabled some individuals to accumulate enough money to begin small businesses, mainly general stores, in the rural area.

Markets of varying size dot the landscape, and these range from Ishiara in the north (the largest market in the District) to the very small centers made up of only a few modest buildings. Markets include various shops devoted to the sale of inexpensive consumer goods--flashlights, blankets, cigarettes, matches, cloth, and the like. A tailor may work in conjunction with a local merchant, setting up his sewing machine in front of the shop where such items as local school uniforms can be produced. Shop proprietors are usually from Mbeere, but several Kikuyu merchants have established businesses and have purchased land at these centers. Bars selling locally brewed honey or sugarcane beer for K.sh. .50, or $.07 per quart (7 shillings=$1.00) as well as European-style beer for K.sh. 2.50 ($.35) brought in by lorry from Nairobi are also ubiquitous in the various markets. Tea shops, called *hoteli*, can be found in each market and offer heavily sweetened tea and milk along with scones or *chapati*. The largest centers contain butcheries and small tanneries, although the slaughter of animals, owing to the problem of spoilage, is irregular and must be carefully timed to the appearance of sufficient numbers of potential customers. Local producers, mainly women, sometimes sell bananas and other garden products in the open areas in front of the shops. At the two large markets of Ishiara and Kiritiri, this open-air selling is formalized in a weekly market day when sellers arrive not only from Mbeere but also from other parts of Embu, Kamba

15

country, and Meru. They must purchase a ticket--really a license to sell--from the market master, an employee of the County Council (District Government) which receives the fees. In the early 1970s the sellers paid a fee of K.sh. .20 to vend their goods, and many hundreds appear in Ishiara each week. They arrive by bus to sell produce or crafts such as clay pots, bows and metal-tipped arrows, or woven baskets. Itinerant merchants who travel about Central Kenya also make their way to the big centers to sell such items as baked goods from Nairobi or clothing, which they neatly display on the ground. Youthful gamblers regularly set up a table in Ishiara where they excite the interest of mostly young men hoping to win money at a variant of a European dice game. The big markets are bustling, crowded places where the large assembly also attracts preachers from the Salvation Army and other denominations seeking new adherents. Their small audience tends to be mostly women and girls.

Settlement and Internal Migration in Nguthi

In an apocryphal legend in Nguthi, Mbogo Kirangi, a prophet (*mūrathi*) of Nditi clan who is said to have lived atop Kanyuambora hill four generations ago, predicts the present order. Spurred on by dreams about the future, Mbogo foretold the coming of Europeans, the building of the Embu-Meru road, increasing cultivation, and the construction of the Kanuyambora market and "white houses" (referring to corrugated iron roofs) at the foot of his hilltop home. He said the Mbeere people would gain what the Europeans had.

When Mbogo made his predictions in the years before the establishment of British control of Embu District, Kanyuambora hill lay above a frontier area only sparsely settled by the Mbeere. Situated as it was near the lands of the Embu and the Chuka Meru to the west and north, the Kanyuambora area was regarded as an unsuitable site for building a homestead owing to its proximity to peoples whom the Mbeere feared as possible raiders. Although the Mbeere historically maintained scattered gardens in this fertile portion of the Sublocation, which exhibits the rich alluvial soils so characteristic of neighboring Embu Division, they

16

preferred to maintain their homes several miles away in the less fertile, lower portions of Nguthi and contiguous Evurore Sublocation. Recalling what they considered the wisdom of their forebears, some people in the 1950s abandoned homes in Kanyuambora for residence once again in lower Nguthi following a Mau Mau raid from Embu which resulted in the loss of some lives and in the destruction of the Kanyuambora market and school in 1954. Yet like their ancestors, these people also wanted to take advantage of the quality of land and the increased rainfall and thus maintained scattered gardens, if not residence, in Kanyuambora, where they have helped realize the prophet's predictions.

Since the 1930s, much internal migration within Evurore Location, especially from the lower elevations to the frontier areas of Nguthi Sublocation, has taken place. An administrative sublocation such as Nguthi combines indigenous, named territorial segments into a single unit. I designate these segments, known in Kimbeere as *matūūra* (sing. *itūūra*) as parishes. The term derives from *gūtūūra*, "to live." Among the Arusha, Gulliver uses this term to denote a similar unit he characterizes as "a socially and geographically defined collection of scattered homesteads, each of which is built on the separate land holding worked by the family which occupies it" (1963:17). Although *itūūra* is translated as "village" by Mbeere speakers of English, that term implies a nucleated quality uncharacteristic of the Mbeere territorial unit, for the constituent homesteads sometimes numbering more than seventy are widely dispersed. The oldest parishes, Kīthecū, Kathimari, Rīakīng'enyi, Ciambingū, Ng'ongi, and Rīakīrīmū were formally organized as tax-paying units in colonial times, as they were traditional, bounded territorial units that had been inhabited and cultivated for generations. Migrants from these parishes, as well as a lesser number from contiguous sublocations, settled the northern and western margins of Nguthi once they felt this former frontier was safe. There they created eight new parishes: Kagongo-Gaceke, Kavengero, Kanyuambora, Gwakaithe, Karigīrī, Imeria, Kanyueri, and Kanganga.

The areas of recent settlement contrast significantly with the older parishes of Nguthi and the parishes of the contiguous sublocation of Evurore. Relatively high in agricultural potential, the land of the new parishes makes possible the cultivation of bananas, maize, mangoes, and tobacco--highly valued crops whose cultivation in the older parishes offers less promise of success. Recently, the introduction of some varieties of drought resistant maize enables farmers in the older parishes to cultivate this highly valued crop along with the millets and sorghum so familiar in the drier portions of the Location. The more fertile, less rocky soils of the upper elevations also receive more abundant rainfall, thus making possible a more secure and varied agricultural base.

In the new areas, the cultivation of perennials such as bananas and mangoes, in addition to seasonal pulses and grains, permits a more permanent settlement pattern. Although particular plots are allowed to revert to fallow as new cultivation begins in reclaimed land, rights to uncultivated land are not relinquished as in true swidden systems where population is sparse in relationship to cultivable land; nor does a change in residence necessarily accompany a change of gardens. Intent to settle in an area permanently is marked by the increasing frequency of dwellings constructed with expensive corrugated iron roofs. Certainly the increasing pressure of population on fertile areas of Nguthi and apprehension that fallow lands, if not closely watched, may invite new claimants have helped to stabilize the settlement pattern.

Although greater rainfall and richer soils in the new parishes permit people to plant a greater range of crops than in their former homes, environmental differences have reduced the significance of stockkeeping. Numbers of cattle, sheep, and goats increase dramatically among people living in the hotter, drier climate of the old parishes in lower Nguthi and the adjacent desiccated plains of Evurore Sublocation. A critical ecological cline thus distinguishes lower areas from the uplands. Although some stock are kept in the latter areas, cultivation predominates as people consciously choose to pursue

agriculture in a setting which they consider inimical
to the primarily pastoral existence marking economic
life at lower elevations. The fear that their
livestock would not flourish in upper Nguthi has
inhibited some Mbeere from migrating from the lower
elevations. An agricultural report prepared in 1938
details the extensive erosion of lower Evurore due to
severe overgrazing, and it strongly suggests that the
herders relocate to elevations above 3800 feet such as
those found at Kanyuambora. The pessimism which has
regularly characterized official assessments of the
agricultural potential in Mbeere is also encapsulated
in this report:

> It is evident that in their present
> milieu the Mbere [sic] in large parts of
> Njamburi's location [Evurore] and parts of
> Kombo's location [Mavuria] have no chance of
> making progress in any direction. Their
> country is barren and inaccessible and they
> obtain very little value for even the reduced
> taxation which is paid in the impoverished
> country in which they live.

> The most promising method of dealing
> with these people appears to be to move them
> lock, stock, and barrel, leaving their
> present land to regenerate [to] bush and to
> become once again the haunt of the elephant,
> the rhinoceros, and the buffalo (Maher
> 1938:40).

Yet the report points out that many people were
unwilling to move because they believed that the more
temperate area around Kanyuambora was inimical to the
health of their stock. They claimed that certain
grasses in the upper area poisoned their animals which,
they felt, could thrive only on the dry, scrubby
vegetation in parts of Mbeere below 3000 feet
elevation. This belief continues to be widely held
around Kanyuambora and contiguous areas of upper Nguthi
where the farmers, although they usually raise a few
goats, contrast themselves with Mbeere herders only a
few miles distant. Ironically, a serious outbreak of
rinderpest in the lower zone spurred the initial wave

of migration to Kanyuambora, where the new arrivals believed crops, if not animals, might more reliably provide subsistence.

As the pace of migration picked up in the late 1930s, a market developed at the foot of Kanyuambora hill, a granite formation rising some 400 feet over the open savanna. The market emerges as a focal point of the Sublocation for it draws people from throughout Nguthi to its several general stores, bar, and tea shops. People may also sell farm produce in the open. It is also the scene of numerous non-economic activities such as a periodic *baraza*, itinerant preaching, an occasional government-sponsored mobile cinema, and legal hearings. In the late 1960s, for example, court officers, litigants and their witnesses, after visiting disputed territories, sometimes gathered in the Kanyuambora market to continue the case with the swearing of a ritual oath, until recently the *sine qua non* of all difficult litigation. Less formally, the market simply represents a convenient place for people to gather and to hear the latest news from other Nguthi residents or from visitors living in other parts of Embu District.

Since it is situated on the loose surface lower road from Embu town to Meru town, the market is also an important staging area for people taking their goods to the much larger market in Embu, the Provincial and District capital some thirty miles westward, or to Ishiara, five miles to the east in lower Mbeere. Nguthi farmers living in the upper reaches especially value their mango crop, and some producers market their fruit in Nairobi, sending it in large crates from the Kanyuambora market, where a local entrepreneur collects it for shipment to the capital. The fertile areas surrounding the market, particularly westward to the border with Embu Division and north to the Thuchi River, along the border of Meru District, support this sort of cash crop enterprise which has in part spurred the recent intense competition for fertile land. The creation of the market itself has figured in land disputes as a subject of intense controversy between different factions claiming to have originally ceded the market land to the County Council (the elected

District governing body which succeeded the old African District Council in the 1950s).

In addition to differentiating their area from the lowlands in economic and environmental terms, people of Kanyuambora and the other new parishes of upper Nguthi also distinguish themselves from their neighbors in terms of attitudes toward change. In the new parishes of Kanyuambora and Gwakaithe, two primary schools associated with the Anglican and Catholic denominations, respectively, draw children from throughout the Sublocation. In addition, Kanyuambora boasts a secondary school which started as a self-help (*Harambee*) school staffed by an American Peace Corps teacher and Norwegian volunteer teacher before becoming a government-supported school in 1973. Economic cooperatives, such as the one for tobacco growers, include some Nguthi farmers seeking appropriate ways to market their crop. Such economic and educational developments have been much less pronounced in the lower areas. As a consequence, Christians, particularly Anglicans, consider themselves "modern" or "progressive" people (*andū a rīu*, literally people of now) interested in education, agricultural improvement, and, for the Anglicans, rejection of beer drinking and other features of Mbeere custom clashing with Church Missionary Society teaching. They contrast themselves with their conservative lowland neighbors whom they regard as indifferent to opportunities to alter more traditional ways of living. Non-Christians in upper Nguthi also perceive the differences, noting that such customary activities as ritual passage into elderhood, placation of ancestral shades, and female circumcision have proven more persistent in the lower areas. Christianity thus conveys much more than a religious attitude; it implies a complex of values associated with the educational, economic, and technological innovations which followed in the wake of the European missionaries. These public professions nonetheless often mask a deep and abiding adherence to customary practice such as female circumcision and the magical ministration of magico-medical practitioners (*andū ago*) whose skill in combatting sorcery-induced illness is still widely accepted. Christians have also publicly reviled oaths in legal procedure, for these rituals, with their mandatory slaughter of goats and consumption of ritually prepared blood, had been criticized by European missionaries. Further, ritual oaths recall the Mau Mau movement, only marginally supported in Mbeere and universally condemned by the missionary and colonial authorities as a primitive, atavistic movement. Yet this very rejection of a symbol of "pagan" procedure in the name of modernity effectively puts Christians beyond the reach of an important customary sanction, and customary legal procedure has thereby been profoundly altered. In sum, professions of Christian faith, whether sincere or expedient, enable adherents to manipulate a variety of claims and evidence unknown in the past as well as to organize factions through new religious symbols.

The Significance of Tribal Designation

In referring to both a people and a place as Mbeere, I am following local usage but not without a critical view of the current fact of Mbeere ethnicity or the nature of the tribal designation. The various ethnic groups in Africa have often been labeled tribes or tribal groups, but in the last fifteen years, especially, anthropologists have closely scrutinized these terms and questioned their conceptual value. Too often, the tribe has been taken as a given, representing a culturally, linguistically, and politically circumscribed unit without considering the wider political processes which have shaped our mode of thinking about this anthropological commonplace. Notable examinations of the concept include those by Helm (1967), Barth (1969), Southall (1970a), Gulliver (1971), and Fried (1975). Well before this spate of important reconsiderations of the concept of tribe, Colson foreshadowed some of the major conclusions of these critics in her important studies of the Makah of the Northwest Coast and the Plateau Tonga of Zambia. In both cases, she questioned the tribal status of these societies outside of the context of the alien administration which organized each group of people and territory in particular ways. Administrative concerns forged a unified identity or implied a political unity where none existed before its derivation from an imposed authority (1951:95-95, 1953:79). Southall

22

cites a number of African examples convincingly showing that the concept of tribe represented by particular named units is similarly a colonial artifact springing from European administration (1970a:33-45). Accordingly, the subjective reality of a traditional tribal identity—people regarding themselves as culturally, linguistically, and politically unified and distinct from other tribes—remains, in some cases, highly dubious.

In Mbeere, colonial processes creating the tribe were at work from the first days of administration. The drawing of administrative boundaries, the use of record books designated "Mbeere," "Embu," and the like, and the imposition of a sort of "national" conception of each tribe emphasizing political autonomy, endemic inter-tribal warfare, and distinctive tribal character traits (enterprising, indolent, etc.) contributed greatly to the tribal formulation. Regarded as indifferent to change and inhabiting. a dry, forbidding land more suited to herding than to cultivation, the people of Mbeere were seen early on as very marginal in the slow evolutionary progress which the colonial administration believed it was setting in motion. In 1970, a European, who had served as a District Officer in Mbeere, remarked to me that "they are one of the ancient tribes." That is, he saw them as backward and unchanging, as if frozen in some putative antiquity. An indifference to progress is only one of several stereotypic views applied to the Mbeere.

Implicit in the tribal concept was the notion that Mbeere culture was homogenous and that the alleged animosity between Mbeere and their neighbors was chronic. Yet Mbeere culture and even language were by no means uniform within the area delimited by the colonial authority and designated as Mbeere. The occurence of some of the same clan names in Mbeere and Embu, Mbeere and Meru, Mbeere and Kamba and the participation of the Mbeere and Embu in the same generation class rituals (Glazier 1976a) and in the formation of some age-sets are indicative of the variegated data showing up the illogic of positing a clearly bounded cultural entity to characterize the

23

people of Mbeere prior to colonial rule. It is highly
unlikely that the notion of tribe as a distinct
cultural unit had the psychological reality for these
people which the colonial view implied. I examine in
the next chapter the complex relationships of both
cooperation and conflict between the Mbeere and their
neighbors, thus pointing up the lack of fit between
ethnographic fact and the concept of tribe.

Various observers noted similarities between the
Mbeere and their neighbors, sometimes designating the
Mbeere a "sub-tribe" of the Kikuyu. As residents of a
large, multi-district area termed the Kikuyu Land Unit,
the Mbeere and the other peoples of Embu District,
Meru, and Kikuyuland were occasionally conceptualized
as a single entity in sometimes amusing ways. In 1940,
very sketchy records of a meeting of the Embu Local
Native Council (the District Commissioner served as
President of this body) indicate that the Council
briefly debated a proposal to aid the war effort by
contributing several thousand shillings toward the
purchase of a Spitfire to be named "Kikuyu-Embu-Meru."
When one elder demured by saying that such a large
expenditure of Council funds might be better used for
famine relief, a second elder admonished the assembly
that money spent in famine relief would count precious
little "if we lose our king." Nonetheless, underlying
the occasional acknowledgment of "supertribal" status
of the Central Kenya Bantu or tribal similarities among
them is the assumption of a more pervasive and
significant distinctiveness.

The subjective reality of Mbeere ethnicity emerged
very strongly at the end of the colonial period. For
reasons that will be examined subsequently, the Mbeere
did not participate in any significant numbers in the
Mau Mau movement and thus stood apart from their Kikuyu
and Embu neighbors. The colonial regime regarded the
Mbeere as staunch loyalists--an estimation which I
think is overstated and self-congratulatory. It is
nonetheless based on the fact that the Mbeere chiefs
were generally able to keep Mau Mau at bay owing
predominantly to the indifference of their people to a
movement fueled by grievances about land alienation
which the Mbeere had not experienced. The colonial

24

government then continued to support people of northern Mbeere in their settlement of fertile lands abutting an area inhabited by the Embu, who were just as eager to lay claim to that territory. Thus it was in competition and struggle at a geographic boundary that ethnicity was not only made explicit but also rewarded by the political authority.

But in other, more recent contexts Mbeere ethnicity has again been encompassed by a "pan-tribal" Kikuyu identity including all of the Bantu peoples of the Mt. Kenya perimeter. Most forcefully articulated by a former chief who is also a local party activist of KANU (Kenya African National Union), the near identity of the Mbeere, their neighbors, and the Kikuyu is asserted along with their singular political interests in an independent Kenya. In discussing the origins of the Mbeere people, the KANU representative went so far as to refer to the famous Kikuyu myth (recounted in Kenyatta's *Facing Mt. Kenya*) of Gikuyu and the Mumbi, the Kikuyu Adam and Eve. I never heard this myth invoked by anyone else when ruminating on Mbeere origins. More overtly, the forging of a strong Kikuyu-linked identity rooted in the anti-colonial struggle has been crystalized in the association of Kikuyu, Embu (including Mbeere), and Meru peoples known as GEMA. In the early 1970s, this association is said to have inspired many oath-taking ceremonies in Central Kenya among men who were required to affirm their support of the continuing political domination of the national scene by the Kikuyu and allied peoples. Sometimes these assertions of collective identity took an ugly turn when, especially in Nairobi, Luo men from western Kenya would be forcibly circumcised by gangs of men from the central area. In Mbeere, the teenage son of a Luo man working as an agricultural instructor fell victim to this outrage in 1970, although the circumstances surrounding the event were probably as much connected to interpersonal antagonisms as to wider political struggles (David Brokensha, personal communication). But the choice of attack clearly indicates the profound symbolic significance of circumcision. In 1980, GEMA was officially banned as it had been alleged that the organization opposed the succession of Mr. Moi (a non-Kikuyu) to the Presidency, following the death of Jomo Kenyatta.

In yet other contexts of perceived group competition and struggle, ethnic identity can again redefine itself. Among school leavers and secondary graduates who have unsuccessfully sought employment in Nairobi, there is a common view that Kikuyu people, owing to what is widely regarded as Kikuyu control of various offices of government and the private sector, enjoy a decided advantage when seeking work. Some Mbeere youth who have sought employment in the capital claim that they apply for jobs speaking Kikuyu rather than Kimbeere. I have heard several young men express their frustration at perceived Kikuyu dominance each time a government of Kenya vehicle passes (identifiable by its GK license plate). They observed the plate and wryly remarked, "government of Kikuyu."

Ethnicity or tribal identity has thus represented a set of shifting cultural symbols circumscribing particular populations at various historical periods. These symbols may be widely inclusive (those who practice male and female circumcision) or narrowly restrictive (speakers of a language designated by its speakers as Kimbeere and believed to be limited to a place called Mbeere). The activation of exclusive or inclusive identity has been set in motion by various competitive struggles for land, employment, political power, and the like. Ethnicity has thus come to represent a set of symbols not only expressing a particular identity but also creating strategies that serve economic or political ends, as such writers as Cohen (1969, 1981) have convincingly argued. In Mbeere, and indeed in much of precolonial Africa, the relatively circumscribed, highly localized nature of the social order rendered broader identities superfluous. The colonial period expanded the scale of social relations in which the ethnic factor became a flexible medium through which the new sources of economic and political competition could be played out.

The social use of ethnic identity is emblematic of other dimensions of Mbeere tradition, which I consider a set of dynamic, instrumental symbols people can effectively exploit for economic and political purposes. In their use of tradition, the Mbeere and various agencies of the government unwittingly collaborated to support institutions and procedures, sanctioned by their alleged place in timeless custom, which would paradoxically contribute to the transformation of the social order. Actions, masquerading as "traditional" or "customary," have facilitated changes that were long resisted. Most notably, the use of custom in justifying land claims upholds the corporate rights of lineages beyond four generations in depth. Genealogical recitation and descriptions of the activities on the land of various putative ancestors have been a recurring feature of the most consequential land cases. Yet historically, it is highly unlikely that anything resembling these large groups, either in their structure or corporate qualities, ever existed. For reasons I shall make clear, this particular rendering of tradition, actually encouraged by the colonial and independent governments, has proven extremely advantageous in the high stakes quest for land under the reform. The manipulation of descent ideology and groups, often shrouding self-interested legal maneuvering, represents the most telling use of tradition for new economic ends.

A related view of customary practice has been explored by several writers including Parkin, who analyzes the mystifying qualities of traditional practices among the Giriama of Kenya (1972). In Giriama society, processes of ecological change have brought profound alterations in the economy, including the emergence of capitalist production based on copra. Parkin examines the ways in which various customary practices, including the witnessing role of elders in law cases and large expenditures for bridewealth, appear to uphold tradition while latently contributing to its demise. This discrepancy between perceived effect and hidden consequence is what Parkin calls mystification. Thus, elders fulfill their customary role as witnesses in supporting claims to land and trees by capitalist entrepreneurs; the latter have gained property mostly through purchase or other means outside of customary agnatic entitlement. As witnesses, the elders continue to support the value of gerontocracy but, by so doing, they also support the growing influence of capitalist penetration which will ultimately undermine the authority of age. Similarly, the monetization of bridewealth and its continuing inflationary spiral require that less affluent farmers sell land and palm trees to the more successful entrepreneurial farmers. In this way, bridewealth continues to support agnatic kinship and the mediating role of elders while latently reinforcing the growing division between capitalist farmers and their poorer neighbors. Thus, Parkin shows how ideological shifts, set in motion by economic change, are unconsciously played out through the existing medium of custom, including rituals and beliefs (Parkin 1972:99-101).

The Mbeere material, while also intimately tied to the changes wrought by capitalist penetration, raises an additional issue--the collaborative construction of tradition by local people and the government. Where Parkin takes custom as a given before examining its various paradoxes, I consider Mbeere tradition, especially that infusing descent group activity and ideology, as problematic. Tradition, in this view, represents an instrumental creation in serving the material ends of kin-based corporations. Through the unwitting cooperation between the government, bent on preserving custom, and self-interested agnatic groups, large organizations well-suited to pressing land claims evolved. Designated as "lineages," these new agnatic groups enjoyed the sanction of the government and of tradition. At the same time, the symbolism of tradition, albeit recently constructed, was then effectively used to pursue large land claims, which in turn are symptomatic of incipient class formation.

Following this introduction, Chapter Two examines the physical features of the land and the pre-colonial historical processes which have shaped Mbeere culture up to the beginning of colonial rule. I emphasize

28

particularly the regular failure of rainfall and the attendant famines and food shortages as critical ecological features influencing a relatively mobile population and its contacts with neighboring peoples. My argument that Mbeere descent groups were historically shallow and only minimally corporate stems in part from the analysis of the highly constraining character of Mbeere natural and social ecology laid out in this chapter. More generally, my contention that some traditions represent recent social construction depends on first establishing the realities of the historical record. This chapter also examines the historic role of the elders' councils as political institutions, since the colonial regime sought to preserve the role of elders precisely at the time when they undermined it through the appointment of chiefs. Analyzing these political changes is vitally important if the contemporary shape of emergent stratification, differential access to land, and tradition are to be understood. Chapter Three describes marriage and domestic organization through time; it also examines how domestic groups organize cooperation and production based on their control of gardens and livestock, how property devolves on house-units within the larger homestead, and how domestic units vary according to their stage in the developmental cycle. Chapter Four examines agnation and the ideology of patrilineal descent in relationship to corporate land-holding. The argument in this chapter is set partially in an ethnographic present prior to the momentous changes instituted by the land reform program which, in the service of contemporary interests, is reshaping popular views of the past. I provide additional evidence, especially concerning funerary rites, to support my contention about the shallow character of the Mbeere lineage historically. I also discuss emergent agnatic groups--large lineages--and what I term "descent coalitions." I argue they are both recent developments abetting the requirements of land claims and effective litigation necessitated by the land reform process. Chapter Five analyzes customary rules of land tenure, including usufruct, tenancy, and sale; it also describes the background to contemporary land reform in Mbeere by discussing the history of government land policy in Central Kenya prior to the extension of that policy to Mbeere. Chapter VI analyzes customary law, particularly concerning land, for it is through customary law that the government sought to adjudicate land claims prior to the registration of title. This chapter also analyzes case material from the Mbeere Divisional Court and from the Land Adjudication Committee formed by local elders to settle disputes. Chapter 7 concludes this study by reviewing some of the consequences of change, particularly the emergence of rural stratification and the use of fabricated tradition in the strategy and organization of lineage groups.

Notes

[1]By the late 1970s an administrative reorganization of Mbeere Division was underway. The new Division of Gachoka was being formed from portions of Mbeti and Mavuria Locations. I will describe the older administrative setup characteristic of Mbeere during the major portions of my fieldwork.

A lower Nguthi garden site, prepared by burning scrub
vegetation, just before the long rains.

A tilled garden in Kanyuambora, prior to planting for the short rains. Mt. Kenya appears in the background.

33

A Kanyuambora family proudly displaying its tobacco
crop.

Kanyuambora Market.

The Salvation Army preaching the Gospel at Ishiara Market.

Women vendors entering the Kiritiri Market.

Chapter Two

The Land and People in Historical Perspective

Ethnographic Context

The Mbeere are one of a number of politically acephalous groups comprising the "Central Tribes of the Northeastern Bantu" (Middleton and Kershaw 1965). Among this large cluster of peoples inhabiting the periphery of Mount Kenya and the contiguous plains south and east of the Tana River, the Kikuyu and the Kamba are the largest in number and by far the best known in the ethnographic literature. Smaller related peoples include the Ndia and Gicugu of Kirinyaga District (formerly a part of Embu District), the Embu and Mbeere, who together inhabit Embu District, and finally the Meru groups including the Tharaka, Chuka, Mwimbi, Imenti, Igembe, Tigania, Igoji, and Muthambi, all of whom inhabit Meru District. Within the last forty years, a sizeable number of Mbeere migrated from Evurore across the Thuchi River to Chuka Division of Meru District, and this represents the largest single migration beyond the original homeland area. Generally, these various groups practice a mixed economy of herding and cultivating, although the emphasis on one or the other economic mode can vary between groups or within a single group. Thus large areas of Ukambani are marked by ecological conditions much more suited to herding than some Kikuyu or Meru highland areas abutting Mt. Kenya; similarly within Mbeere the low plains stretching along the Tana River across from Ukambani offer stockkeepers a more suitable environment than they can find among their agricultural neighbors to the north and west in Mbeere.

Linguistically and culturally, the Mbeere are most closely akin to the Embu. Patriclans, shallow lineages, age-sets, and dual generation classes define the fundamental features of pre-colonial social organization in Mbeere and Embu. The Kikuyu and most of the Meru peoples maintained similar institutions, but these differed in important ways from those of the

39

Mbeere and Embu. The Kamba, lacking both age-sets and generation classes, appear most distinct among these peoples.

The name "Mbeere" derives from the ordinal number, *mbere*, meaning "first" in most of the languages of these central Kenya groups. The Mbeere refer to themselves as the "first people" (*andū a mbere*), for they believe that they were the first people of a larger migration to enter the lands south and east of Mt. Kenya. Lambert's effort (1945, 1950) to relate the migrations of the Mbeere to those of their Bantu neighbors and to suggest dates for these large scale movements from the 14th to the 18th centuries concentrates on a purported coastal origin. The alleged coastal beginnings of these peoples at Shungwaya, or Mbwa, figures prominently only in the oral traditions of the Meru. Their migration to Meru, according to a legend ubiquitous among the Meru peoples, required crossing a body of water. Those groups crossing during the daytime became the white clans, those crossing at sunset became the red clans, and those crossing at night became the black clans--a tripartite division of clans still recognized in much of Meru. Yet among the Kamba, Kikuyu, Embu, and Mbeere, a division of clans into three groups does not exist. Further, although I found some few informants who were familiar with the Meru legend of migration from Mbwa, none could systematically relate it to Mbeere origins. They only grant that perhaps the Mbeere originated at that point, too. This tale has little relevance for historical inquiry into Mbeere migration. Saberwal finds the legend equally unimportant in the investigation of Embu history (1967:31-33). Munro (1967) points out that Lambert himself presented evidence supporting the view that only the Meru demonstrate close historical links to the coast; some of the Meru peoples, compared to their neighbors, for example, speak languages much more closely related to the languages of the coast, suggesting more recent historical ties to coastal peoples. His linguistic argument for coastal origins is much more convincing than a naive effort deriving history from myth and purporting to pinpoint the location of Shungwaya as one might attempt to locate

Eden (Fadiman 1973). Munro hypothesizes that the Kikuyu, Embu, and Kamba did not originate at the coast, but rather moved out of Tanganyika in a course which took them directly into Central Kenya simultaneously, or perhaps prior to the movement of the Meru peoples (1967:27). This suggestion more plausibly accounts for the observed linguistic, historical, and social organizational variation between the Meru and their neighbors.

Although the Mbeere were likely not part of the inland migrations of the Meru as recounted in the Shungwaya narrative, a simple alternative is not warranted. That is, evidence derived solely from equally condensed accounts, told by informants attempting to characterize an alleged collective movement of people calling themselves Mbeere, reduces the complexity of the migration, which most certainly occurred in different waves. Accounts of the migration of clan or lower order segments present a fuller picture of successive movements of peoples into Mbeere and adjacent territories.

Clan histories recount migration into Mbeere from one of two directions. Some clans suggest Meru for their origin and point as far away as Tigania in the Nyambene Hills as the specific source of their ancestors' migration to Mbeere. Elders of other clans look in the opposite direction, to the south and west, for their origin point in the vicinity of Mwea, Mbeti, and Ithanga. Historical and archeological research may at some juncture establish definitively whether the peoples from northeast and southwest originally derived from a common source. Once they departed from the farther reaches of Meru, according to clan traditions which cite quarrels and especially food scarcity as the stimuli to migration, these "proto-Mbeere" moved southward into present day Chuka; there they crossed the Thuchi River near Igambang'ombe to fan out across what was to become the land of the Mbeere. Significantly, Igambang'ombe has been commemorated as the northeast dispersal point of the Mbeere in the periodic *nduiko*, or investiture ceremonies, which marked the passage of ritual authority from one generation-set to the next. Now commemorated only through oral tradition, the ritual recreation in the *nduiko* of the original migration through Igambang'ombe was observed for the last time in 1932 (Glazier 1976a:317).

To the southwest, forbears of the Mbeere maintained a periodic contact, mainly through skirmishes over livestock, with the Maasai. Oral tradition especially glorifies the Mbeere experience at Ithanga and on the Mwea Plain as a time of immense livestock wealth. But Maasai incursions eventually decimated the Mbeere herds and forced them to migrate to their present home where horticulture, together with herding of small stock, became their characteristic way of life. The Mbeere vision of their prosperity at Mwea attributes to Kaviū Nthiga, a prodigious culture-hero, qualities of enormous physical strength and leadership, which insured Mbeere pastoral success. According to some versions of the Kaviū story, his son Nthiga, a fierce but vulnerable leader, succumbed to the Maasai because of the treachery of his Maasai wife whose extreme ardor weakened him greatly. She also proved to be a spy, as well, reporting Mbeere secrets to the Maasai, who eventually turned this strategic knowledge to advantage in soundly defeating an enervated Nthiga and his Mbeere warriors. Seizing the vast herds at Mwea, the Maasai successfully drove the stockkeepers to the northeast where they became cultivators, while attempting, without success, to regain their former pastoral greatness. Yet, in the story, the Maasai, for whom the Mbeere hold a respect springing from both fear and admiration, taught the Mbeere circumcision customs through their mutual contact at Mwea, and those customs define in part the Mbeere identity. The Mbeere became convinced that in male circumcision lay the extraordinary strength and power of the Maasai, and indeed, other cultural similarities between Mbeere and Maasai suggest a history of regular contact between the two peoples. Relatedly, it is said that the belief in circumcision as a source of physical strength also contributed in part to Mbeere and particularly to Embu decisions to resist European incursions. Thinking that the white interlopers were uncircumcised, the warriors were inspired to fight until they realized the full devastating effect of European firearms upon them.

Like Igambang'ombe, Mwea drew the ritual attention of Mbeere generation-sets during the investiture ceremonies. Specialists performed sacrifices at Mwea to increase livestock. These sacrifices were carried out before an assemblage of generation class members from throughout Mbeere, who then returned home for local sacrifices. Mwea, as a dispersion point of the remaining Mbeere clans, was thus commemorated (Glazier 1976a:322). In contemporary songs and stories, allusions to Mwea connote the prosperity borne of pastoral wealth, yet recall the prelude to stunning defeat and loss, bringing forth a world resembling the less glorious cultural present.

Assessing the historical accuracy of Mbeere accounts of their migrations and origins requires further research joining the historical to the archeological record. My concern here, however, is the theme of the food quest, stimulated in narrative accounts either by defeat or famine. The theme pervades Mbeere descriptions both of the historic movement of people on their land and of the extensive settlement of frontier areas, such as Nguthi, within the last two generations. Scarcity and hunger are most frequently cited as well in etiological explanations of the emergence from single units of the two generation classes, Nyangi and Thathi, and the two divisions of patriclans, Thagana and Irumbi. Indeed, depictions of famine have infused the oral tradition with themes of loss and starvation. Noteworthy here are the locally popular ogre tales in which monstrous projections of chronic but difficult to satisfy human needs take form in a demi-human creature which ruthlessly stalks his human prey. He is driven by an uncontrollable, animal-like hunger, which can only be satisfied by the consumption of human flesh. (Gorfain and Glazier 1978).

Ecological Zones

The earliest written descriptions of the Mbeere and their territory create a picture of poverty and desolation unmatched by other peoples of what was to become Embu District. In the main, colonial

43

administrators prepared these reports as they were the first European observers of the people and their land. Such nineteenth century explorers as Krapf and Chanler, who travelled in east central Kenya, did not venture into Mbeere but rather skirted around it by way of the Tana River. Typical of the early descriptions of the Mbeere landscape is the following brief statement by R. G. Stone, District Commissioner in 1916: "The Emberre [sic] live in a stony waterless country and their crops are poor. They were formerly rich in cattle, but lost most in tribal warfare." Reiterated in subsequent colonial reports, this view of the Mbeere not only emphasizes the harshness of local environment but also victimization at the hands of their neighbors. Both points require qualification.

Incomparable as much of the land of Mbeere is to the temperate highlands of Kikuyuland and upper Embu to the west, it is hardly surprising that early observers emphasized the marginal economic potential of much of the land, especially due to water problems. Particularly striking are the immense stretches of stony, waterless landscape supporting only a scattered pastorally oriented population. But despite early descriptions focusing on such marginal portions of Mbeere, the territory is by no means geographically uniform, although rainfall represents the most critical limiting factor in Mbeere ecology.

Although every part of Mbeere at various times experiences severe food shortages brought on by either rainfall failure, exhausted soils, stock disease, overgrazing and diminished pasture land, or some combination of these factors, ecological diversity points up important internal economic and demographic differentials. This diversity affects not only the relative emphasis on hoe farming or herding in particular areas but also, concomitantly, the distribution of population and the value of land. In addition, the impact of periodic rainfall failure varies with ecological setting, and competition for productive, relatively well-watered land is in part a function of people's desire to live in economically more secure circumstance.

44

Except for a western land boundary with Embu Division, Mbeere Division (including Evurore, Nthawa, and Mavuria Locations only) is defined by river boundaries. To the north, the Thuchi River marks the boundary of Embu and Meru Districts, as it represents the northern margin in Mbeere proper. The Tana River runs along both the eastern and a part of the southern boundary; the Thiba River, which has its confluence with the Tana on the southern margin of Mbeere, forms the remaining part of the southern boundary. The land which lies at the northern and western margins of Mbeere is notably more productive agriculturally. With more rainfall and better soils than eastern and southern portions of Mbeere, this area sustains higher population densities, more permanent settlements, and more opportunities for the production of cash crops. By contrast, the eastern and southern areas are more pastorally oriented, supporting a poorer, more scattered population.

Within this ecological gradient running roughly northwest to southeast, three distinct zones can be identified (Brokensha & Glazier 1973:190). The first lying at an average altitude of 3500 feet which includes upper Nguthi, receives about 40 inches of rain annually. Land in this zone offers the highest potential for agricultural development in Mbeere. With its fertile soils and relatively greater precipitation, this zone supports a range of crops such as maize, cowpeas, pigeon peas, lablab beans, and millet, as well as such important perennials as bananas and mangoes, which in part make possible a more sedentary population. In addition, cash crop production has met with some limited success. In this zone, Kiang'ombe, the highest hill in Mbeere, rises to an altitude of 5817 feet. Although people keep some cattle, sheep, and goats in this zone, these animals do not flourish under the environmental circumstances of higher altitudes. The first efforts by the colonial administration to encourage Mbeere of lower altitudes to migrate to this more fertile agricultural zone adjacent to Embu Division were met with the reluctance of pastoralists, who claimed that their livestock would suffer (Embu District Annual Report 1933). The people of Nguthi identify in their area a variety of grass

45

called *kanyūra*, which they say is fatal to their stock, especially cattle, and it does not grow in the distinctly pastoral areas.

A second zone lying between altitudes of 2500 and 3500 feet is less favorable to agriculture than the higher zone. Rainfall ranges from 25-40 inches annually, making the cultivation of the banana a risky endeavor since it requires at least 35 inches of rain per year (O'Connor 1967:35). Yet millet (both finger and bulrush) and sorghum do reasonably well under conditions of limited rainfall and poor soils, as they require only about 14 inches of rain in the growing season (O'Connor 1967:29). Maize, pulses, and root crops such as cassava and arrowroot also grow in this zone. Beginning in 1929, the government pushed cassava cultivation in Mbeere as a hedge aginst famine. It resists drought better than other cultigens and can survive insect attacks and disease (O'Connor 1967:7). Farmers normally plant cassava in scattered bunches in gardens predominantly devoted to other crops. In addition, cotton has been a promising although not fully developed cash crop in this zone.

A third zone with average elevations under 2500 feet lies well toward the eastern and southern reaches of the Division. Its forbidding desiccation due to annual rainfalls averaging less than 25 inches makes cultivation a highly marginal undertaking. The natural vegetation of baobab, acacia, cactus, and dry grasses are apt indices of an ecological zone most suitable for stockkeeping. Here population is small and scattered. Maher, who recommended the sustained effort to resettle Mbeere, based his conclusions on observations in this zone. Zone 1 offered the promise of hoe farming whereas Zone 3 was so badly eroded, parched, and overgrazed that any economic activity was regarded as highly tenuous (Maher 1938:40).

The cycle of food production in Zones 1 and 2 follows a regular pattern, discernible twice a year and timed by the expectation and appearance of the rains. The task of clearing bush areas to make gardens or to reclaim old fields from fallow normally falls to men, who often resort to burning as a labor-efficient means of eliminating the natural floral cover. Many men in so doing disregard the frequent instructions of Agricultural Officers who warn of the destructive effects on the top soil of burning. At the onset of the rains, the major planting activity begins for men and women, and cultivators take great care in calculating whether a downpour marks the beginning of the rains or represents only a false start. Planting in the latter case may well result in germination of cultigens which may then likely dry out before the regular rains begin. Yet rainfall in Mbeere is so erratic that no one can be certain about the quantity or timing of the rains.

Using the *panga*, a long knife akin to the machete, Mbeere cultivators break up the soil, planting their favored seasonal crops: maize, beans, pigeon peas, cowpeas, green grams, bulrush millet, and sorghum. Farmers neither plant in rows (because of the difficulty of making neat furrows without a plow) nor cultivate a single crop in one garden. The pattern of intercropping has developed as a strategy for reducing the chances of crop loss due to environmental threats, particularly moisture stress. By not restricting a single crop to one garden, the farmer can spread the risk of loss by cultivating the same plant in different microenvironments represented in multiple garden holdings. Commonly, maize, which has become a preferred crop among the various grains, is grown with cowpeas, pigeon peas, or beans. In the older parishes, particularly, millet or sorghum and either cowpeas or pigeon peas may be planted together. Because of the chronic danger of rainfall failure, even in the newer upland parishes, farmers may plant the more drought resistant millet along with maize.

In recent years, ploughs have been used in the flatter, less stony Zone 1 area by some individuals who have sufficient cash to contract for the service of either a government-owned tractor or a privately owned plough and ox team. Few people can afford the 40 shilling per acre cost of hiring the ox team to plough a previously cultivated field; if much bush has grown on a fallow area which a cultivator is reclaiming, the cost runs to 80 shillings per acre. Rental on the tractor is even more expensive. Planting by hand with the aid of the *panga* thus remains the predominant mode of cultivation. Once the germination of the seeds begins, cultivators spend increasingly long hours in their gardens, devoting themselves to the task of weeding and subsequently protecting the maturing grains and pulses from the depredations of such pests as birds and vervet monkeys. Some people erect wooden platforms in their gardens which they sit atop for hours to survey the crops; from time to time they crack a sort of leather strap or simply hoot to frighten away the animals. Men and young boys frequently make use of the bow and arrow to attack the monkeys which prey on the new crops. Labor expenditure during the planting season is so great that a cultivator who is working a garden beyond the immediate vicinity of the homestead may build a simple hut at the edge of his garden rather than return each night to the main homestead.

During the agricultural cycle, some people may maintain more than one garden under cultivation. But although 75% of 180 informants claim at least two gardens, few would attempt to cultivate more than two in a single season. In peak periods of labor demand, such as during the harvest period following each rainy season, people seek the aid of various categories of kin, both agnates and affines, as well as other neighbors. On a particular day, a group of such helpers gather at the garden to render assistance, and, at the conclusion of the work period, will be paid by their host with several gourds of freshly brewed beer, usually made from sugarcane or honey. The host will be expected to offer his labor, on the same terms, on a similar occasion. In recent years, however, such cooperation has diminished (David Brokensha, personal communication).

Although subsistence agriculture is the prevailing economic mode in Zones 1 and 2, cash crop production has gained momentum in recent years. Cotton and tobacco, particularly, have drawn the most attention in Mbeere. Yet the venture appeals only to a small minority of farmers. Air-cured tobacco, for example, grows well in Nguthi, but the requirements for successfully raising a crop demand careful planning and intensive labor. Farmers must cure their own crop, which necessitates their constructing a tobacco barn--a major outlay in labor because they are typically much larger and elaborate in their construction than the traditional hut for habitation. Many who demur at the construction of the barn and the yearly investment of time in the cultivation and harvesting of a non-food item explain that labor expended on tobacco detracts too much from the more important cultivation of seasonal food crops. The fear of hunger is a persuasive deterrrent to risky activities during the growing season which will not directly eventuate in a food harvest.

Two rainy seasons separated by periods of little or no precipitation establish the rhythm of social and economic life in east central Kenya. The long rains normally commence in March and run their course by the end of May, at which time a dry season begins. By early October, under normal circumstances, the short rains commence continuing periodically through November or December. Thus the Mbeere expectation is for two harvests per year, although these will vary in yield depending almost solely on the quantity and timing of the rains. Marked internal variations in rainfall in Mbeere as well as distinct variations at a single recording station from year to year must also be taken as "normal." All too frequently diminished amounts of rain during a growing season, the irregular occurrence of precipitation in the rainy season, or complete absence of precipitation in the interval between rainy seasons has brought on crop failure and famine.

Reliable rainfall diminishes along an ecological cline running from the northeastern portions of the District, which approach the slopes of Mt. Kenya, to the southern and western portions, which constitute Mbeere Division. In the extreme reaches of the latter area, Zone 3, altitude drops below 2500 feet in the dry Tana River plains where rainfall averages less than 25 inches annually. Embu town, on the other hand, lies at 4790 feet, and its rainfall, although sometimes erratic and widely variable from year to year, averages over 52 inches of rain annually. Yet rainfall in the town plummeted below 35 inches in eight different years between 1930 and 1967 and in two years between 1970 and 1977. During the latter period, the highest annual rainfall, 67.5 inches in 1972, was followed by 33.6 inches in 1973, which approximates the lowest reading of 33.1 inches in 1975.

Intermediate between the extremes of elevation within the district lie two points in Evurore, Kanyuambora and Ishiara, which provide data illustrating both the close connection between rainfall and altitude and the variability in annual rainfall. For the years 1958-72, rainfall at Kanyuambora averaged about 43 inches, but in at least four of those years 35 inches of rain fell. Kanyuambora lies at 3700 feet of elevation some thirty miles east of Embu town. Only five miles east of Kanyuambora along the lower Embu-Meru road lies Ishiara market, yet the ecological differences between the two sites are striking. At an elevation of 2750 feet, Ishiara lies nearly 1000 feet below Kanyuambora, and a similar dramatic attenuation in average rainfall and concomitant reduction in reliability parallels the drop in altitude. For the years 1956-72, Ishiara received an average of 32 inches of rain; during five of those years, it fell below 30 inches, and in three different years below 20 inches. Variations in rainfall at a single station appear most clearly in data for April and November, the expected peaks of the long and short rains, respectively. In Embu town, rainfall ranges from 3.4 inches to 22.3 inches in April, and from 5.2 inches to 25.4 inches in November for the period 1964-69 (Eastern Province Planning Team 1969:1). At Kanyuambora, April rainfall has varied from 3.46 to 20.90 and November rainfall from 8.10 to 20.6 during the years 1967-72. Data on monthly variations in Ishiara are not available. Kiambere market which lies in southeastern Mbeere in Mavuria is intermediate between Kanyuambora and Ishiara on the ecological cline, and rainfall variation for April and November during the years 1967-72 ranges from 0.1 to 14.37 and 4.47 to 18.05, respectively. Table I summarizes the rainfall and altitude data.

A failure or significant decline in rainfall creating widespread loss of crops and hunger marks what the Mbeere term *yūra* (pl. *mayūra*), famine. The

Table 1
Rainfall and Altitude

station	altitude	mean annual rainfall	#yrs. under 30"	#yrs. under 35"	#yrs. under 40"	April range	November range
Embu town	4750 ft.	52 in. (1930-67)	5 of 37	8 of 37	12 of 37	3.4-22.3	5.2-25.4
Kanyuambora	3700 ft.	43 in. (1958-72)	1 of 15	4 of 15	8 of 15	3.46-20.9	8.1-20.6
Ishiara	2750 ft.	32 in. (1956-72)	5 of 17	10 of 17	13 of 17	n.a.	n.a.
Kiambere	3450 ft.	35 in. (1965-72)	2 of 8	4 of 8	6 of 8	0.1-14.37	4.47-18.05

Sources: Embu District Annual Reports 1930-1967
Embu District Agricultural Reports 1956-1967
East African Meterological Department Rainfall Records

These figures are consistent with Porter's contention (1965:410) that in East Africa the general relationship between altitude and precipitation is covariant, and variation in rainfall increases as mean annual rainfall decreases.

frequency of ubiquitous shortages is borne out both by archival records, notably Embu District Annual Reports, and by the Mbeere recitation of famine chronologies. Like the annual age-sets named in commemoration of some noteworthy event affecting Mbeere during the year of formation, particular names commemorate famine periods. For example, in 1971, the last named famine year I recorded (notwithstanding the shortages of 1973, 1975-1976, and the early 1980s), people designated the year as *yūra rīa kīro*, or simply *rīa kīro*, meaning the "famine of the kilo." This name grew out of the government's decision to adopt the metric system, and those fortunate enough to be able to purchase maize did so on the basis of metric weights. Rainfall in that year reached 36.7 and 31.3 inches in Kanyuambora and Ishiara, respectively, only slightly below average for each area. Also, precipitation during the April and November peaks reached 12.5 and 9.09 at Kanyuambora, and 12.3 and 7.7 at Ishiara. These figures for Kanyuambora fall only slightly below averages for the peak months calculated for the years 1965-71; for Ishiara, the 1971 figures exceed averages for the peak months calculated for the years 1961-1971. Rainfall at Kiambere fell below the annual average in 1971, although the April figure far exceeds the average for that month. The following table summarizes this profile:

Table 2

Comparison of Rainfall in Peak Months of Famine Year, 1971, with Averages for Peak Months

	Kanyuambora	Ishiara	Kiambere
April '71	12.5"	12.3"	14.27"
April average	14.1 (1965-71)	7.5 (1961-71)	4.63 (1965-71)
November '71	9.09	7.7	4.5
November average	12.5 (1965-71)	7.1 (1961-71)	9.6 (1965-71)
1971 Total	36.7	31.3	28.44

Despite the importance of adequate rain during the months of the rainy season, precipitation during the remainder of the year is also critically important. In 1971, no precipitation was recorded during the months of January, February, July, August, and September, thus accounting for the famine. Although these months fall in the "dry" season, small amounts of rain must fall during these months in the three sample areas if there is to be a reasonable harvest. Even with moderate rains during the rainy period, previous or subsequent months in which precipitation fails completely will threaten crops owing to insufficient moisture in the soil. Seasonal crops such as the various pulses, millet, sorghum, and maize are most susceptible to moisture stress. During the first six months of 1973, Kanyuambora recorded 17.8 inches of rain against the average of 31.2 inches for that same period; for Ishiara the figures are 11.0 and 18.1, and for Kiambere 13.4 and 18.1. The District Agricultural Officer thus reported grim findings, especially in the lower sublocations. His June 1973 report in part reads:

> The division is out to experience yet another difficult year . . . All the annuals with the exception of one or two types have almost been wiped out of the *shambas* [gardens] by the prevailing drought conditions. The most seriously affected crops included maize, beans, grams, corriander, and cowpeas. From the outlook of the prevailing weather conditions the situation of food continues deteriorating day by day . . . . If the short rains fail, there will be no alternative but to declare the area as a real disaster area (Embu District Agricultural Report, June 1973).

The consequences of ruined annual crops such as those named by the Agricultural Officer are especially serious in Mbeere where they constitute an estimated 80% of general subsistence. In the 1973 drought, for example, most of the Mexico 142 pea bean crop, cultivated for both cash and subsistence in each growing season, perished on the vine; it had limited

53

success at the higher elevations. Of 131 acres planted in Evurore Location during the first half of 1973, 106 acres (81%) were lost. For Mbeere Division, including Evurore, Nthawa, and Mavuria, 1988 of 2571 acres (77%) were ruined (Embu District Agricultural Report, June 1973). Moreover, perennials, unless they are particularly deep rooted trees such as the mango or paw paw, may prove vulnerable to severe drought conditions. During the first half of 1973, the banana, an especially important and valued crop in the upper areas, was "dwindling away in health and vigor in growth" (Embu District Agricultural Report, June 1973). Shortages in supply were apparent in the markets. Finally, desiccation destroyed pasture land and "vegetation favorable for animal consumption" decreased in nutrient value quite consistently (Embu District Agricultural Report, June 1973).

At other times, drought has combined with other natural calamities, such as locust swarms, to devastate crops in Mbeere and beyond. Locusts were particularly destructive in 1928 and 1929. The 1929 Annual Report for Embu District indicates that approximately 90% of the grain crop of Embu and Meru was decimated by the insects and that the partial failure of the long rains further reduced yields (1929:14,58)

Erratic and variable rainfall in east central Kenya has thus led to a series of famines. These can be approximately dated through collation with both official rainfall statistics and District reports documenting food shortages. Some of the names the Mbeere confer on the famines are poignant reminders of suffering regularly endured over the generations. Other names simply recall events taking place at the time of a particular shortage. The famine cycle appears to be roughly every five years, although shorter intervals are not uncommon. Brief shortages may not be named, yet together with outright famine, these periods of hunger appear ubiquitous in Mbeere history. Doubtless certain names escape the memories of informants, as recollections of particular times of hunger become assimilated to accounts of the severest famines in the same manner that the smaller annual age-sets come to be identified with large ones close in time. Variations in the famine names from one part of Mbeere to another also constrain the data available, making the task of constructing a composite chronology difficult. Further, like age-set and generation-set chronologies, famine chronologies are often telescoped; that is, informants may compress chronologies by skipping over particular names. Table 3 presents a composite picture of Mbeere famines or food shortages and their dates, based on informant accounts and documents. Some of these famine names also appear among the Embu (Mwanīki 1973). Normal reference in discourse to a given famine requires prefixing *rīa*, of, to the name, but this has been dropped in the chronology. Little but the names of the four earliest famines is available to date them, but their severity probably marked them as especially memorable. Lambert recorded an Embu account of the Mbaraganu famine which took many lives. He dates the famine to about 1810 on the basis of its co-occurrence in tradition with the investiture of the Iria generation which he establishes through a reconstruction of generation-set succession in postulated intervals of thirty years (1945:397). His dating, however, remains highly speculative.

Table 3

Mbeere Famines and Shortages

Famine	Meaning of Name	Date of Famine or Rainfall	Failure
kīro	kilo Kenya's conversion to metric system.		1971
gatūmba	"isolating the stomach" People did not share.		1964
ndeke	airplanes Food relief brought by air.		1960
Mageneti	Emergency The colonial regime declared it in response to Mau Mau.		1953

55

Table 3   (continued)

Famine	Meaning of Name	Date of Famine or Rainfall Failure
kamavindĩ	short for karĩa mavindĩ They ate bones.	1949
mĩanga	cassava People had only cassava to eat.	1943
thuti	lust for food	1939
njũthĩrĩrĩa	people ate alone	1933
ndorio	scarcity of food	1929
ngige	locusts Locusts destroyed crops.	1928
gatanthoni	end of shame, reserve The quest for food led people to act indecorously to obtain it.	1919
kĩthioro	twist in road It refers to the building of the upper Embu-Meru road.	1918
kavuria	? In Embu Division, it is called Ndwiga wa Ngaara, a personal name.	1909
karĩa ndwara	They ate skins. The famine was part of the East African rinderpest pandemic.	1898-99
ngwaci	sweet potatoes People ate only sweet potatoes.	1893
kathĩrĩ	?	?
kĩng'ang'a	?	?

Table 3 (continued)

Famine	Meaning of Name	Date of Famine or Rainfall Failure
kīverio	no cooperation	?
mbaraganu	?	1810?

Ethnic Relations and the Cycle of Hunger

Here I consider interethnic relationships, reserving for subsequent chapters an analysis of Mbeere social organization and its adaptation to the features of the land and the natural environment I have described. Yet the relationship between the Mbeere and their neighbors -- the social environment -- has also been markedly constrained by ecological factors.

In the precolonial era, periods of hunger prompted both warfare and the quasi-military *tubū*, a trading scheme between the Mbeere and their neighbors. The Mbeere maintained regular contacts with their Kikuyu, Embu, Kamba, and Chuka neighbors, although raids sometimes occurred among these groups. Temporary alliances were also struck to raid another group. Warriors most frequently sought livestock, but also took female captives whom they subsequently married or exchanged for bridewealth. The final raids in this part of Kenya occurred about 1898 when the Kamba made a large foray into Mbeere in order to seize cattle. They crossed the Tana River into what is now Mavuria where they proceeded as far as Nyangwa in the west central part of the Location. Other contingents fought in Evurore. Fighting as they seized cattle, the Kamba ultimately retreated back across the Tana. The Mbeere warriors rallied around the remarkable Ciarūme (a name implying manhood from the masculine root, *-rūme*), a formidable woman who not only had mastered martial skills but also proved a capable leader. They crossed the Tana into Kamba country, and recovered the livestock which had been seized. This episode coincides with a serious famine and rinderpest outbreak which swept Ukambani and portions of Kikuyu, Embu, and

57

Mbeere. Among the Kamba were many women, brought along to help carry off the booty; some were killed but others were captured to be subsequently married to Mbeere men, especially in Mavuria.

Although the Kikuyu and Embu historically raided the Mbeere, a major engagement a few years prior to the Kamba incursions pit the Kikuyu, Embu, and Mbeere against the Chuka. The encounter probably occurred no earlier than 1893. In 1969, a very aged man in Mavuria, a member of the Ngũngi age-set formed about 1892, described the Chuka raid. The martial actions of his age-set are inscribed in its name, Ngũngi, which glosses as "platform," in reference to hiding places constructed in trees from which warriors could launch fusilades of arrows against the Maasai. A brief portion of the old man's account of the Chuka raid follows:

> When we went to raid Chuka, we were mixed with the Kikuyu and Embu so that we could defeat Chuka--to kill them in order to get cattle, goats, children, and women for selling. Our warriors formed six lines with the Kikuyu and Embu. We didn't fight them then because we had joined together. Men went between the lines. These were the war leaders (njama ya ita). Each went through the lines saying, "It is the moon" (nĩ mweri). This was so we wouldn't kill each other mistakenly. The warriors answered, "It is the sun" (nĩ riũa). All war leaders said, "It is the moon," and all warriors answered, "It is the sun." If he delayed in answering, he was killed, even if he were a Mbeere.

> There were people chosen from every parish who formed the njama ya ita. One parish might furnish ten of these people. They were chosen by the warriors to go to a medicine man (mũndu mũgo). He gave them instructions. Warriors came from all over because they were informed by the njama ya ita about the day of the raid. They would assemble on a plain such as Mwea, and the warriors would carry out the medicine man's

instructions: "it is the moon; it is the sun."

We were badly beaten at Chuka. All of our brave warriors were killed. As for myself, I jumped over a small river called Naka. I followed a cow track and separated myself from the other warriors. I wanted them to follow me but they refused, and I followed the cows by myself. I found some people in the trees. The enemy had climbed these trees. It was the Chuka, and I kept quiet. They were talking about how they would kill us. I passed them without saying a word. I went and found a goat in an enclosure of banana leaves. Some people were talking on the other side of the river. I observed them and thought that these were our warriors. Then I shouted, "it is the moon."

They kept quiet. They stopped talking, and I called again, "it is the moon." They all ran toward me. I decided to jump into the river to escape with the current. If I was killed, they would not get my sword and shield which would be washed away. But I jumped over the river. I tell you Ngai [God] was with me. When I did that, they said I was a Maasai. I ran and met some warriors and shouted, "it is the moon; then I heard, "it is the sun." Then I felt good. We fought again. We drove them back; after driving them back a short distance, we were driven back again. After being driven back, a person near me was shot with an arrow. He was a very handsome man (*mūndū mwega*). He was shot dead. We fought to save him, but he did not awaken.

The war leaders charged with organizing and directing the warriors also negotiated the temporary alliances which produced concerted military action such as the Chuka raid. Mbeere war leaders and their counterparts among neighboring Kikuyu, Embu, or Kamba groups could also confront each other with plans for staging a *tubū*, which I shall gloss as "market."

The arrangements both for a market and for a raiding alliance were strikingly similar. In each case, war leaders consulted medicine men (*andū ago*) to determine an auspicious day and to mark out, in the case of the raid, workable strategies which might insure success. For the market, a medicine man prepared magical treatment to guarantee that a large number of people would participate, bringing with them as many goods and foodstuffs as possible. Further, the medicine man sought to insure that the market would remain peaceful; this was a special concern owing to the presence of warriors and war leaders from different, and at times, mutually hostile groups. In striking a temporary accord for trade, Mbeere war leaders trekked to neighboring peoples carrying special sticks painted in alternating bands of red, black, and white with grass separating each color section. The sticks symbolized peaceful intentions, yet in their very designation as *mūraagi*, their potential use as weapons and the very ambiguity of the encounter was recognized. *Mūraagi* represents a play on words, for it is phonetically close to *mūūragi*, the usual term for "killer."

The Mbeere war leaders made overtures particularly to the Kikuyu, Embu, and Kamba, and, for the Mbeere of Evurore, to the Chuka and Mwimbi of Meru. In times of famine and crop devastation, the Mbeere sought to trade livestock for such foodstuffs as beans, sugarcane, bananas, and maize produced by the cultivators of the agriculturally more productive areas closer to Mt. Kenya. The Mbeere also traded iron-rich soil, so common in their territory, to the blacksmiths from neighboring areas; or valued products of the iron-working industry such as axes, produced by the ubiquitous Mbeere blacksmiths, were traded directly. With the Kamba, the Mbeere traded pottery, iron implements, and occasionally millet and sorghum for livestock and sometimes beads.

From time to time, the elaborate preparations of the medicine men and war leaders for a peaceful exchange would prove ineffectual as over-zealous warriors "shocked the market" (*kūmakia tubū*). That is, particular warriors, unable to observe agreed on restraints, might suddenly seize goods and foodstuffs brought by the trading partners without offering items in exchange. Defending their booty by waving swords over the newly accumulated goods, the warriors might kill those who resisted. Although probably a rare occurrence, violent outbreaks required added preparations for future markets. For example, the war leaders from a group feeling itself the victim of treachery and duplicity required assurance, often in the form of a ritual oath from visiting warriors who were sworn to renounce violence through "shocking."

Intended as an economic exchange during times of acute famine, the pre-colonial market grew out of an ecological setting characterized by a complementary although overlapping distribution of resources among neighboring cultivators and pastoralists. Rainfall variations in this part of Kenya, microvariations in ecology, and the exploitation of a variety of cultigens and livestock resulted in a differential impact of famine conditions.

The frequency of famine also prompted migrations, both within Mbeere and beyond. A folk etymology of the term "famine," *yūra*, points to its derivation from the verb *kūūra*, to be lost, or to run away. Thus people not only lose the products of their livelihoods during famine but also migrate in order to find more favorable economic circumstances in areas less stricken by food scarcity. Some Mbeere migrated to Embu, Kikuyu, and Chuka, intermarrying and remaining in the new area. Others betrothed their daughters in these areas in order to get bridewealth. Women represented real wealth, exchangeable for other scarce resources. The Mbeere frequently use the vocabulary of the market place to describe marriage arrangements in which a woman is "bought" (*kūgūra*) or sold (*kwendia*). Affinal ties thus created represented yet another means of striking a relationship which could be exploited in times of scarcity. In some cases, these previously established affinal connections provided the basis for establishing a *tubū* market. The ramifying ties of kinship between the Mbeere themselves and neighboring

61

peoples provided a mode of social reintegration following migration.

Periodically, refugees from famines in Ukambani migrated to Mbeere, settling among local clans and achieving incorporation into Mbeere society through a ritual rebirth known as *gūciarana*, "to be born together" or *gīciaro*. Joining Mbeere clans through ritual means, Kamba migrants acquired land under customary law and settled into local communities as normal residents. The absorption of Kamba migrants was also facilitated when they joined Mbeere clans such as Cīīna, which traces historical connections to Ukambani. The pace of migration into Mbeere and other parts of Embu District picked up considerably in the 1940s, stimulating competition for cultivable land which was previously virtually uncontested.

The man who participated in the late nineteenth century raids into Chuka also actively took part in the market arrangements as both a medicine man and a warrior. Although he states that he did not engage in trading relationships with Meru people, informants from northern Mbeere suggested that such ties were sometimes struck with their geographically close neighbors, the Chuka. The following account focuses on the relationships between the Mbeere and the Kikuyu, Kamba, and Embu.

Since my father was an important man [*mūnene*, literally a big man; a term which has come to mean chief] he produced the medicine (*mūthega*) for making successful markets that would be attended by many people. I too used medicine to produce new markets. The medicine for Kiritiri was produced by my brother; he also produced the medicine for Ngumi. I prepared the market at Nganduri. I also prepared the one beyond Kambevo which was held with Embu people. My family (*mūciī*) was responsible for all of these markets.

To prepare these markets, we first held a meeting as is done today. We chose five or

62

ten war leaders to inform the people of the other group about the market. The leaders painted their sticks and went there. They would go to different homes once they arrived. Each leader went to the home of someone he knew was important. The leaders stayed away for about three days and then returned. They told the other people about the day of the market. These things were done during famines.

When the day came, the people who had food carried very much of it to the market. The medicine was very strong, and so people brought many things to the market. The medicine is still here in my bag. We gave knives, goats, bags, cattle, and axes and got food in return.

If some of the people at the market started a fight, others would run away in fear, leaving what they had brought to the market. The warriors who remained collected the things they wanted. Once when I was a warrior I filled one grain-store (mūrūrū) with food from a market. I sold some of that food and kept some of it for cooking. Two small bags of food cost a goat. I could also buy cattle. One cow cost ten goats, and I could pay ten goats or three or five goats plus some food.

We had these markets with the Kikuyu, Embu, and Kamba. I never witnessed such markets with the Chuka, Tharaka, or Meru. With the Embu we held markets where we could buy sugarcane, yams, arrowroot, bananas, and potatoes. With the Kamba, we held markets where we bought beads, goats, and cattle. I bought three cows from the Kamba. We only went to Tharaka once in order to buy goats, but that was not a market.

When the market was "shocked" people could be killed -- Mbeere, Kikuyu, or others.

Food and goats were seized in quantity. Some people collected goats and goods, then used their swords to defend what they had accumulated. But very soon we would try to have another market with those people. The leaders would again paint their sticks and set off for Kikuyu, Embu, or Kamba. They would persuade the other people to hold a market and would agree sometimes to swear an oath that the new market would not be "shocked." They swore that anyone who "shocked" the market would be punished. And once such an oath was taken, the next market would not be "shocked."

Then there were some people who went to live with those who had food during the famine. They went with their families. Some sold their daughters to Kikuyu men. The people at that place then could not mistreat us because we had sold them our daughters. Other Mbeere went there to live. And we could not mistreat people who supplied us with food.

The person who prepared the medicine for one of these markets got more food than others. If I produced the medicine but was not given what I wanted, I would cause the next market to be "shocked" with my medicine. I still retain that medicine. I shook it saying, "May all the Kikuyu, even those who live far away, attend the market with much food to feed the children of Mbeere." As I shook the gourd, the powdered medicine poured out. Then the Kikuyu attended the market in great numbers.

I was a warrior, and then I was a medicine man. But now we have stopped having markets and wars.

Schneider (1979:90) has recently suggested from his Turu studies a complementarity in the effects of drought on herders and grain producers. Farmers without significant livestock holdings maintain surplus grain supplies which can be sold to herders for maximum gain during droughts. The latter have likely reduced their own production of grain in order to concentrate on their herds from which they can realize higher prices. But in drought, the value of grain appreciates and transactions between herder and grain producer result in a redistribution of livestock as grain is traded, thus producing egalitarian effects. Certainly, the redistribution of goods is a latent theme in my informant's narration. He also emphasizes the high value of grain during the *tubū* market. The Mbeere redistribution also rewarded market organizers disproportionately--the medicine men who insured a successful, non-violent trading cycle and the warrior leaders instrumental in carrying word of the market beyond Mbeere. Through their greater control of goods, they garnered prestige and the possibility of contracting plural marriages and forming independent homesteads. Although economic relations were largely egalitarian, the control of trade by important warriors and elders could effect "big man status." Indeed, the earliest appointed chiefs were drawn from this pool of indigenous *anene*, "big men." As inhabitants of a land best suited to the herding of small stock and rich in iron-bearing soil which supported an extensive forging industry, the Mbeere were geographically well-situated to benefit from trade with their primarily horticultural neighbors, the Kikuyu and Embu. Yet trade also flourished with the Kamba, who were also primarily stockkeepers. The Kamba were a ready source of larger stock as well as goods such as beads, which came up through Kamba country from the coast.

The complex relationship between the Mbeere and their neighbors thus grew out of both competitive and cooperative activities stimulated to a great extent by environmental pressures on the food supply. Warfare and markets provided two modes of resource reallocation during periods of shortage, which also stimulated intermarriage and resettlement within or beyond Mbeere. The "market" in women, especially in famine times, mediated relationships since they were "sold" for food. Cooperation was also facilitated by close linguistic ties, shared customs such as male and female circumcision, and similar organizational features such as patrilineal descent and an age organization. Between Embu and Mbeere, for example, there exist some common age-set names, clans, and generation-sets. Moreover, Mbeere and Embu united during the periodic investiture ceremonies marking the assumption of ritual power by a new generation. This picture thus belies any effort to interpret precolonial interethnic relationships as either pervaded by animosity or integrated without discord. Rather, relationships between the Mbeere and other peoples of Central Kenya, based on an idiom of shared tradition and on ecological complementarity, took shape in their collective response to environmental pressures on resources.

The Mbeere Polity: Age-Sets, Generation Classes, and Elderhood

Prior to European rule, Mbeere political organization conformed to the broad type social anthropologists variously term segmentary, acephalous, stateless, or uncentralized. Under these rubrics are subsumed very different polities including true segmentary lineage systems, such as the Nuer, and age organizations, yet all share an absence of central leadership and formal hierarchy. In Mbeere, principles of agnatic kinship and particularly age organized political relations in the settlement of civil strife and in the maintenance of order. This organization of political relations did not constitute a single overarching framework but rather a series of local arrangements centered in assemblies of elders (*kīama*, pl. *ciama*) throughout Mbeere. It is difficult to define precisely the geographic area from which a council drew its membership and in all likelihood the range of effective action, although highly limited, was variable. This area was certainly co-extensive with the limits of regular social relations, which centered in the homestead, parish, or group of contiguous parishes. Yet occasional matters of broader significance could draw together elders from a more extensive area. A council carried out its activities in a domain probably more narrowly circumscribed than the modern sublocation.

Principles of age institutionalized within an organization of age-sets defined a model of social advancement based on the life cycle, yet it also gave ample scope to the recognition and advancement of men of all ages who showed special abilities. Indeed, Mbeere social structure defined appropriate behavior within a highly flexible framework which could accommodate a range of alternative actions. Thus a man of uncommon rhetorical skill or one especially adept at arbitration might serve in an *ad hoc* assembly, even if he had not yet passed through the elderhood rite. Recognition of the keen political sense of some young men is succinctly stated in the proverb, "Knowledge (in the sense of lore, customary law, and practice) is not exclusive to old age" (*Kĩrĩra tĩ ũkũrũ*). Even generational status, seemingly ascribed at birth, might be manipulated (Glazier 1976a:315). Age-sets took shape for young men 18-20 years old on average, when they underwent initiation rites culminating in circumcision. The sets in different locales cooperated on an *ad hoc* basis for military forays. In no sense did a regular military organization coordinate warrior activity throughout Mbeere, and indeed raiding could occur between different areas within Mbeere.

The initiation rites carried out annually solidified a group of male coevals by celebrating the death of childhood and their collective rebirth as brothers and as adults. Men of a single age-set might address the father of any member as "father," and further extend this term to all the men of the fictive father's age-set. In like manner, the children of any man of an age-set were addressed as son and daughter by that man's age mates, and fraternal solidarity was enhanced by the prohibition of marriage between a man and the daughter of an age mate. Other kinship usages of a particular individual could be taken over by his age mates as the age organization was itself cast in the idiom of descent ideology.

Once formed, a name emblematic of some notable event during the year was conferred on the annual set and, together with other recently circumcised youth, the young men, known as *aanake* (warriors, youth), settled into an indeterminate period of warrior service. After marriage, warriors would retire but would still retain a collective identity commemorated by their unique age-set name and fraternal solidarity. Age-set names are inconsistent from one area to another, further pointing up the numerous local stages for social action. Thus no single "Mbeere-wide" ritual established an age-set, but rather a number of uncoordinated local rituals were significant, at times drawing together Mbeere and Embu in set formation, particularly in geographically transitional areas.

Although age-set formation was predicated on the performance of collective rites, the character of the age-set changed following members' retirement from warrior activity. At that point, the career of an age-set no longer unfolded in corporate activity nor did it advance, as a unit, through higher grades beyond that of warrior. Instead, advancement through age grades occurred individually, depending as it did on particular events in the life cycle of individual age-set members as well as on distinctive individual capabilities. In this respect, the Mbeere age-set system differed markedly from the more corporate organizations characterizing such East African peoples as the Nandi (Huntingford 1953), Arusha (Gulliver 1963), Maasai (Jacobs 1965), Samburu (Spencer 1965), Karimojong (Dyson-Hudson 1966), and other Eastern Nilotes.

At marriage, a young man normally retired from the warrior grade and would enter elderhood *de facto* without any particular rite. Known as *mūthuri* (elder male) rather than *mwanake*, this designation simply recognized his status as a married man. In formal terms, he was not yet recognized as a suitable candidate for the elders' council. But once his eldest child, either male or female, was about to be circumcised, he and his wife would undergo a rite of elderhood known as *kuma kīama* (to come forth from the council). The immediate significance of this rite lay in conferring on the man a formal entitlement to participate in council activities. It did not mark accession to office. As an elder, or member of the council (*mūkīama*), he joined with others in forming a pool of elders from which could be drawn an *ad hoc* assembly to settle disputes. This council, *kĩama kĩa mũcingara*, represented the first level of elderhood beyond which most men did not move.

At a second level, a select group of men of advanced age highly respected for the power of their curse constituted the *kĩama kĩru*, the black council. This name connotes the obscurity of its secrets, opaque to all those who had not been initiated into this council. It was also known as the "council of the ring" (*kĩama kĩa ngome*) because members were identified by the goat skin ring worn on a finger of the right hand. Assemblies drawn from this council might hear especially difficult cases such as those requiring compensation for homicide, or they might administer particularly potent oaths. Although assemblies from both councils made much use of supernatural sanctions embodied in various oath-taking procedures, oaths administered by the higher council were particularly fearsome because those whose age put them closer to death are widely believed to issue especially devastating curses. Their power also derived from a putative sexual purity, for they were believed to be beyond an active sexual life, which, unless otherwise suspended at critical phases of ritual, can vitiate the intended results of symbolic manipulation.

When the *ad hoc* assembly of either council met, it did not constitute a judiciary nor did it function in an executive capacity to enforce decisions. Men in these assemblies exercised influence without the authority of office; they carried out their task through argument, persuasion, and compromise, often backed by the supernatural sanction of their collective curse or the oath of a disputant. Widely respected as they were, councilors from senior age-sets could not even guarantee that the hearing for which they had been called would be held. Individual disputants might simply choose not to appear on the appointed day, thus delaying settlement. Roberts (1965) has noted a close relationship between the existence of such supernatural sanctions and weak secular authority, and this relationship obtained in the Mbeere political order prior to European rule. Although it was possible for elders to endorse the use of physical force by younger

69

war leaders against recalcitrants, this option appears to have been infrequently used as intense public opinion was brought to bear on miscreants. Also, the assembly permitted an airing of mutual grievances and encouraged reconciliation of antagonists, if only in their mutual renunciation, while under oath, of future sorcery. Although the assembly might cite established norms of propriety in their arbitration, the elders were equally constrained by a pragmatic interest in re-establishing social equilibrium without exclusive reference to precedent or binding custom. Practically speaking, arbitration based on precedent would have been very unlikely as each assembly, even within a single parish or group of parishes, was variable in membership since it was the prerogative of disputants to call elders to hear their case. Continuity of assembly membership within a local area nonetheless existed since the value on calling able councilors insured the regular participation of certain individuals. Their objectives in settling disputes inevitably compromised between widely articulated principle and what would be accepted by antagonists.

Agnatic kinship also played a key role in the settlement of disputes within the domestic group or shallow lineage. In these contexts, elders, at once agnates and initiates into the councils of elders, performed their accustomed role as mediators. Such an agnatically-based assembly might be designated a council of the homestead or family (*kīama kīa mucii*); it might set out to restore order and, if necessary, administer oaths in order to re-establish social equilibrium. In these kin-based gatherings, as in other elders' councils, criteria of elderhood and skill combined to qualify one for active participation, which became all the more binding when one's agnates were disputing. Indeed, the principles of seniority and agnation converged in the position of homestead head, *vis a vis* his domestic group. Yet it is not possible to state categorically that only agnates participated in the settlement of domestic or lineage conflict, for a pragmatic flexibility governs the various domains of Mbeere social and political life. Here, rhetorical skill, persuasion, and an ability to reconcile conflicting interests extended a man's reputation well beyond his own parish, and he could be called upon to participate in elders' councils otherwise constituted by a group of agnates. Indeed, flexibility in the Mbeere polity militated against the fulfillment of political roles exclusively based on ascriptive statuses such as position in a kin group or in an age-set or generation-set (Glazier 1976a:319).

Like their Kikuyu and Embu neighbors, the Mbeere gave wide latitude to people of demonstrated ability if they exercised their talent in accord with the public good, which at the same time brought particular individuals immense prestige and recognition. It was a sign of great honor for an elder to be seen returning to his homestead from a legal case carrying a portion of an uncooked goat, which was his due as a councilor. This value on individual action and achievement within the customary political framework set the stage for the protracted conflict between these peoples and the colonial power bent on containing aggressive local initiative, manifested most significantly in the drive for landed entrepreneurship. Although numerous European observers attributed this phenomenon to the encroachment of European ideas and the concomitant attenuation of traditional "communal" values, they little recognized that these indigenous societies were preadapted to the exercise of spirited individualism by virtue of a traditional political system which did not concentrate power or thwart men of recognized ability. Without formal office, authority, such as it was, diffused outward to all men who could, if they were capable, exercise influence with little regard to their position in a kin group or in the age organization.

Anthropologists have conventionally categorized the stateless societies of East Africa in terms of two types. One type, the segmentary lineage, is illustrated by the classic case of the Nuer (Evans-Pritchard 1940), but it also subsumes other Western Nilotic groups such as the Lugbara (Middleton 1965). The second type, based on the presence of an age organization, typically occurs among the Eastern Nilotes. East Africanists have generally agreed that somehow fully developed segmentary lineage systems and cyclical, corporate age organizations do not co-occur

71

within a single society. This is not to say that age
and lineage principles are absolutely dissonant but
rather that "the full and dominant development of the
one is incompatible with the other" (Southall
1970b:184). Thus the Nuer segmentary system co-exists
with an age organization but the latter is little more
than a classificatory device defining seniority and
juniority without any scope for corporate action in any
social field. It is rather the Nuer segmentary lineage
which is functionally significant in shaping political
relations. By contrast, an age organization represents
the fundamental feature of Maasai social structure to
the virtual exclusion of segmentary lineages. In the
Mbeere case, it is less a matter of mutual
exclusiveness between age and lineage principles and
more a question of equally weak principles, especially
in comparison to their respective elaboration among
Eastern and Western Nilotes. The Mbeere most closely
resemble the Embu in this regard (Saberwal 1970), but
they cannot be taken as representative of other Mt.
Kenya Bantu groups, which exhibit considerable
variation in age organization and lineage structure.

The Mbeere age organization encompasses two
distinct sets of principles for recruitment into
independent groups of solidary males. These groups are
age-sets, closely keyed to chronological age, and
generation classes. The generation classes and their
constituent generation-sets were predicated on
genealogical generation so that all of a man's sons,
regardless of their age range, were in his generation
class and in the generation-set immediately below his
own. A single generation-set thus comprised males of
all ages based on the genealogical fact that polygyny
can result in an age range of thirty, forty or even
fifty years between the eldest son of a senior wife and
the youngest son of a junior wife. In the next
generation, age discrepancy can become even more
dramatic, yet genealogical generation remains the basic
principle defining each generation-set. The generation-
set obviously bears no relationship to a particular age
range, even one that is approximate, since the
principle of genealogical generation inevitably links
together men of vastly different ages. At any one
time, two generation classes, internally stratified

into generation-sets, organized sacrifices and exercised primarily ritual and symbolic functions. Dichotomous principles, crystallized in the dual generation classes and in the linking of alternate generation-sets within a single class, closely parallel similar patterns in Eastern Nilotic age organizations, which Southall believes are "particularly compatible with elaborate complementary symbolic identifications, usually dichotomous . . . " (1970b:32). The structure and symbolism of the Mbeere generational system have been described in detail (Glazier 1976a).

Historical relationships and cultural borrowing between the Mt. Kenya Bantu and their relatively close neighbors, the Eastern Nilotes, have long been recognized and without question encompass various features of their age organizations. Thus the Mbeere generation class, Nyangi, is certainly related to the Nandi age-set, Nyongi (Huntingford 1953). The Kikuyu generation, Maina, which appears as one term in the generational alternation, Maina/Mwangi, is also a Nandi age-set. Further the Nandi system consists of seven successive-sets; each of these recruits for fifteen years during which time circumcision rituals initiate new members into the set. After fifteen years and a period of closure, a new set begins recruitment. The sets, such as Nyongi and Maina, maintain unchanging names and reappear every 105 years to begin a new cycle. A likely Mbeere connection to this form of cycling appears in the Thathi generation class where the first named set, Kinyari, appears seven generations later. Having done such historical reconstructions in the 1970s, long after the Mbeere age organization began to fall into disarray and when informants were pressed to recall details that were no longer socially significant, I recognize the highly tentative nature of tracing particular relationships between the Mbeere and their various neighbors. But the general fact of such relationships can hardly be doubted.

In social structural terms, Eastern Nilotic cycling systems and the Mbeere generational system are very different. For the Eastern Nilotes, entry into an age-set was predicated on undergoing the circumcision rite, which normally placed a newly initiated man in the second set following his father's. For the Karimojong, five age-sets, each with a span of five or six years, join together in forming a generation-set. Two generation-sets exist at any particular time, and they are complemented by two additional generation-sets which eventually succeed the extant ones, thus forming a continuing cycle of four generation-sets (Dyson-Hudson 1966:156). For both the Nandi and Karimojong, the cycling of age-sets or their grouping into larger units brings chronological age and generation into line. But as noted for the Mbeere, the generational system is severely skewed, emphasizing genealogical generation leading to generation-sets which include males ranging in age from infants to the very elderly. Bearing no relationship to demographic factors or to chronological correlates of seniority and juniority, generation-sets and their parent generation classes instead represent the object of much symbolic manipulation related to complementary dualism, alternation between rain and drought, and totemic representations of the seasons (Glazier 1976a:319-325).

Independent of the generational system and more immediately articulated to issues of political order were the age-sets. Known in Kimbeere as *irua*, which literally means circumcision, an age-set was constituted of young men circumcised in the same three to five year period. Informants claimed that an age-set was named and recruitment to it closed when elders so determined. They cited military considerations as the important factors constraining decisions about recruitment. Certain sets which were particularly large or well-known might lend their names to temporally adjacent sets, thus blurring distinctions between contiguous groups. Women circumcised during a particular period would also take the name of the age-set, but as organizations of male warriors emphasizing life-long fraternal solidarity of initiates, the age-sets were decidedly male institutions. Taking the name of a notable event, personage or natural phenomenon marking the year of initiation, the set assumed a position of seniority or juniority in relationship to all other annual sets, and a set maintained its

74

collective identity during the life span of its members. Unlike the named generation-set, which changed its designation during its movement from junior to senior to retired status, and also maintained an alternation name, the age-set ultimately became known by a single, unique name as distinctive as the object it commemorated. Moreover, the age-set provided a ready means of establishing the relative chronological ages of men in a society where principles of seniority and elderhood were instrumental in shaping the character of social relations. A man's age was, in effect, his age-set designation, slotting him into a group which assumed its place in the chronological sequence of sets. Circumcision, and hence entrance into an age-set, represented the *sine qua non* for the attainment of full political rights and jural adulthood. A man was then recognized as a legitimate potential founder of an independent homestead and ultimately could participate in councils.

In keeping with the flexibility which informs so much of Mbeere culture, rights and duties associated with particular age statuses might be operable before an individual had ritually attained the appropriate position. Thus a strong uncircumcised youth, who had not yet been initiated because his family was unable to begin the cycle of prestations these events required, could nonetheless be called on to serve as a warrior. Such an occurrence was certainly no more extreme than the activities of the famous woman warrior, Ciarūme. The period of warrior service, ideally encompassing the time between circumcision and marriage, might also extend to young married men, especially if local demographic factors created a shortage of warriors.

Following the organization of a newly formed age-set and its consignment to the warrior grade, particular Mbeere age-sets could no longer be identified with fixed age grades, as the life cycles of individuals within a set became the arbiters of movement into elderhood positions. Set identity was not invoked to legitimate participation in an elders' council; only the fact of elderhood itself came to represent the major social criterion for participation.

75

Is it possible to account for the Mbeere system of non-collective advancement of individuals from warrior to elder grades in contrast to the corporate movement of age-sets among the Eastern Nilotes? Within any homestead or domestic group, the attitudes and relationships between a father and his sons and between older and younger brothers reiterate the patterns defining the relationship between seniors and juniors in the age organization. Since men of a given age-set consider themselves like brothers and in turn consider men of their fathers' sets as fathers, the usages built up in the domestic circle provide the model for age organization relationships. It is perhaps for this reason that men who have established independent homesteads wherein they become senior males *ipso facto* enjoy the greatest prestige and seem to predominate on elders' councils. In noting a similar pattern in the Kikuyu data and taking a social structural approach, Eisenstadt remarks that the domination by family heads of activities associated with elderhood indicates that "the two integrative principles, the one based on age and the other on family seniority, are incompatible, one negating the other" (1956:127). This view anticipates similar positions of Southall (1970), Baxter and Almagor (1978), and Schneider (1979), although the latter, especially, also considers ecological factors. In other words, to the extent that an individual over the course of his life is increasingly implicated in the affairs of family, domestic group and lineage, the role of his age-set, apart from age grading per se, correspondingly diminished.

Moving beyond the familiar social structural arguments about incompatibility of age and descent principles, I would argue that ecological factors may account for the non-corporate character of Mbeere age-sets. A mixed economy of horticulture and herding with reliance on small stock rather than cattle represents the key feature shaping the Mbeere system. The specific needs of small stock as opposed to cattle complement sedentary cultivation because small stock do not require extensive pasturage that for cattle usually necessitates periodic transhumance. Small stock, especially goats, subsist well on scrub vegetation, as they "browse by preference, even where grass is present and use far less water than cattle . . ." (Dyson-Hudson 1966:58). As a result, a migratory pattern is not essential for keepers of small stock, which can remain in settled areas through the year, including the driest periods. Moreover, special efforts to protect small stock at night need not be taken as the animals of normal herd size can be kept inside huts within the homestead. Cattle, by contrast, must be kept in special kraals built in order to protect the animals from predators. Small stock thus require less specialized labor output and do not call for the services of young men to take the stock to distant pasture or water. Small stock, by contrast, are best herded around the home throughout the year, and sheep and goats predominate in Mbeere herds. Informants further emphasize the Mbeere trade in goats rather than cattle at the periodic *tubū* markets and how small stock were the usual medium of sacrifice.

Given the dominant role of small stock over cattle, the military role of Mbeere age-sets ought not to be overemphasized. The age based cattle-oriented societies of East Africa, including those with substantial numbers of small stock, focus their raiding activities on cattle as these animals represent repositories of greater value than do goats and sheep, which increase more rapidly. Slaughter of the latter also impinges on fewer social relationships owing to their small size and highly limited range of distribution. Mbeere warriors were as likely to act as a local military force facilitating or deterring various efforts at self-help as they were to engage in long distance raids for cattle.

The cattle-keeping complex which shaped the values and social organization of many Eastern Nilotic people was thus transformed by the Mbeere into a horticultural/small stock economy which placed a premium on the close and continuing attachment of young men to their domestic groups while maintaining at least some martial values as much related to ideas of maleness and circumcision as to actual military forays. Domestic groups have been the locus of economic life,

77

and a young man's goal of becoming an independent homestead head is constrained by the need to gain small stock, especially for bridewealth, from his father. Unlike the common tendency of Eastern Nilotic peoples at certain times of the year to merge herds belonging to separate stock-holding units for purposes of common pasturage, small stock within Mbeere remain in distinct herds controlled within single homesteads. There are no occasions for a number of herds to be joined since goats and sheep do not require a transhumant cycle. A young man sees to his own best interest by sustaining continuing bonds with his agnatic line. Mbeere age-sets thus organized themselves without pulling against agnation and the manifold constraints of a farming and small stock economy controlled by senior males of domestic groups.

The forces of change, particularly the creation of chiefs and other forms of political hierarchy, rapidly undermined the age organization. Writing of the Mbeere age-set system in 1945, Lambert remarks that Mbeere elders claimed that "the whole system has now fallen into disuse owing to the virtual demobilisation of the warriors and the modern disinclination of youth to be regimented" (1945:434). Although youths circumcised up to the early 1950s might still receive a commemorative name, the formal age-set organization, replete with customary responsibilities of a military nature, had been on the wane for at least two decades prior to Lambert's remarks. Not bound to their sets by a succession of collective rituals advancing coevals through the various grades, Mbeere males, in contrast to their Eastern Nilotic counterparts, could more easily enter into the emerging system of patron-client ties coming to define the relationship between chiefs and headmen, on the one hand, and their constitutents, on the other.

Chiefs and headmen early on had to contest their position with elders whose customary role fell under the shadow of these newly empowered political appointees. The elders exercised an informal advisory role *vis a vis* the chiefs and headmen but only enjoyed formal recognition by the government for a brief time, although the government regularly looked to the elders for various pronouncements on law and custom in support of policy. Young men, on the other hand, were caught in the struggle between elders and chiefs and served as chiefly retainers and messengers. Attempting to gain from their association with the imposed authority while also deferring to the elders, young men who would have entered warrior service a short time before began to seek aggrandizement in new ways. Where warrior service might have propelled them into "big man" status through control of goods secured in raiding or in the *tubū* markets, patronage from a chief or headman might also elevate one's position.

Elders continued their attempts to exercise control over their juniors as in periodically defining which junior age-sets were permitted to drink beer. It is probably for this reason that elders of Mavuria, hoping to influence their new chief in 1912, supported eighteen year old Kombo over a considerably older candidate (Embu Political Records 1912:103). Also, pressure for a lower circumcision age to increase the labor supply of young men forced youth into the colonial economy at the expense of their participation in age-set activities. Mbeere herds, unlike those of the Maasai, were never of sufficient size to insulate large numbers of men from the labor market; that is, the Mbeere had too few animals to convert into cash for tax payment. Their labor thus helped chiefs in meeting government demands while at the same time assisting their families in meeting tax payments, thus further bonding youth to their homesteads and agnatic lines. In this way, the latter principle was strengthened at the expense of the horizontal ties of age, and the elders' efforts to dominate young men was correspondingly diminished as the latter entered an expanding social field.

The Establishment of Colonial Rule: Local Political Change and the Eclipse of the Age Organization.

Two military expeditions, in 1904 and 1905, set out to establish colonial rule in Embu District, but that goal was not accomplished until a final punitive patrol was launched in 1906 (Low 1965:25-26). According to Mungeam (1966:161-162), efforts to establish a government station were immediately prompted by two considerations. First, some Mbeere had gone to Murang'a (a Kikuyu District more often known as Ft. Hall in colonial times) as a delegation seeking protection from the government. When they were returning home, an Embu raid decimated their party. Second, two separate European partnerships were seeking leases on forested areas of Mt. Kenya contiguous to Embu territory, and authorities in Murang'a believed that a government station was essential before these could be granted. The Embu station would thus protect European interests and indigenous people ready to accept the government. Embu resistance would therefore have to be quashed. The government also claimed that the Embu were themselves boasting that they were too powerful to be subdued. According to my Mbeere informants, the Embu were very resistant to Europeans, whom the Embu believed to be uncircumcised and therefore weak. Some Mbeere also claim that in response to a European request to the Embu that they not fight, the Embu responded by sending a large bag of finger millet and claiming that their warriors were as numerous as the grains of millet. The Mbeere also say that Embu bravado even extended to discounting gunfire as no more than the popping of maize kernels the whites were roasting. The Embu soon learned the catastrophic results of attacking men armed with guns. After a month of moving through Embu country and putting down all resistance, the European expedition killed 407 Embu and confiscated 3180 cattle and 7150 small stock (Mungeam 1966:163).

Shortly after the expedition of 1906, one of the earliest official accounts of the people of the Embu-Mbeere area appeared as a letter to the Principle Secretary of State for the Colonies. The writer described the countryside and the response of the inhabitants to the establishment of British rule following the recent patrol's success in putting down the last armed resistance. Having set off from Murang'a, the author met with various groups as he traversed the District from Kutus (a small trading center named for Chief Gūtū) to Karue, a dramatic

granite hill which surveys the vast expanse of
territory from Mt. Kenya southwest through the lands of
the Embu and Mbeere:

> On the 17th (August) I arrived at Kuroki
> [sic] Hill, a well-marked bluff in a commanding
> position in the Embu country, from which a
> magnificent view of the whole country from the
> Kenya Forests to the Tana and the Mumoni Hills
> was obtained. A number of elders and their
> people had come in to meet me. To these I
> spoke at length on their behavior since our
> occupation of the Province which had finally
> necessitated our taking action against them.
> They were informed that so long as they hold at
> peace with each other and their neighbours they
> would have nothing to fear, but that we were
> determined to put a stop to their cutting up
> caravans, raiding women, and attacking all who
> approached them. They admitted their past
> misdeeds and promised to behave well in the
> future, to admit caravans to their country and
> to cease from molesting neighbouring tribes.
> They seemed satisfied when I told them that a
> veil would be drawn over the past and that they
> would be admitted as children of the Government
> . . . It is a peculiarity of the Kikuyu and
> kindred tribes that once they are conquered and
> have admitted our superiority they settle down
> once and for all and become good subjects . . .
> (Public Record Office, Colonial Registry,
> August 31, 1906).

Yet fearing a reversion to "their former condition
simply from absence of any sign of authority over
them," the writer urged the establishment of a
government station near the Rupingazi River, replete
with a company of King's African Rifles. Around this
station subsequently grew Embu town and District
Headquarters. Thus began the long period of colonial
rule which transformed the texture of social life
beginning with the cessation of armed encounters
between various peoples of the District.

Not the least of these changes was the centralization of authority and the creation of a political hierarchy of local subchiefs and chiefs, who served under the European District Commissioner. Moreover, at the beginning, councils at several levels of administration were built on a customary form (the *kĩama*) and gained official recognition in their support of the chiefs and subchiefs. As the head of an administrative apparatus which the British attempted to construct out of what was perceived as indigenous authority, the District Commissioner could actively intervene in local affairs, as he wielded powers considerably beyond the ideal of indirect rule.

Pre-colonial political power among the Embu and Mbeere, distributed as it was among age-set elders who were also homestead heads, concerned some of the earliest European observers critical of peoples whose political institutions diffused rather than concentrated power. Customarily, political action depended not so much on one's ability to coerce through force or through the authority of office but rather on one's ability to influence people and on his attainment of elderhood. Elderhood underpinned the customary political system built largely on unquestioned gerontocratic principles. Above all, the early Europeans were struck by a seeming power vacuum they regarded as enigmatic; it was unacceptable as a base on which they might erect a colonial edifice. The previous writer, for example, in describing the Embu noted that

> their tribal constitution is defective as the chiefs and elders are not always obeyed . . . The absence of influential chiefs will possibly be a difficulty in the way of administration at first but administration will be introduced gradually and with a District Officer permanently established in the country and with a small force to support his authority this difficulty will soon be overcome, and these tribes up country should settle down as the other natives in the Province have done (Public Record Office, Colonial Registry, August 31, 1906).

An observer in 1926, even more explicit about the problems of administration in an acephalous polity, compared the peoples of Kenya unfavorably to the Baganda, whose centralized political structure represented a model for the imposition of indirect rule:

> The indigenous system of government in Kenya previous to British occupation was of a very nebulous character. Functions of government were . . . performed by irregular chieftains and indeterminate Councils of Elders . . . Nowhere in Kenya was there any chief who could command the respect accorded to the Kabaka [of Buganda], nowhere was there any ready made organization which could be converted into an administrative machine (quoted in Read 1972:173-174).

With the imposition of an alien administration backed by irresistible force, people of Embu District settled into an accommodation, sometimes uneasy, with the new authority.

After the establishment of the Embu station in 1906, the colonial regime set out to organize local administration along the lines previously laid down in Kikuyuland. The government appointed as headmen noteworthy individuals who commanded respect in their local areas. Yet in no sense had these men been chiefs exercising authoritarian rule over wide areas prior to the intrusion of the Europeans. They entered the civil administration as salaried public servants directly accountable to the District Commissioner and possessed of political power theretofore unknown. A 1911 report from the Embu District Commissioner to the Provincial Commissioner on the capabilities of various Mbeere chiefs emphasizes their role as tax collectors and reserves for special praise those who could perform this task promptly and with a minimum of opposition from their people. In these early days, the difficulties of an appointed chief or headman (subsequently called subchief) asserting his authority over a population unaccustomed to such coercive

83

importuning were apparent in periodic popular resistance to tax payment. In April, 1910, the Assistant District Commissioner, Orde-Browne, who ironically would write *The Vanishing Tribes of Kenya* (1925), launched a punitive expedition resulting in the burning of a number of huts in Kathera Sublocation (Evurore). Occasional local opposition to administration seems to have continued until 1913. Those chiefs capable of controlling "turbulence" in their areas or, more likely, who happened to administer people resigned to the government from the outset, were particularly valued and received special praise in district reports.

The new administration initially established the councils of elders as a judiciary and as an advisory body to chiefs and headmen. But after a brief period of participation by chiefs in council judicial activities, (sanctioned by the Native Authority Ordinance of 1908), chiefs officially lost their judicial responsibilities, which had been extensive. Phillips, in his excellent report on native tribunals, notes for this early period that "although the jurisdiction of a 'council of elders' was recognized, the influence of the chief seems usually to have been dominant" (1944:14). The formal proscription of the judicial role of chiefs and headmen was sanctioned by the Native Tribunal Rules of 1911 and the Native Authority Ordinance of 1912 in an effort to return authority to the elders' councils. In so doing, the colonial administration recognized chieftaincy as an alien institution and thus attempted a closer approximation of the ideals of indirect rule. Under the influence of the new Governor, Girouard, who had previously served in northern Nigeria (Sorrenson 1967:45), the Attorney General wrote in 1912:

> Only such Councils of Elders as are constituted under and in accordance with native laws and customs and are recognized by the Governor can exercise jurisdiction over the members of a native community. No change in the constitution of a native tribunal should be made except with the concurrence of the members of the community affected (quoted in Phillips 1944:14).

84

The Native Tribunals, organized by division, gained formal recognition and were "entrusted with the settlement of all civil disputes between natives with slight powers in criminal cases" (Embu Political Records 1911). The tribunals, like the *ad hoc* councils they were modeled on, settled cases through customary law. Yet ironically, the divisional tribunals, established after 1910 in an attempt to institute a purer form of indirect rule, differed in important ways from the traditional councils, which were restricted in authority, informal, and very numerous. Their locus of action was highly circumscribed and, as *ad hoc* assemblies, the elders' positions as councilors did not exist beyond the hearing of a particular case. By contrast, all of Mbeere was represented by a single Native Tribunal, more formal in its constitution and predicated on a fixed membership quite unlike the organization of elders' councils. And in its procedures, the Native Tribunal utilized judicial and punitive powers far in excess of those exercised by the traditional councils with their customary emphasis on mediation, restitution, and reconciliation.

Although a growing specialization of district administration into judicial and executive functions remained the ideal, chiefs continued to intervene in the activities of tribunals. Phillips remarks that chiefs after the 1911-12 reforms

> still retained their executive power and were inclined to resent the curtailment of their authority in regard to judicial matters. The result was that the tribunals still tended to be subservient to the headmen, and if they did try to assert their independence they found themselves powerless to enforce their judgments (1944:14).

In regard to Embu District in particular, a statement by the District Commissioner, Lindsay, in 1935, stressed the significant power of the chiefs in matters of appointment to the tribunals:

The elders now forming the existing tribunals
are really chosen by the chiefs and
missionaries, however much we like to think
that they are elected in open *baraza* [public
meeting] by the people. They are composed of
pagan and mission members who often have no
recognition as qualified adjudicators in the
eyes of the people. Owing to the system
whereby certain members are elected by specific
communities (e.g., pagan, Protestant, Roman
Catholic) these members show a tendency to
regard themselves as champions of their
community interests rather than as
disinterested adjudicators (quoted in Phillips
1944:79).

Moreover, the influence of chiefs and subchiefs
continued to be felt in the informal councils of elders
which attempted to mediate minor disputes, although
these truly indigenous institutions were not part of
the civil administration after 1910. They would never
again play a formal role in the machinery of government
despite efforts to duplicate their functions in the
tribunals.

By 1924, tendencies toward centralization and
specialization in the civil administration grew even
stronger with the passage of a new Native Authority
Ordinance. It created the Local Native Council (LNC)
as a district-wide governing body composed of chiefs
and other district representatives appointed by the
District Commissioner, who also presided over the
Council. At its inception, the Embu LNC drew eight
representatives from Mbeere including Chiefs Kombo,
Rumbia, and Njamburi of Mavuria, Nthawa, and Evurore
Locations, respectively. Also on the Council were
chiefs and other elders representing the other peoples
of Embu District. The 1924 Ordinance concentrated
government, enabling it to work through a single body
meeting regularly at District Headquarters in Embu town
rather than through the various elders' councils
scattered throughout the District. The District
Commissioner's authority in Council appointments and
his presiding role insured that the LNC would be a
tightly controlled instrument of the government. The

elders' councils continued in an advisory and consultative capacity for chiefs and subchiefs, but their customary influence was diminished both by chiefship itself and the Mbeere tribunal. The LNC, with the District Commissioner as President, further increased its responsibilities when it evolved into the African District Council in 1951 under the sanction of an Ordinance of the same name. Like its predecessor, the African District Council (ADC) consisted of the President and African members, many of whom were nominated by the District Commissioner; it continued to address local concerns such as taxation, famine relief, marketing and trade, education, health, roads, and agriculture. The ADC eventually grew into the contemporary County Council, the elected district governing body. The power and control of intrusive government thus impressed itself on the Mbeere and other peoples of the District from the earliest days of the colonial era. The comment of a member of the LNC following an earthquake in 1927 is emblematic of the widely held view of government power. Because the people found the event very disturbing, he urged official action to prevent a recurrence of the tremor.

District administrative control extended from the LNC to the judiciary (tribunals), which was part of the local government rather than the court system. Only in the 1960s did local judiciaries become incorporated into a national court system, thus overturning an old dual structure established in colonial days. Although local councils persisted into the independence period, they served only in an informal advisory and mediating capacity with little authority. Since early in the colonial period, their customary role has increasingly been curtailed by the emergence of new legal and executive institutions.

Accordingly, the balance of location power shifted dramatically to the side of the chiefs who could easily dominate the local elders' councils and the tribunal. Chiefs continued to intervene in local disputes, although they were officially enjoined not to do so once the Mbeere tribunal was set up. Decisions of the latter were ultimately unenforceable without the support of the chief. The power of chiefs could also be exercised through the LNC, for they were among its most active members. The 1939 District Handing Over Report, for example, indicates the extent to which chiefs dominated the LNC and exercised power in their own constituencies. District Commissioner I. R. Gillespie thus noted that of 17 LNC members (9 nominated, 8 elected), 13 were chiefs. He also stated, without further explanation, that people felt unhappy about the disproportionate number of chiefs on the LNC yet did not like to vote against them. Empowered with coercive authority to make arrests and to seize property, namely livestock, in default of taxes, chiefs gave an entirely new dimension to political relations in transforming the previous diffuse, gerontocratic order. Each chief's camp became an outpost of the central district administration, which maintained a taut rein on its appointed chiefs for whom tenure in office was immediately contingent on effective exercise of authority in collecting taxes, conscripting labor, and maintaining order.

As a chief's power depended on support from the District Commissioner and the civil administration, it also was bolstered from below by a cadre of local supporters. At the outset of colonial rule, District Commissioner Horne instituted a system of "tribal retainers" (*njama*). The term *njama* in certain vernacular contexts (e.g., *njama ya ita*, war leaders) connotes a military role also made clear in its Swahili rendering, *askari*, soldier, which appears in various District reports. These retainers made arrests on behalf of chiefs and also served as messengers between District Headquarters and outlying locations (Embu District Record Book 1907-1946:98). As they received gratuities and acted predominantly in the service of the administration at its lowest level, the retainers began to act independently of the elders' influence, thus arousing popular suspicion. Moreover, as agents of the headman, or subchief, to whom the *njama* reported, the latter were locally regarded as spies, or at least as individuals who could not be trusted. Their growing independence from customary constraints was marked no more dramatically than in conflicts over their consumption of alcohol, which had traditionally been controlled by the elders, who permitted drinking only for retirees from warrior service. The third meeting in 1925 of the newly formed LNC expressed this concern in noting that "in the old days, drunkenness was not common because of fear of raids now . . . not a threat" (Local Native Council Minutes 1925). A resolution was passed mandating a 30-shilling fine or one month in jail if men of particular age-sets (younger than Gatumo which was initiated about 1918), not yet given permission to drink by the LNC, consumed alcohol. Despite the resolution, supported by Kombo and other chiefs, the LNC noted over the years that many violations occurred as it continued to rule periodically on which age-sets were entitled to drink beer. But such rulings were in effect no more than a recognition of a *de facto* state of affairs. Other tensions between elders and young people, including retainers, surface periodically in official records, and these range from concern about the younger men seducing women (Embeere [sic] Record Book, Division III 1915-1918) to the spread of European dancing "with a consequent breakdown in manners and customs" (Embu Local Native Council Minutes, January, 1941:9). Although the chiefs lamented widespread drinking as well as other problems, they nonetheless became the direct beneficiaries of the loosening of customary controls these changes respresented.

Not only did the institution of chieftaincy weaken the councils of elders and indeed the very principle of elderhood itself, it also provided the basis for a new system of stratification with chiefs usually rising to the top. They were among the first individuals to receive a regular salary, although it is highly unlikely that their economic success rested solely on a monthly wage. Embu salary schedules were likely very similar to those described for the Kikuyu chiefs whose official earnings were pitifully small in light of their responsibilities (Tignor 1976:53-54). The Mbeere chiefs, like their Kikuyu counterparts, grew wealthy through accumulation of livestock, land, and unofficial gratuities exacted from individuals seeking some favor. Moreover, Kombo of Mavuria, as well as a number of Evurore chiefs, were able to become polygynists (although few men are) which added to their personal domains through wide-ranging affinal alliances and bridewealth payments from the marriages of their daughters. Kombo toward the end of his life had thirty wives, a shop in Kiritiri market, and two homes--one near Kiritiri market and one in Mwea, where he kept most of his livestock. When former Evurore chief Mwandiko, who had six wives, early in 1970 mused to Kombo about the possibility of investing in a bus as a prudent way to make money, Kombo demured by saying women are the best buses. He meant, of course, that daughters borne of many wives are an even more valuable investment, for they not only are vital in the portage of water, firewood, and other items of the domestic economy but they also marry in exchange for cash. But this bit of traditional wisdom followed his own manifold successes over the course of forty-seven years in a very untraditional position.

In Evurore, the considerably less triumphant careers of a succession of chiefs could hardly match Chief Kombo's extraordinary tenure, marked by active collaboration with the civil administration and strong control over his location. In one way or another, various Evurore chiefs, from the earliest days up to the 1950s, managed to run afoul of the government. Eight Evurore chiefs served from the beginning of colonial rule to the eve of independence. In the same period, Mavuria was served first by Kombo's father, Mūnyīrī, who died in 1912; then Kombo assumed the chiefship and dominated the office until 1959, when he was succeeded at his retirement. The various District Political Record Books and the Annual Reports are elliptical about the shortcomings of particular chiefs and simply indict them with charges of "inability to obey orders (Embu District Annual Report 1941:2-3), "ineptitude," or "rumours . . . of irregular activities" (Embu District Annual Report 1946:2). But some of these chiefs were not without personal successes. Chief Samson, for example, remained in office from the turbulent days of Mau Mau up to independence and, in so doing, used the Mbeere African Court to make large land claims in Nguthi. During the early 1960s, he and his clanmates were embroiled in a series of court cases, all of which they won. At the same time, the Chief's classificatory brother was one of two court members rendering decisions, and the

90

Chief's son was the court recording secretary and sometime court member. These aggrandizements resulted in a highly factionalized community in upper Nguthi, where the Chief and his kin cultivated and made their homes. The antagonisms continued into the land reform period when these important court decisions became pivotal in guaranteeing the success of the Chief and his agnates in the land adjudication proceedings.

The institution of chiefs directly altered the political fabric of precolonial life and was closely associated not only with an emerging system of economic stratification but also with other sources of factionalism. For example, chiefs also played an important role in assisting the activities of missionaries, who created enduring schisms throughout the District. The LNC had to approve applications for the building of mission stations and schools, and the chiefs, most of whom were non-Christian, cooperated or at least passively assented. A more typical response, consistent with the emerging pattern of chiefly power and patronage, was the attempt by chiefs actively to control missionary influence, albeit indirectly, by coopting those converts especially esteemed by the missionaries. In its 1935-36 Annual Report, for example, the Church Missionary Society noted that Rev. Comely of Embu District found many problems regarding "beer drinking and heathen customs," especially in Mbeere where "a recent development is that a chief will appoint a capable leader, who is a Christian, to be a headman or to do some work for him." The report continues by noting that "in distant districts, the churches may be influenced in this way, and their hands weakened" (1935-36:62).

No Mbeere chiefs after the first two decades of colonial rule actively opposed missionary activities, although these were not as extensive as in neighboring Kikuyuland. The female circumcision issue shows the full extent of chiefly compliance with missionary pressure exerted through the colonial administration. Chiefs certainly collaborated with the administration in numerous other contexts, but the circumcision issue is particularly pertinent in showing the willingness of chiefs to repudiate, verbally if not in practice, even the most integral features of customary life.

Throughout the colonial period, missionary condemnation of various practices reached its most impassioned level in regard to female circumcision. Attacks on female circumcision among the Kikuyu did much to politicize the population and provided one basis for the earliest anti-colonial political movements and breakaway churches in Central Kenya (Kenyatta 1938; Rosberg and Nottingham 1966). Missionary outrage, if less sustained than in Kikuyuland, was nonetheless felt in Embu District and acted on by the administration. In 1930, the LNC directed registered female operators to restrict their cutting to the removal of the clitoris only while leaving the surrounding tissue intact (Local Native Council Minutes 1930). In an effort to give this LNC by-law even more force, the administration in 1932 secured the support of "ruling elders," that is, the senior members of each generation class. The support of generation class elders seemed especially important to the government since 1932 witnessed the accession ceremonies of juniors into senior status within the Thathi class and seemed to present an opportunity for the reiteration of customary rules. Their support would bring "tribal custom" into accord with administration policy. But missionary condemnation, even of the limited operation restricted to registered circumcisers, continued. Without any overt opposition from the Embu District chiefs, the government was eventually persuaded to ban the operation altogether. It was only expedient for such defenders of tradition as Kombo, who staunchly believed in the importance of female circumcision, to concur in its interdiction. In 1956, the operation was proscribed in an Embu African District Council Resolution which stated that "this Council prohibits the uncivilized practice of female circumcision in Embu District and declares it henceforth to be an offense against native law and custom" (Embu African District Council Minutes, November, 1956:4). In reality, no rite was more consistent with customary practice nor more infused with moral imperative. Accordingly, it was driven underground, for operators and ritual participants faced fines and prison sentences. Christians at least nominally supported the ban and condemned as backward those who practiced the operation. After only two years, the prohibition was rescinded for "public opinion couldn't accept the female circumcision ban [and] jails were filled" (Embu District Annual Report 1958:5). This episode is the starkest example of administrative naiveté in attempting to justify policy fiats in terms of "native law and custom." The division of local opinion about the value of female circumcision is indicative of the schisms created by missionary influence in communities already growing factionalized over land issues and chiefly patronage.

An old man of the Ngungi ya Itara age-set. Initiated
in the 1890s, this set mobilized warriors for the final
livestock raids before the establishment of British
rule in Embu District.

Ex-senior Chief Kombo wearing several medals awarded
him by the colonial government.

A notable elder

Honey being transferred from a collecting container to a tin.

Grandparents and grandchildren in their sorghum garden in lower Nguthi.

A Kanyuambora man gathering up beans in a half-calabash.

Women planting maize in expectation of the long rains.

Girls beating millet to separate grains from the unusable portions.

A woman grinding millet.

An elder in council.

Elders pondering the anthropologist's diagrams of the age organization.

Chapter Three

Domestic Groups

In the last chapter, I examined how environmental
factors, particularly erratic rainfall and consequent
famine or shortage, constrained Mbeere relationships
with their neighbors and affected the incidence of
warfare, *tubū* markets, and marriage across ethnic
boundaries. Mobility has been a major theme in Mbeere
history and, until recent decades, limited attachment
to the land. In this chapter, I discuss the social
organization of production and reproduction. I examine
social relationships within a much more restricted
social field, namely, the domestic group. The
distinction between domestic group and non-localized
kin group, which I take up in the next chapter, is now
a familiar one in social anthropology. It follows
Fortes's analytical distinction between the domestic
and the politico-jural domains (1958). What is at
stake here is the difference between the internal
organization and activities of a group and its external
relationship to other groups of the same or different
social scale. The domestic group is "the workshop . .
of social reproduction" (1958:2) and insures continuity
through a cyclical process which confers social meaning
on birth, maturity, and death. The developmental
process in the domestic group culminates in its own
social demise and subsequent replacement by other
domestic groups. Each domestic group is further
enmeshed in a web of institutions--the politico-jural
domain--transcending the purely domestic field of
social relations yet influencing these relations. Thus
these social fields, although analytically separable,
interpenetrate, and in regard to the politico-jural
domain established through patrilineal descent and
common interest in land, the developmental cycle of the
domestic group provides a model of social segmentation
which the Mbeere use in thinking about and discussing
lineage relations. But for the present I am concerned
with how the Mbeere organize themselves on the ground,
so to speak, how domestic groups are founded, how
property is allocated and used within the domestic

105

group, and how social roles operate for production and consumption in this domain.

In the present chapter, I am also concerned with the nature of change in the domestic group. It has become axiomatic in social anthropology that an understanding of domestic groups will remain elusive if we restrict ourselves to synchronic models attempting to "freeze" the domestic group at a moment in time. The concept of "developmental cycle" of course implies temporal change, and the value of diachronic analysis of such local groups has been well-established through a number of important studies in African social anthropology beginning with Fortes (1949) and including Gulliver (1955), Goody (1958, 1976), Stenning (1958), Gray and Gulliver (1964), and Rigby (1969). The kind of change informing these studies includes formation, development, and ultimate fission of domestic groups whose structure, though altering through time, is eventually recapitulated in the growth of new domestic groups spawned by the fission of the old group. The changes occurring in the developmental cycle of the domestic group constitute what the Wilsons call "social circulation" (1945:58-59); here alterations in the personnel of groups occur as a result of the normal processes of aging, leading people to assume new statuses at different points in their lives. The crucial point is that social circulation does not result in a change in social positions or their interrelationship. The shape of the domestic group rather depends on the stages of the life cycle of its membership, and it can only be understood through models not predicated on assumptions of fixity in household or family units. Thus a Mbeere domestic group formed by a newly married man and woman who have left the homestead of the man's parents will differ markedly from three generation domestic groups for whom fissioning is imminent; yet over time the former may come to resemble the latter through the operation of what Vogt (1960) calls "recurrent processes."

A second dimension of change examined in Chapter Two and informing this entire study contrasts with recurrent process. It is what the Wilsons have simply termed "social change" (1945:58-59), and Vogt calls

106

"directional process" (1960). In this second aspect of change, the focus is on social structural transformation in which the content of particular social roles alters and the relationship between roles assumes a new form. Indeed, new roles may develop as in the colonial era when chiefs emerged in previously acephalous societies resulting in wholly new political arrangements and social sanctions. Here we see something more than simply changes in personnel or cyclical episodes in the history of a particular group or institution. While it is certainly possible that structural change may follow in the wake of climatic or environmental alterations, social structural change in Mbeere has proceeded most rapidly and dramatically as a result of the colonial experience. Domestic groups thus can be understood only if we are also alert to the historical forces that have impinged upon them.

The Homestead

I use the term homestead, as one translation of *mūciī*, to designate the physical dimension of the domestic group. It is an approximate rendering of the broader vernacular term, which also includes the domestic group itself. Moreover, *mūciī* may also be applied to a group of close agnatic kin, who, although they are not co-resident, lived together prior to recent fissioning of their natal domestic group. Such individuals would normally be full or half brothers but would at least descend from the same grandfather and would thus constitute what I am calling a shallow lineage. Members of the same *mūciī* normally identify themselves by prefixing the phrase *kwa andū a* (from the people of) to the name of the homestead head with whom they reside and to whom they are agnatically related.

The homestead represents a collection of huts, kraals, and granaries, sometimes surrounded by a makeshift fence, stockade, or hedge, but more often set off from neighboring homesteads only by surrounding gardens, fallow lands, or bush. Fences and stockades became less prevalent with the cessation of raiding and diminished stockkeeping. Mbeere homesteads, while broadly similar in appearance, do not conform to a

107

single plan. Few restrictions, except material ones,
limit the manner in which people site and construct
their homes and associated granaries and kraals.
Nonetheless, a single rule scrupulously observed by the
Mbeere requires that the entrance to a hut not be
constructed on the east-west axis. It is widely
believed that illness or death will result if sunlight
enters a hut directly from east or west. Mbeere
sorcerers reputedly utter curses invoking the demise of
their victims by metaphorically likening growing
weakness and ultimate extinction of life to the dimness
of the sun at first light or, particularly, at sunset.
The final course of the sun may especially augur these
misfortunes and hence explanation for hut orientation
emphasizes avoidance of a direct siting of entrances to
the west.

Hut construction primarily makes use of mud,
wattle, and thatch, although a growing number of people
build more permanent dwellings using corrugated iron
roofing. The simplest dwelling consists only of wooden
poles closely staked out in a circle ten to twelve feet
in diameter on top of which a simple wood roof frame is
added preparatory to thatching. Such dwellings require
only a small investment of time and no investment of
money, since materials are readily available in the
bush. They are commonly found in homesteads and in
gardens where people may sleep owing to the distance of
the cultivation from the main home. The interior of
the circular thatched hut consists of a single,
unpartitioned space in which the most prominent
features are a hearth in the center and a traditional
bed (ūrīrī) consisting of a raised platform of wood.
Sometimes, a more protected hut of the same form may be
built with the addition of a wattle framework which can
be covered over with mud.

The most elaborate dwellings depart from
traditional huts both in design and materials.
Consisting of two to four rooms, the more modern house
assumes a rectangular shape and utilizes mud walls,
which are given a more finished appearance by the
addition of a plaster-like coating made of ash and cow
dung. Although these houses may be roofed with thatch,
it is more desirable to use corrugated iron roofings.

Because the roof materials must be purchased, this house-type is more likely to be found at the homesteads of teachers, government employees, or others with some cash income.

Dwellings of whatever type are subject to rapid deterioration owing to rain erosion of mud walls and termite damage to wooden supports. The cumulative effect of these chronic problems is of course collapse of the hut or mud house. Although the walls of the latter can be periodically replaced with mud, frame deterioration due to insects is much more serious. After approximately seven to ten years, dwellings are in danger of collapse unless they are at least partially reconstructed.

In social terms, new house-types and the investment of time a larger construction demands reflect a growing sedentariness and a concomitant change in the organization of some families. The widespread use of perennials, especially such tree crops as bananas and mangoes, and the more recent expectation of legally inviolable land titles combine to fix people's association with particular pieces of land in ways uncharacteristic of much of Mbeere history. Moreover, a male family head may no longer require his own hut, independently of that customarily built for his wife and children. A very rigid delineation of male and female roles and a certain segregation of tasks both domestically and beyond characterize much of traditional social life, and the organization of domestic space, including separate living huts for mature men and women, marked these restrictions. The more recent multiroom dwelling explicitly delineates a family unit at the same time that formal and exclusive male organizations such as age-sets have declined. Correspondingly, the sexual taboos that at times separate spouses and constrain male-female relations have loosened.

Dwelling construction requires the work of both men and women, although a sexual division of labor marks most of the requisite tasks. If a simple, circular hut is to be built in the traditional style, men will gather the wooden poles and women will collect

109

grass for thatching the roof. Men arrange the poles and construct the framework for the roof. Thatching is ideally an exclusively male task hedged with a taboo (*mūgiro*) which threatens the vitality of any man whose wife thatches a hut. If the hut is to be plastered with mud, women will carry out the additional task of hauling water and will participate with men in this aspect of construction. For this task and for larger scale construction of rectangular dwellings, labor proceeds through work parties composed of neighbors, non-resident agnates, or affines. On these occasions, the host will brew beer as an immediate form of reciprocity for the help rendered, and, in addition, may in future expect a request from any of these people for assistance in hut construction, bush clearing, harvesting, and the like.

Domestic Production, Marriage, and the Matricentric Household

The primary constituent unit of the domestic group is a matricentric household known in Kimbeere as *nyūmba*, "house." Within a homestead, the term refers to a married woman's hut where she resides with her unmarried daughters, both circumcised and not yet circumcised, and her uncircumcised sons. Once her sons are circumcised and thus culturally regarded as sexually mature, they may build their own huts within the homestead or reside with their older brothers but must certainly cease living under the same roof as their mother. Additionally, *nyūmba* designates a lineage consisting of people who claim patrilineal descent from a common ancestor, usually more than two generations removed from the senior members. The Mbeere recognize in the identity of terms for these distinct groups similar social processes at work in the growth and fissioning of families, on the one hand, and descent groups, on the other. Thus they see an analogue in the separation of matricentric households within a single homestead and in the social cleavages leading to the formation of descent groups. Indeed, a matricentric unit itself contains lines of fracture which widen when each brother in a set of full brothers establishes his own homestead.

The economic and social characteristics of the matricentric house suggest what various writers following Gluckman (1950) have termed the "house-property complex." Found among a number of eastern and southern African patrilineal societies, the house-property complex establishes the rights of a group of sons to gardens and animals utilized by their mother but assigned to her by their father. The operation of the house-property complex is particularly clear in a polygamous family, where the sons of each wife represent a distinct unit based on their entitlement to property controlled by their mothers. Inheritance is thus patrilineal, although rights to property are passed on through women who, paradoxically in Mbeere and in most other societies with the house-property complex, cannot own productive property outright. Women do not inherit land or livestock from their fathers but rather gain use rights in gardens and herds from their husbands soon after marriage when they play a major productive role in the domestic economy of the homestead. A woman assumes responsibility not only for growing staples, including planting, weeding, and harvesting, but also for storage and preparation of food for herself, her husband, and the dependents of her house. She usually maintains her own granary, and her husband will likely contribute to its store from the harvest of his own garden. A man can maintain his own granary, using it as a reserve in case of shortages, when he will give grain to his wife or wives. Women may also choose to market a small portion of their crop locally and to keep the proceeds for their own and their children's use, although her husband may ask her for the money, especially if he shares her garden or at least assists her in preparing or working the land, driving away birds as the grain matures, or harvesting. But for a man to use such funds for his other wives or children is regarded as unseemly, and the money he does provide each house ought to come from his own wage labor, craft specialty, sale of livestock, or cash crop production.

The house-property system also governs the distribution of livestock, and the rules of allocation and use of domestic animals are well-illustrated when the dispositon of bridewealth in livestock is examined.

Bridewealth prestations in the form of livestock fall under control of the house of the bride, and these animals cannot be utilized by her father for purposes which do not serve the immediate benefit of that house. Such livestock is earmarked as bridewealth for the bride's full brother and cannot be used for that purpose by a classificatory brother or even by her father to secure an additional wife. Some informants say that if bridewealth goats are kept in the house of her mother's co-wife, the married girl will succumb to illness (*kūvitana*) if her father and that woman have sexual relations. The unity of the matricentric house finds further expression in the use of increasingly common cash bridewealth payments for school fees for the bride's full siblings.

Kinship terminology also marks the matricentric house as a distinctive unit within the homestead. Full siblings are terminologically distinguished from half siblings as well as from children of classificatory fathers. The following diagram shows the terms of address used by either a male or female speaker toward these various "brothers" and "sisters":

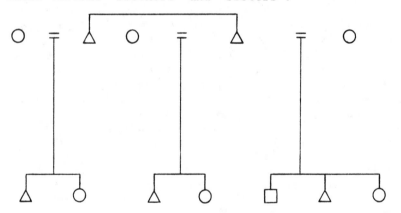

| mūrū wa
baba | mwarī wa
baba | mūrū wa
baba | mwarī wa
baba | male or
female ego | mūrū wa
nyanya | mwarī wa
nyanya |

Terms of Address for Full, Half, and Classificatory Siblings

Figure 1

Sometimes classificatory parents may be addressed by appending *mūkūrū* (older) or *mūnini* (younger) to the kinship term depending on his or her age in relationship to biological father and mother. The terms for full sibling literally mean son of mother and daughter of mother; terms for half siblings or offspring of classificatory fathers, however far removed collaterally, gloss as son of father and daughter of father. Within the virilocally based domestic group full siblings are clearly separated terminologically from the offspring of other houses as well as from children of other classificatory fathers in the dispersed lineage. Terms of reference are equally consistent with this system of classification.

The nearly autonomous character of the matricentric house and its distinctive place in the domestic group also stand out in the relationship between co-wives. The likelihood of tension between co-wives is widely noted and the uneasiness of the relationship is linguistically marked in the term for co-wife, *mūiru*, which literally glosses as one who is jealous. Jealousy (*ūiru*) motivates people to commit sorcery (*ūrogi*), and a woman is especially sensitive to obvious advantages her co-wives may enjoy. Such advantages may include differential favor shown by the husband to one wife or even differences in the number of children co-wives have borne and raised without mortality. A taboo against a woman suckling the child of a co-wife (or indeed any child other than her own), despite her position as classificatory mother to these children, is rationalized as safeguarding hapless children against a sorcery-induced illness borne of jealousy. But the taboo also symbolizes the estrangement between co-wives and the irreducible social bond between natural mother and child. Because the interests of co-wives may be opposed in the assignment of gardens and livestock or in the expenditure of money by their husband, a woman is well-aware of the productive and reproductive differences among the matricentric units of her co-wives. The following excerpt from my field notes is illustrative:

I usually find Mbogo in his garden about half mile from his homestead. The garden overlooks a deep gorge through which runs the Thuchi River, dividing this part of Mbeere from Chuka Division, Meru District. He maintains a small hut at the garden and is frequently in the company of his second wife-- Ciarūviū. Mbogo was born in Kathimari parish, but says he has no gardens there. He maintains three gardens in the vicinity of his homestead. His first and third wives cultivate the gardens just near the large dwelling area of the homestead near Kanyuambora. The large garden here at the Thuchi is divided in half--one part for Mbogo, and one part for Ciarūviū. All of the gardens have banana trees for the use of each wife. He divided his own garden in half because he wants to keep all the sugarcane [which does not grow in the gardens near the homestead] in his garden; it can then be taken freely by any of his children. If the sugarcane were in the garden of his second wife, he explains, only her children would be entitled to it and that would create jealousy among the wives.

Yet amidst the symbols of estrangement and the possibility of diverging economic interests of co-wives, cooperation also characterizes this complex relationship. Although each wife maintains a granary for storing grain harvested from her own garden, co-wives may cooperate in planting, weeding, and in carrying out other domestic tasks, particularly drawing water and gathering firewood. In cases of illness, particularly, one woman may enlist the aid of her co-wife, although the latter is under no legal obligation to comply with requests for assistance. No publicly recognized sanctions can be exerted on an uncooperative co-wife, although the pervasive belief in sorcery and its likely occurrence between co-wives discourages at least overt anti-social acts. Cooperation may also extend to food sharing but once again women have no legal claim, as co-wives, on the food and livestock belonging to the houses of others. Even a husband cannot freely take food from his wife's granary unless

114

he has contributed to its store. Consumption thus appears more socially circumscribed than production, marked as it is by a diffuse anxiety about the always nefarious activities of ubiquitous sorcerers whose favored vehicles for conveying their dangerous magic is food and beer. Since many Mbeere recognize ambivalence in even the most intimate relationships ("it is your closest friend who will poison you"), they feel constraint in all aspects of consumption and consequently observe a marked etiquette in its many facets. Production, on the other hand, in its various phases from bush clearing, to planting, to harvesting, may necessitate some degree of less intimate cooperation and entails considerably less ambivalence in its accomplishment.

In the event a woman has no full brothers, the integrity of her mother's house and patrilineal inheritance from the father through the widowed mother is maintained through the fictive marriage of women. That the Mbeere regard the union between women as a marriage when a bridewealth transaction has occurred is clear from the conventional terms of marriage (ūthoni) which they utilize to describe the formation of the relationship. Men discuss their marriages using the active voice of the verb "to marry" (kūvika) or "to buy" (kūgūra); women, on the other hand, use only passive voice forms as they discuss their marriages. Thus a woman never marries but rather is married or is bought by a man. The exception occurs in cases of widows past childbearing, who have borne daughters only. Such elderly women control bridewealth livestock paid for their daughters but, lacking sons, cannot bequeath the estate in a conventional manner. That the livestock do not devolve to classificatory sons such as those of co-wives attests to the importance of the house-property complex. Using some of the livestock in her herd, a widow can marry a young woman who will cohabit with an agnate of the older woman's deceased husband. The young woman's sons can then inherit the wealth of the house, as they are considered descendants of the house, born legitimately because their mother's marriage was effected by transfer of cattle from that social unit. The following diagram depicts a case of woman marriage:

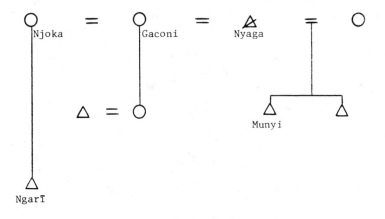

Fictive Marriage of Women

Figure 2

Gaconi, widow of Nyaga, bore one daughter who married
and left home after her husband began paying marriage
livestock to Gaconi and Nyaga. Following the latter's
death, Gaconi "married" Njoka. Njoka bore a son,
Ngarī, who will inherit the livestock and land of
Gaconi's house. Gaconi had used some of the stock of
her house to "buy" Njoka. Munyi, son of Gaconi's co-
wife and residing in a different homestead, fathered
Ngarī who calls him "young father". This
classificatory term normally designates biological
father's younger brother. The child is regarded as a
descendant of Gaconi's fictitious son; the child is
also a member of Nyaga's patriclan and the legitimate
heir of Gaconi's house property. Neither Munyi nor his
full brother are entitled to inherit either the land or
livestock associated with Gaconi's house as the all-
important fiction of descent from Gaconi and Nyaga is
maintained. Accordingly, the child calls the old woman
cūcū (grandmother), and his own mother, Njoka, calls
her maitu (mother), a term a woman normally uses to
address her mother-in-law. It is important to note
that in this case Gaconi became a surrogate husband
because she was beyond her child-bearing years. Had

116

she been able to bear children, it would have been possible for her to enter a leviratic union with one of Nyaga's younger agnates in order to produce male heirs. Children borne of such unions are considered those of the deceased, and the males can inherit his property. Their genitor, as in the case above, is in a classificatory category and is addressed as "younger father." Both the levirate and the fictive marriage of women insure lineal inheritance in the context of a house-property system while nullifying the lateral transmission of property.

Although the domestic economy of homesteads may derive from both subsistence farming and livestock, the balance in Nguthi weighs heavily toward cultivation as the economic mainstay. The number of livestock is both uneven through Mbeere Division, tending to cluster in the lowland areas of Zone 3 in the east, and irregularly distributed from homestead to homestead within a single sublocation. Table 4 summarizes a survey of stock ownership, including cattle, goats, and sheep, in randomly selected homesteads in the upland parishes of Kanyuambora and Kavengero:

Table 4

Stock Holdings In Kanyuambora and Kavengero

average number of small stock (sheep) and goats) in all homes	6.3	average number of small stock in homes with small stock only	11.7
average number of cattle in all homes	2.3	average number of cattle in homes with cattle only	8.1
average of all stock in all homes	7.9	average number of stock in homes with stock	14.7

N = 37 homesteads
      17 homesteads with no livestock
      10 homesteads with small stock only
       2 homesteads with cattle only

These figures include all the livestock controlled by members of sample homesteads and maintained in the parishes of Kanyuambora and Kavengero. Because of a widespread belief that livestock are more vulnerable to disease in the upland parishes, some stockkeepers, although a minority, divide their herds, maintaining some of them at the homes of agnatic kin close to Ishiara market and lower Nguthi. Three people from three different homesteads in this sample maintained a portion of their herds in this way, although I came across no instances of upland residents maintaining livestock for kinsmen in the lower parishes. Resort to cattle trusteeship with non-agnates as Rigby reports for the Gogo (1969:52-53) and non-agnatic bond friends as Gulliver describes among the Jie (1955) has not developed among the less pastorally oriented Mbeere. Among the latter, the preponderance of small stock in the domestic economy does not necessitate the kinds of extra-domestic cooperation in herding and transhumance which reliance on cattle entails.

The stock census in Kanyuambora and Kavengero assumes greater meaning when seen in relationship to the human population. In the homes of the livestock sample, the average homestead population is 7.9, including men, women, and children. In all homes in the stock census, the average per capita holding of stock is 1.0. Among stock-owning homesteads only, the average is 1.83. These figures parallel data of a very gross kind provided in a 1969 official stock census for each location of Mbeere. In that survey, Evurore Location, with a population of 16,495, accounted for 6700 cattle and 8000 sheep and goats; the per capita stock holding based on these data is .89 (Eastern Province Planning Team 1970:14). Compared to pastoral peoples such as the Gogo, whose stock holding averages 2.52 stock units per capita, thereby exceeding that of the Nuer (Rigby 1969:50), Mbeere reliance on livestock in the upland parishes is considerably less. The comparison between Mbeere and Gogo suggests an even greater discrepancy in per capita holdings than first appears, because Rigby has utilized the concept of "stock-unit", a veterinary department convention whereby one head of cattle or five head of small stock equals one stock unit. Thus the Gogo per capita

118

holding is 2.52 head of cattle, or approximately 12 small stock, or some equivalent combination of the two.

The risks of economic loss in stockkeeping are great, and the threat of disease especially serious. A herd of average size can be wiped out in a few days, and the unusually devastating outbreak of the 1890s, which swept much of East Africa, and the outbreak of the early 1930s are remembered as particularly dramatic phases in local history. Tick-borne diseases, such as East Coast fever, have proven especially perilous for herders who, until very recent years, could not avail themselves of cattle dips. In addition, rinderpest and anthrax have menaced herds at different times. For those who maintain livestock, animals represent a source, albeit tenuous, of great pride, and the stockkeepers themselves often voice a realistic fear that their animals may precipitously die. Nonetheless, people tend not to slaughter animals routinely nor to market them except to meet emergency demands. Hoping to increase the size of their holdings in the face of ubiquitous pitfalls, they much prefer to maintain their animals. Yet animals do circulate or are consumed through bridewealth payments and are slaughtered at rituals. They may be sold for cash to purchase grain, either for consumption or planting, especially after famine or shortage. In addition, payment of school fees drains meager resources and may require a stockkeeper to sell animals either for a person of the homestead or for agnatic kin in other homesteads. It is not unusual to find a young person faced with onerous school fees trying to persuade a stockkeeping kinsman to sell an animal so that school obligations can be met.

Any person within the homestead may herd domestic stock either in bush land within the parish or in neighboring parishes. Rigid sex and age restrictions apparent in much of Mbeere life, either in the form of dangerous taboos or in more diffuse proscriptions unbacked by mystical threat, do not obtain here; but men, and especially uncircumcised boys, predominate as tenders of homestead herds, which may include animals associated with different houses. When an individual derives some cash income from employment, the stock may be tended by a hired herder, usually a young boy, for fifteen to thirty shillings per month depending on the number of livestock. Most of these hired herders are local youth, but I have noted some from as far away as Buluyia in Western Kenya. In the previous sample, where twenty homesteads held some livestock, seven homesteads made use of paid employees to maintain their herds. Consistently among stockkeeping homesteads, adult men and women prefer to expend the major portion of their labor on farming. Accordingly, they allocate responsibility for stock herding to youth not yet mature enough to devote sustained attention to farm work (Enos H. N. Njeru, personal communication). Herding requires only a modest amount of attention and few physical demands; thus, the minimal requirements of herding are not considered beyond the capacities of uncircumcised youth, uniformly regarded as immature and generally incapable of making sound judgments.

Beyond cultivation and, secondarily, stockkeeping, the domestic subsistence economy has also utilized other strategies, including hunting game and gathering wild vegetables. Much of the game over the years has migrated from Nguthi where the human population has grown in size and density. Moreover, government efforts to eliminate poaching along the Tana River have discouraged Mbeere archers, who now find few outlets for skills previously honed in warfare or hunting. The exploitation of wild food plants, on the other hand, proves important, especially during famine or prior to harvest (David Brokensha, personal communication). One wilderness food source which has been significant for the Mbeere is honey ($\bar{u}\bar{u}k\bar{\imath}$), valued both in its own right and as a source for beer production, particularly on ritual occasions. Men control honey culture exclusively, including the carving of beehives ($m\bar{\imath}at\bar{u}$) from logs, tying them atop trees in the bush, and collecting the product in special wooden drum-like containers ($ithembe$) of their own manufacture. Once it is gathered, men control the distribution of honey and can turn it over to their wives for fermentation, although men sometimes participate in beer-making. The hives and containers are part of the moveable portion of a man's estate which will be inherited by his sons according to his bequest.

Mbeere homesteads tend to be built up out of an agnatic core of male kinsmen and their in-marrying wives who form their own matricentric homes within the homestead cluster. But only a minority of these matricentric units comprise polygynous unions, despite polygyny remaining an ideal for some men. Although I shall point to some of the indigenous constraints limiting the frequency of polygyny, various social changes have also discouraged plural unions. Included here are the influence of schools, missions, and a new system of values engendered by economic consumption of goods and services both within and beyond Mbeere. Thus one finds an increasing emphasis on the accumulation of resources in order to purchase land or consumer goods, or to pay children's school fees, and this attitude is often seen to conflict with older ideals supporting plural marriage and numerous progeny. These value changes are occurring among both men and women, and for the latter, particularly, the devaluation of polygyny is linked to what is perceived as a generally improving lot for women, at least in their relationship to husbands. Concomitantly, as both the form of, and expectations within marriage come under scrutiny, the major legitimation of marriage--bridewealth--also is under some challenge, as I shall indicate. Moreover, as people link polygyny to large families, its lessening hold on younger people is likewise bound to new concerns about limiting family size in order to distribute always limited resources among fewer children; they will thereby enjoy greater access to education, material goods, and the complex of changes closely associated with schools and churches.

In order to gauge the frequency of plural marriage and its occurrence within different age groups of men, I collected data on the marriages of 211 living males. The statistics derive from genealogical and census data collected in three parishes in Nguthi, the primary research site, and in two parishes in Mavuria. Both areas are very similar in the extent of mission activity, in the availability of schools, and in their general profile. This information is summarized in Table 5:

Table 5

Incidence of Polygyny

Approximate Age of Men	Number of Wives							Total Men
	0	1	2	3	4	5	6+	
20-30	15	41	1	-	-	-	-	57
30-40	-	36	7	-	-	-	-	43
40-50	1	32	6	1	-	-	-	40
50+	1	37	25	2	2	-	4	71
								211

Analysis

Ages	Wives Per Man	Per Cent Polygamist
Total	1.3	23
30-40	1.2	16
40-50	1.2	18
50+	1.8	46

A relatively low incidence of polygyny among men in their younger and middle years reflects heavy obligations to pay bridewealth for first wives and to assist younger brothers and sons with bridewealth payments. Over the years, the Local Native Council attempted to fix bridewealth at what was regarded as a fair level (although not binding) and settled on 800 shillings and fifty to seventy goats or their equivalent (one cow in lieu of ten goats, one bull in lieu of five goats). In addition, the bride's father and brothers might require sugar, honey, and assorted gifts, including dresses and coats for the bride's classificatory mothers. School fees for the bride's younger siblings may also be sought. (This was an issue in the case presented in the Appendix.) If the bride has attended secondary school, then her father and brothers might require more bridewealth. If she has not gone to primary school, bridewealth may likely be negotiated downward.

Whatever the amount of bridewealth, payment is protracted for both ideological and material reasons, and it is not unusual for a man to complete payment for his mother after the death of both parents. It is commonly believed that full payment while a woman remains young will seriously threaten her childbearing capacities and, if she does have children, it is feared that they may be especially vulnerable to disease. Thus payments ought to be completed only after a woman has passed beyond her childbearing years. But in addition, material factors necessitate the extended payment of bridewealth because what is required normally far exceeds an individual's economic resources at a particular time, which is apparent if average herd sizes are compared to the requirement of seventy small stock or equivalents. Also, extending the payment of bridewealth livestock in a setting of periodic and sometimes severe outbreaks of disease creates networks of cross-cutting obligations between homesteads resulting in a continuing circulation of livestock. The consequent dispersion of animals in different homesteads and parishes may reduce the absolute number of animals which perish in an epidemic, and protracted obligations can provide one means of rebuilding herd size. During disease outbreaks, men request their affines to delay a livestock payment or otherwise to pay cash in place of the animals they would transfer.

The possible addition of a monetary requirement for bridewealth as well as frequent demands for coats, dresses, or other consumer goods has increased the gross value of bridewealth over the years. Paying for the education of a daughter, in the view of many parents, increases a woman's value and justifies their adding the cash requirement to the normal livestock demand. Men often use the language of the marketplace to discuss the marriages of their daughters suggesting that the idea of "wife-purchase" (Gray 1960) accords with the Mbeere view of betrothal. Parents and brothers seek cash for an educated girl and consider it compensation for the cost of both her upbringing and her school fees. A man who is employed, then, clearly has an advantage in seeking a wife, particularly an educated one, for whom money will be demanded. It is further reasoned that any woman, once she is married, will bear children for a patrilineage other than her own, and high bridewealth both legitimates the children and compensates a woman's parents for bestowing on her husband's descent group genetricial rights in her children. The high bridewealth in Mbeere accords with Goody's observation that "the relative size of payment is . . . linked with the quantum of rights transferred" (1973:3).

Since 1931 when Evans-Pritchard proposed the term "bridewealth," it has become customary in social anthropology to avoid the earlier designation of "bridesprice" in describing marriage prestations moving from the husband's group to the wife's, and I have been following this conventional usage. Gray's analysis of Sonjo marriage (1960) in economic terms, wherein he argues for the appropriateness of the term brideprice, represents a noteworthy current of thought running against the tide of anthropological opinion. A recent critique of what is awkwardly called "economistic" interpretations of bridewealth argues that although bridewealth has economic implications, these are distinct from commerical transactions. The latter perspective, the author suggests, offers little general applicability (Comaroff 1980: 10-11). Yet in considering the position of women in society and its relationship to marriage prestations, it is important to take account of local views which articulate commercial motives and conceptions regarding bridewealth.

The term bridewealth has come to be generally regarded as the proper gloss for a set of transactions considered outside the context of buying and selling goods. Although Evens-Pritchard early on recognized the ubiquity of bridewealth as an "economic value" (1934), he could say flatly in 1951: "It is no longer necessary to show that the African payment of bridewealth is not a purchase" (1951:89). In the wholesale acceptance of the bridewealth designation in the two decades between Evans-Pritchard's initial statement and his latter remarks, social anthropologists were doubtless reacting to the many superficial, crudely biased accounts of African societies written by those missionaries and colonial officials whose distorted characterizations of African life also pictured women as chattel. In proposing the substitute term, Evans-Pritchard in fact observed that, in considering women as commodities, one could hardly exaggerate the "harm done to African peoples by this ignorance" (1931:36). Social anthropologists have also generally been disposed to cast native peoples in a favorable light, which could less easily be done where women seem to represent little more than property, as the term brideprice implied.

The analytic problem surrounding these transactions still remains for anthropologists confronting data from societies such as Mbeere where the circulation of goods legitimates marriage. Especially in view of the ways in which the Mbeere themselves talk about marriage in terms of the buying and selling of women, the issue of brideprice or bridewealth and specifically the economic implications of marriage payments seem all the more pertinent. Chiefs Kombo and Mwandiko, quoted earlier, explicitly considered women an investment value in much the same way they thought about purchasing a bus. In the folk view, informants emphasize the compensatory nature of bridewealth. After marriage, a daughter's labor contributes to her husband's homestead, and bridewealth reimburses her parents for relinquishing this economic good. As Mbeere men tersely put it in proverbial form: "A man does not give his daughter like an arrow." They mean that for each daughter who marries, there must be a return, whereas an arrow often misses its target and is lost.

The inflated bridewealth for educated women similarly finds justification in economic terms, for it is argued that her costly school fees ought to bring some return—either from her directly if she secures employment or from her husband in the form of bridewealth. From the perspective of some Mbeere men, women are thus of more or less value in economic terms based on their fathers' expenditures on their behalf.

A number of young men in Mbeere secondary schools who wrote essays for me on the topic, "What I Believe About Bridewealth," also casts such payments into a commercial framework, which the writers felt resounded to the benefit of Mbeere women. Thus, it was argued, high bridewealth helps to insure that men will treat their wives well, for they are made valuable through the outlay of scarce resources which men can acquire only with great difficulty. Appreciating the investment value of his wife, a husband was said to spurn abuse and mistreatment of her. By contrast, a few students objected that payment for a woman gives a man absolute rights of ownership legitimating any cruel treatment he wishes to inflict. Both views are informed by a consideration of the perceived consequences of thinking about women as property.

High bridewealth in the folk view is commonly regarded as the source for strong pressures stabilizing marriage owing to a man's reluctance to return any bridewealth once it has been given over to him for his daughter. He therefore exerts considerable influence on her if she wants to leave her husband. In the event of marital discord, a woman's only option customarily was to return to her parents. Indeed, the Mbeere speak of divorce in reference to women almost exclusively by using the verb "to return home" (kwĩnũka), and it was

126

incumbent on her father to yield the bridewealth so that his son-in-law could marry again. But such a return could be facilitated by the woman's remarriage in which case her father served as an intermediary in the transfer of livestock from one man to another. I have no evidence to suggest that, independent of divorce and remarriage, women circulated between men, but given the penalties for adultery (a fine of livestock against the offending man), the major issue is not so much an act of illicit sex itself but rather an uncompensated violation of the husband's nearly absolute right over his wife. A woman, on the other hand, is not entitled under customary law to seek compensation or even divorce if her husband engages in an adulterous relationship.

The calculation of economic equivalence between women and sometimes their children, on the one hand, and livestock, on the other, underlies customary legal notions about other aspects of betrothal, affiliation of children, and marriage termination. If children were borne to a union and their father wishes to continue affiliating the children to himself after divorce, he is entitled to only a partial return of bridewealth. In either case, customary law gives sole discretion to the husband in determining custody of children. Children born out of wedlock to a woman who subsequently married belong to a woman's descent group unless separate provision is made for them by her husband. He must pay his father-in-law if he wants to affiliate those children; otherwise eventual bridewealth for the woman's daughter must be paid to her grandfather rather than to her mother's husband. Similar matrilateral claims on women can be exerted when bridewealth payments have not been forthcoming. In one instance, a man betrothed his sister's daughter, while she was still a child, so that he could receive livestock in lieu of what was overdue from his brother-in-law.

The economic conception of marriage also emerges in the *tubū* context. These precolonial markets prompted a lively trade in foodstuffs, livestock, iron ore, and women "for selling." Domestic slavery was not practiced among the Mbeere or their neighbors, nor did

the Mbeere experience any but the most sporadic contact
with Arabs and coastal Bantu seeking slaves in the
interior. It is thus not possible within the Mbeere
context to compare this clearest form of a market in
people to conceptualizations and processes of
matrimonial transactions. Nonetheless, Mbeere
perspectives and practices regarding marriage payments
are intimately implicated in economic issues, for the
transfer of rights in persons entailed by marriage
occurs through prestations establishing an individual's
value in terms of livestock, money, and commercial
goods. It is precisely because kinship systems in
Africa customarily control the disposition of rights in
their members and transfer these rights among
themselves that Miers and Kopytoff (1977:12) have
recently noted the similarity between these practices
and conventional Western views of slavery, thus
necessitating considerable rethinking about the nature
of slavery in Africa.

Goody has also addressed these issues in regard to
slavery, marriage, and the entire matter of rights in
people, as they relate to land and technology in
Africa. He considers the problem mainly in the context
of state societies but his insights are also applicable
to stateless systems. Although they lacked chiefs,
stateless political orders such as Mbeere can produce
"big men" who gain informal followings and enjoy
considerable prestige and influence despite the absence
of formal office and institutionalized authority.
Goody contends that political domination in Africa
derived from control over people and not land, given
the abundance of the latter and the absence of large
populations pressing on it. Accordingly, controlling
access to land did not serve as a basis for political
power or economic differentiation in pre-colonial
Africa, unlike the developing feudal pattern of
medieval Europe. A very limited technology, which did
not include the plow or wheel (and consequently few
differences between people in terms of their access to
food), underlies the African pattern. In Goody's view,
the control of people at the base of political power in
Africa included both women and slaves, and state
societies with superior military organizations,
including cavalry in the Western Sudan, raided

acephalous groups for slaves, who could then be traded (1971:32,72).

In Mbeere, raids resulting in the capture of women provided some warriors a ready means for additional livestock acquisition through selling their captives. Alternatively, a warrior could marry the captive himself, thereby escaping the pressing task of paying bridewealth and obviating the need for his father's assistance; he was, accordingly, closer to the point of founding his own homestead. Several agnatic lines in southern Mbeere very near the Tana River count uterine links to the Kamba, for a number of Kamba women were captured in the final skirmishes between the Mbeere and the Kamba early in this century. Their marriages to Mbeere men conformed to established patterns, except for the absence of payment, and the Kamba women were routinely absorbed into their husbands' homes. Raids for both women and livestock could enhance the position of any warrior just as a polygynous elder with large herds and at the hub of numerous affinal exchange networks could likely exert greater influence and garner more prestige than his less affluent counterparts.

Unlike economically valuable women, male captives were not actively sought in raids and no permanent class of strangers developed in Mbeere. Settlers from beyond Mbeere have historically entered from such places as Kamba country and Meru, usually because they were fleeing from famine. But they gained legitimacy by adoption into Mbeere clans, thereby transforming their status from strangers to indigenes and never assuming client positions in the Mbeere system of unranked clans. In considering when an economic value can be attached to persons, an interesting problem arises in the occasional cases of warriors who were in imminent danger of being slain but were spared. If an enemy could find an old woman and address her as mother as he clung to her, he might gain sanctuary from battle. Her giving him milk, as if to accept him as her child, signaled a willingness to ransom him. It is unclear how the captive's family was informed of his fate, but it is likely that word could be carried by Mbeere warriors in much the same manner that they arranged *tubū* markets with impunity. Here, the interstitial role of the old women past childbearing could be turned to mediation as they "sold" an enemy back to his home.

The relationship between high bridewealth, marriage stability, mode of descent and other social structural features has been extensively discussed by various Africanists including Gluckman (1950), Fallers (1957), Mitchell (1961, 1963), Lewis (1961), and Lloyd (1968). Gluckman argued initially that divorce would be low in patrilineal societies such as the Zulu and Nuer because corporate patrilineages were the basic units of social structure, and they could only be replenished through marriage. That is, a rule of clan or lineage exogamy prevented women from perpetuating their own patrilineages. Thus a lineage maintains temporal continuity only if it can gain rights to the reproductive capacities of women from other lineages, and these rights are won through the payment of large bridewealth, symbolizing and legitimating the transfer of these rights from one lineage to another. The Zulu say "cattle beget children" meaning that certain rights *in personam* flow from the bridewealth transaction. Specifically, a patrilineage gains genetricial rights, as a corporation, to the children of in-marrying women. These rights are transferred in perpetuity, insuring that all the children of in-marrying women, including adulterine children, belong to the lineage. A number of secondary marriage practices such as the levirate, sororate, ghost marriage, and fictive marriage of women are consistent with this transfer of genetricial rights, and stable marriage makes high bridewealth possible rather than vice versa. Gluckman also argues that corporate control of genetricial rights in bilateral societies such as the Lozi, where divorce is much higher than among the Zulu, is not an issue since lineages do not exist and residence determines economic and political status. Similarly, divorce is also high in matrilineal societies where conjugal rights and genetricial rights are divided between two different descent groups. Since a woman's children, regardless of their father's lineage affiliation, always belong to her descent group in a matrilineal society, paternity is socially less significant, bridewealth is very small, and genetricial rights create a schism rather than an enduring bond between husband and wife.

Since Gluckman first examined this problem, anthropologists have further refined their understanding of the jural dimension of descent and have expanded the ethnographic record against which theories of marriage stability can be considered. It is now clear that rights attendant to patrifiliation and descent among the Zulu and Nuer, although also present in a number of other African societies, cannot be taken as generally characteristic of patriliny in Africa. Fallers (1957), for example, has shown that genetricial rights among the Soga are not corporately held and the house-property complex as well as other social practices by which a woman might be absorbed into her husband's patrilineage do not exist. Divorce rates are correspondingly very high. Similarly, Lloyd (1968) argues that genetricial, uxorial, and jural rights are analytically separable, and their particular distribution between the descent groups of husband and wife directly affects the stability of marriage. Thus, the patrilineal Yoruba, who transfer uxorial and corporate genetricial rights to the husband's patrilineage at marriage, nonetheless manifest a high divorce rate because jural rights surrounding a woman continue to be held by her descent group. She continues as a member of her own group and exercises rights in it. Her husband's lineage, despite its claim to all of her children, does not absorb her.

Among the various societies examined by these Africanist social anthropologists interested in marriage stability, the Zulu bear the closest relationship to the Mbeere, for both societies include such features as patrilineal descent, the house-property complex, fictive marriage of women and other secondary marriage practices such as the true levirate. In addition, the Zulu and Mbeere maintain high bridewealth and corporate control by a husband's lineage of genetricial rights over all of his wife's children. He is thus pater to any adulterine offspring his wife may bear. The Mbeere woman is not subject to the jural control of her natal lineage, nor does she exercise jural rights in it. In addition, she cannot build an independent house at her father's homestead nor are her agnatic kinsmen responsible for any debts or legal responsibilities she may incur. Like the Zulu, the Mbeere exhibit a very low rate of divorce, although economic and social changes have reduced the stabilizing effect of traditional structural features, which markedly constrained individual choice now exercised through labor migration, wage employment in the rural area, and economic changes profoundly affecting the fabric of traditional society. Nonetheless, marriage continues to represent a process of absorption of a woman into her husband's kin group where her sons, through her, establish their economic status. Marriage data in four parishes reveal no divorces among women with at least one circumcised child. Once a young man is circumcised, he reaches the point when he can assume his rights in gardens overseen by his father, and, although he may gain cultivation rights in land controlled by his mother's agnates, such rights are temporary and cannot be transmitted to his sons. When a young woman is circumcised, she approaches the age of marriage and her agnates do not wish to lose the bridewealth her marriage should insure. This loss might be realized were she to follow her mother to the latter's home. It further appears that the duration of marriage and the birth of children, except among younger parents, inhibit divorce, although my data are not altogether clear on this point. If a woman returns home with her children, her husband is entitled to demand not only the return of his bridewealth but also compensation for each child, which then would entitle his affines to affiliate the children with their patriclan and descent group. This rarely occurs, however, and people adamantly state that circumcised youth would not follow their mother to her natal home.

At marriage, a woman leaves her parents and agnates to join her husband in a new domestic group. Although she continues to maintain strong emotional ties to her natal home and kinsmen, especially to her mother, these loyalties are no longer exclusive, for she assumes new domestic obligations to her husband. Yet the possibility for role conflict is small, for her ties to parents remain sentimental and personal whereas those to her husband additionally exhibit structural significance. In regard to the possibility of role conflict for women who marry into patrilineal groups other than those into which they are born, Gulliver (1963:141) notes the following:

> The difficulty . . . is largely avoided where a woman relinquishes her membership of, and rights and responsibilities in, her natal patrilineal groups (i.e., those of her own father and brothers), and is incorporated as a full and permanent member of her husband's groups . . . . If, however, a married woman retains formal membership in her natal group, and continues in some degree to exercise rights and obligations there, whilst she is progressively involved with her husband's and son's group, then the area of ambiguity is larger, and the possibilities of role conflict and divided loyalties are likely to be important in their effect on her social activities.

In Mbeere, a woman utilizes productive resources, establishes her home, and enters the market to sell food crops by virtue of her position in her husband's homestead and descent group. Although she continues her association with parents and her natal group through visits and cooperative labor, her jural rights and obligations squarely fall within her new domestic domain and the larger descent group within which it is embedded. As a consequence, the issue of divided loyalty on the part of the Mbeere woman does not arise, for she in effect relinquishes membership in her father's group as she comes to identify herself and her interests in terms of her husband's group. This particular structural feature helps to stabilize marriage and provides a rather stark contrast to the patrilineal Yoruba whose system of marriage and descent, otherwise strikingly similar to Mbeere, provides for a woman's continued membership in her natal group where she exercises jural rights. Divorce among the Yoruba is correspondingly high as the brother/sister bond competes with the husband/wife bond to the peril of stable marriage (Lloyd 1968:79).

133

What I identified in the field as divorce closely
followed Mbeere conceptions about the jural termination
of marriage. It did not include all of those cases of
husbands and wives who simply do not reside together.
For example, a senior wife beyond her child-bearing
years may join her eldest son at his homestead leaving
her husband with his junior wife. This choice may
instance an individual preference and not necessarily
represent a case of non-cooperation or marital discord.
In numerous cases of outright conflict, a woman may
return to her parents home for an extended period of
time, but such a return does not in itself constitute
marital dissolution. Rather, it may represent an
indefinite separation, or a prelude either to possible
reconciliation with her husband, especially if she has
children, or to repayment of bridewealth, thus marking
formal divorce. Just as Europeans distinguish
separation from divorce, so too do the Mbeere, who
regard the termination of marriage as contingent on the
return of bridewealth, which then suspends conjugal
rights of the man and woman as well as his exercise of
genetricial rights to children the woman may
subsequently bear. I thus count as cases of divorce
only those instances in which bridewealth has been at
least partially repaid. A total return of bridewealth
does not occur if a man wishes to affiliate his wife's
children to his clan and descent group. In this
instance, he will relinquish from the returned
bridewealth several head of small stock for each child,
although requirements vary and amounts are negotiable
between affines.

In his discussion of marriage stability and social
structure, Mitchell (1961:256) brings together data on
divorce from thirteen Bantu societies. The lowest rate
is 3.5% among the patrilineal Kgatla followed by 9.4%
among the patrilineal Shona. While Mitchell shows that
certain aspects of patriliny, which resemble the Mbeere
system, tend to stabilize marriage, their stabilizing
effect depends on continuity in social structure. But
the Mbeere, like so many other African peoples, are
increasingly enmeshed in social relationships both
different from and sometimes antithetical to those
defined by patrilineal descent alone. Different

loyalties, choices, and attitudes, including skepticism about the value of bridewealth itself, now have diminished the encompassing influence of agnation and affinity. In the absence of numerical data on marriage among differing age groups over an extended time period, it is impossible to determine the relative effects of structural as opposed to historical or contingent influences on divorce rates. The higher rate of divorce, which I have found, among people below the age of 30 may reflect the weakening hold of patriliny and its attendant stabilizing effects. On the other hand, marriage among young people is of insufficient length for the process of absorption of a woman into her husband's descent group to occur. Children will not have been circumcised nor will the economic position of jurally minor sons yet be realized in their descent groups. Correspondingly, the absence of divorce among people with at least one circumcised child indicates that marriage may grow more durable through time when the structural pull of Mbeere patriliny can exert its full force on in-marrying women. Overall, my impression is that the structural forces of patriliny very effectively stabilized marriage historically but now a vast array of social changes significantly undermines that cohesive influence.

Women's status in Africa, including the relative ease of divorce, and its relationship to colonial and post-colonial economic changes raises complex questions often pervaded by ideological bias. The domestic realities of Mbeere and indeed of numerous other East African societies historically show women consistently subordinated to men, first as their daughters and sisters and then as their wives. If traditional society circumscribed the choices men could make, customary constraints were even more limiting of women's prerogatives within and especially beyond the domestic domain. But while class lines are growing more distinct in Mbeere, the possibilities of an enhanced position for some women are increasing. With the emergence of a series of new sources of prestige ranging from schooling to wage employment in the city to cash crop production, there has been a concomitant weakening of customary controls, including those which limited women's prerogatives. A woman, for example, can press court suits, including divorce, against her husband, thus bringing in the formal authority of an unknown magistrate. Moreover, women can now more readily refuse to enter secondary unions, such as the levirate, should this prove irksome to them. Rather than remain among her husband's kin, she might simply board a bus and return home with her children, as did the young Kikuyu widow of a former chief. Additionally, the out-migration of Mbeere males to wage labor in towns has bolstered the already well-established position of women in agriculture. Women continue overwhelmingly to cultivate, and in the absence of husbands, they now actively and of necessity make important decisions about land use and, increasingly, sale. Some participated in the demarcation of land when their husbands were absent. Although customary rules of land tenure gave virtually no scope to decision-making by women in regard to anything but usufruct, land registration has now insured that women will at least be entitled by statuatory law to acquire and to dispose of land independently of any male. Through trading and growing cash crops (some women have joined the tobacco coop), women may accumulate enough money to purchase land. Furthermore, women have before themselves examples of female achievement in such official capacities as public health workers, community development officers, and in 1977, as assistant agricultural officer for Mbeere Division and as Divisional Officer for the recently formed Gachoka Division.

Types of Domestic Groups

The social composition of domestic groups is variable, ranging from elementary families of husband, wife, and children to three generation extended families numbering more than thirty people. The agnatic core of the homestead is bound together by the diffuse obligations of patrilineal kinship and the authority of the senior male, who actively controls the disposition of land and perhaps livestock. In examining the varying forms of Mbeere domestic groups,

I have found it useful to distinguish types of the
family identified by Tait in his study of the Konkomba
(1961:184). Tait follows Konkomba designations closely
in using the term family synonymously with house. I
have similarly glossed the Kimbeere term *mūcii̇̄* to
indicate the localized family or domestic group as well
as the homestead itself in its physical aspects. The
following typology represents a slight variation of
Tait's:

1. elementary   husband, wife, and children
2. polygynous   husband, wives, and children
3. extended   husband, wife or wives, and
                        children, including unmarried
                        sons and daughters, married
                        sons and their wives and
                        children
4. expanded   husband, wife or wives,
                        their children, and his full
                        or classificatory brothers
                        and their wives and children

Although plural marriages might be found among types 2,
3, and 4, only type 2 is termed "polygynous"; in this
context, polygynous families are always two
generational, and offspring remain unmarried minors.
By contrast, extended families may or may not contain
plural marriages and the sons have begun to marry.
Expanded families may also contain plural unions, but
the distinguishing feature here is a fraternal pair at
the agnatic core of the domestic unit. This typology
emphasizes the position of a married senior male and
his relationship to siblings, offspring, and women who
join the domestic group in accordance with a virilocal
rule of residence. Although other kin may associate
themselves with the homestead, its character is
dependent on an agnatic core and in-marrying women.

Since Fortes's now classic work (1949) emphasizing
the temporal dimension in the study of social
structure, social anthropologists regard the numerical
distribution of types of domestic groups not so much
"as deviations from a modal or from an ideal type"
(Goody 1958:3), but rather as phases in the
developmental cycle of domestic groups. In this shift

from a synchronic to a diachronic perspective, it is possible to chart the variable career of domestic groups in particular societies. This developmental view leads, then, to an examination of the numerical distribution of various forms of the domestic group and the variables which in turn account for these family frequencies. As succinctly stated by Fortes, the tripartite phases of the developmental cycle proceed as follows:

> First there is a phase of expansion that lasts from the marriage of two people until the completion of their family of procreation. The biological limiting factor here is the duration of the wife's (or wives') fertility. In structural terms it corresponds to the period during which all the offspring of the parents are economically, affectively, and jurally dependent on them. Secondly, and often overlapping the first phase . . . there is the phase of dispersion or fission. This begins with the marriage of the oldest child and continues until all the children are married. Where the custom by which the youngest child remains to take over the family estate is found, this commonly marks the beginning of the final phase. This is the phase of replacement, which ends with the death of the parents and the replacement in the social structure of the family they founded by families of their children, more specifically, by the family of the father's heir amongst the children (Fortes 1958:4-5).

These universal processes, intimately linked to the life cycle itself, unfold in various ways in different societies depending on a concatenation of such factors as patterns of inheritance, the use and control of productive resources, the stability of marriage, and the like.

A survey of 118 homesteads in Nguthi reveals the following distribution of types of domestic groups:

Table 6

Profile of Domestic Groups in Nguthi

	number	proportion of sample	mean no. of people
elementary	52	.44	6
polygynous	6	.05	8.5
extended	55	.47	12.3
expanded	5	.04	6.5
total	118		overall mean 8.3

The relative infrequency of polygynous groups is consistent with the earlier data on plural marriage indicating that polygyny is not widely practiced by men below the age of 50. By the time a man is most likely to marry for a second time, he will very likely be living in an extended family in which sons by his first wife have already married and perhaps have fathered children, thus creating an extended domestic unit. The paucity of expanded units suggests that the pattern of inheritance represented by the house-property complex creates fracture lines along which domestic groups are likely to break apart. Expanded families thus appear to be highly unstable. The opposition between women's houses in a homestead is at all times clear, even when all children of the homestead are minors, for each woman maintains her own gardens, hearth, and animals. Social divisions within a single house, except for the ranking of sons by seniority, are less clear. But when the father dies, the various claims of male heirs of a single house become manifest, not only in the relationship of this house to others of the homestead but also among the house heirs themselves.

Although these men continue to share residual rights in land held by the wider descent group, they are immediately interested in dividing their father's land, part of which in turn they can assign to their wives. The present shortage of land and the intense competititon for it may well create quite diverging

139

interests among a group of full brothers, especially if the eldest brother attempts to control his siblings by virtue of his succession to senior status. Although inheritance within a house in principle follows a *per stirpes* rather than a *per capita* rule, the seniority of the eldest son confers some advantage, especially when he has minor brothers for whom he serves as a guardian. Additionally, the eldest son, in succeeding to his father's position as homestead head, assumes a custodial role over uncultivated lands claimed by his father. This position enables him to allocate these bush areas to his brothers on their attainment of majority, essentially marked by their marriage. Moreover, this customary assumption of the prerogatives of seniority is usually supported by the wider descent group, especially if the father made a public declaration of his wishes prior to his death.

In the event that a man's surviving sons are all minors, his brother will assume the role of their guardian as well as tender of their estate, which should devolve to them when they reach adulthood. If the distribution of garden lands and other portions of the estate has been contested after the father's death, then these distinctive concerns may be further compounded by acrimony and fears of sorcery. One individual, for example, noting the infrequent coresidence of brothers and their wives and children explained that mutual jealousy, particularly over property, leads brothers to establish separate homesteads. Distance, both social and physical, he argued, is more conducive to highly valued respect (*gītīo*) and will likely diminish dangerous jealousy, which always motivates sorcery.

A man's succession to his father's position additionally entails the care of his mother and any younger co-wives with minor children. He may inherit these co-wives and, consistent with leviratic practice, any children they bear will be regarded as those of the deceased. The senior son's position finds further expression in his assumption of major responsibility for negotiating his full sisters' marriages and for assisting younger brothers with their bridewealth. In both instances, his role is similar to his father's.

He commands extreme respect from his sister's husbands, which is the due of senior affines; and with his brother's wife, a formal relationship is created which precludes his inheriting her should his younger brother die. By contrast, younger siblings enjoy a casual and informal relationship with the spouses of older brothers and sisters.

Forms of inheritance and the house-property complex significantly constrain domestic organization and limit its lateral extensions, thus accounting for the small proportion of polygynous and expanded families. On the other hand, the large proportion of elementary and extended families in the sample of domestic groups points to a process of lineal growth followed by eventual decline after the death of the homestead head on whom sons are primarily dependent for access to land, which in turn makes possible the formation of their own families. The availability of land in the past had been catalytic in the hiving off process as young men not only stood to inherit land from their fathers but also could claim uncontested bush land as initial cultivators. Over the years, however, the possibility of cultivating unclaimed land has diminished in the wake of the land scramble. Since the recent conflicts over land are largely waged between descent groups, the shortage of land, created less by population pressure and more by exaggerated claims, has weighted agnatic ties with a new functional load. As a consequence, the fissive tendencies in the developmental cycle are in some degree counterbalanced by new pressures for cooperation in the wider order of descent groups.

External Factors and Paternal Authority in the Domestic Group

Mbeere domestic groups grow, divide, and grow once again through the recurrent effects of structural forces, but these groups are also subject to the influence of such external factors as labor migration and wages, education, and the system of values they imply. These factors will become increasingly important in shaping domestic groups. Here I wish to note a decline in paternal authority and concomitant

141

independence of sons.

Paternal authority not only depends on the cultural values which underpin it but also follows from a father's control over the disposition of productive resources in the domestic economy including testamentary rights over the familial estate. Exercise of these rights can serve to reward an obedient son or to punish an errant one. But with the growth of employment opportunities outside of Mbeere, men can earn money and utilize it independently of their fathers' control. At least one man from thirty-nine homesteads in the domestic group survey, or 33% of the homestead sample, was working for wages outside of Nguthi, and numerous others resident in the Sublocation had been labor migrants earlier. In Nairobi, an organization of Mbeere workers has been formed to assist newcomers as well as to disseminate news from the rural area. Cash incomes are used for local improvements at home, including building metal-roofed dwellings, payment of school fees for one's children and siblings, purchase of consumer goods, and care of parents. As parents have customarily looked to sons for support in old age, they continue to do so in the hope that a son's income will provide added security in an economy increasingly dependent on cash. Thus parents generally encourage labor migration, although the money it provides may also diminish paternal authority and the value on filial piety. Sons may purchase land or contribute money to the litigation costs of other descent groups in exchange for an award of land should the case be won. Additionally, money gives a man more room to manuever in marrying, for paternal assistance in accumulating bridewealth is less important when a man can pay affines directly or otherwise purchase livestock for them. At the same time, fathers lament this growing independence and attempt to reassert authority by their power to curse or to threaten disinheritance, although this latter sanction lacks force if a son has managed to purchase his own land or is cultivating parts of the estate before his father's demise.

Shortly before leaving the field in 1970, I attended an elders' assembly which had been convened to settle a dispute between an elderly medicine man, Njiru, and his only son, Ireri. The father and son aired their mutual grievances before five of their clanmates after Ireri physically assaulted his father and smashed his gourd of beer. For his part, Njiru had cursed Ireri. His curse was deemed particularly serious because it threatened Ireri not only with physical death but also with social death as Njiru said that Ireri would produce no more sons. That both men had been drinking led the elders to attribute such a foolhardy curse, which would also deny the continuity of Njiru's own line, to the old man's intoxication. The exact sequence of events leading up to the case was not completely clear, but prior to this hearing both men on a number of occasions exchanged verbal abuse and had at least once fired arrows at each other. Ireri some years before had married and established his homestead a short distance from his father's. After working in Nairobi, Ireri quarreled with his father, who felt that Ireri should give him some money. When Ireri began to raise tobacco, his father again sought money from his son, and mutual recriminations periodically surfaced. Njiru, shortly before the case, threatened suicide because of his son's disobedience as well as the beating suffered at his hand. The elders decided that Ireri should come forth with a male goat which would be killed and eaten in atonement for his assault against Njiru; the latter, it was decided, would be required to retract his curses using the first stomach (gītathira) of the goat, which is believed to cool (kūborobia) states of ritual danger. Moreover, the father would be asked to swear that he would never again curse his son.

What follows is an edited text of the ndundu, the deliberation by the elders following the disputants' testimony. It is a particularly apt representation of Mbeere cultural values supporting the father-son relationship. Because Ireri already attained majority and cultivated land provided by both his father and the lineage, the discussion of property transfer from father to son centered on moveable property such as beehives. There were no other sons to inherit the property, and the elders did not consider disinheritance as an option for Njiru, who never raised

143

the issue. Among the five Mūkera clanmates of Njiru and Ireri, three men were from their lineage and two, including Nderi, a former Nguthi subchief, were from another lineage.

Nderi: Ireri is annoyed with his father for throwing ashes and shooting an arrow. [Njiru cursed his son by throwing ashes and saying, "may Ireri be lost like these ashes."] Who is bad?

Nthiga: They are both bad. When Njiru drinks beer, he causes trouble. When Ireri drinks, it is the same thing.

Nderi: The arrow was shot, a gourd was broken. We want you to tell us what we shall do. This is your home. [Nthiga does not live in the homestead of Njiru but is of the same lineage.]

Nthiga: We must make them swear they will not do these things again. That is an oath.

Mirongo: Ireri is born of Njiru. Njiru helped him marry a wife. Ireri will provide a goat and that is where we shall get the stomach to pick up the ashes for the retraction of Njiru's curse. Njiru is a parent, and he cannot throw his child away.

Njenga: Njiru was slapped and knocked down. We shall tell him to provide a goat because he beat his father and knocked him down.

Mirongo: He also broke the gourd.

Njenga: If we do not settle this fairly, he will still beat his father and the other people will start beating their fathers. We shall give Njiru an oath using that goat. We shall tell him to swear that he will not say that boys will not be born in his home.

Nderi: He will also swear that he will not curse
              Ireri ever again.

Njenga: It wouldn't be bad even if he is killed
              by such an oath. But his son also did
              something very bad. He broke the gourd
              instead of drinking from it. If we don't
              ask him to provide a goat, Nderi will be
              beaten by his son. I shall be beaten as
              will other parents. Ireri will provide a
              goat and the stomach. [Njenga's words
              were to prove tragically ironic when, six
              years later, Nderi was beaten to death by
              his classificatory son, who was angered
              over his allocation of land prior to
              registration; as an important lineage
              leader, Nderi was very influential in
              determining the way land was to be
              distributed.]

Mūturi: Njiru will provide a *mbūva* [a larger
              gourd of beer]. We shall not tell him to
              swear that he didn't shoot an arrow
              because he will die if he swears that
              way. He will swear that he will not
              throw ashes or soil and that he won't
              curse his children. Ireri will provide
              the goat because he beat the elder. He
              beat Njiru twice in my presence; the
              first time Ireri slapped Njiru and the
              second time he used a stick.

Mirongo: It is a bad thing to beat a parent. Let
              this man provide a goat so we may defend
              ourselves from our sons.

Nderi: Ireri said that Njiru said that boys will
              not grow here. That curse will affect
              the entire home.

Nthiga: Njiru said that if it were a girl, she
              would not do these things.

Nderi: That is a bad thing for a parent to say.

Nthiga: Who would inherit the property if you don't have a boy?

Nderi: The property would be taken by other people. One man was cursed that he would not have a boy. Has he a boy now, although he has four wives?

Following the deliberation of the elders, these men called Njiru and Ireri to inform them of the results and to review the case. Although all the men recognized culpability by both father and son, they emphasized the obligations of a son to his father and admonished Ireri not to abuse his father. As fathers of adult children, they especially concerned themselves with filial obligations.

Mirongo: Ireri has called us and he is born. Njiru has called us and he fathered Ireri. What could you be proud of if you didn't have a son? Who can inherit your property if you die? Ireri, is there a child who comes from the sky like a drop of rain? You will bring a goat and Njiru will bring a *mbūva*. Njiru, I don't want you to lose your child. Ireri, I don't want you to be thrown away by Njiru.

Njenga: We have decided this because you beat the old man, although we know that Njiru made a mistake in throwing soil. Even if you appeal anywhere else you will be told to provide a goat because you beat your father. Even if you go to London you'll be told to bring a goat. With the goat, Njiru will take the oath, "may this oath kill me if I throw soil again and curse my son."

Nderi:	Ireri, you are annoyed and you have beaten your father. Do you know that you are an elder, and this person is weak? You beat him and after that you poured out his beer. You've made a mistake. Maybe that is the reason he throws soil.
Mūturi:	Another man cut his son with a *panga* after he broke his father's gourd.
Nderi:	If it had been Mirongo, he would have shot his son with an arrow.
Mirongo:	Ireri, you can shoot Njiru and be left with his beehives, but they will not be blessed. I want Njiru to bless you when he dies. I want him to bless you so that you have boys. I want him to bless the beehives for you.
Ireri:	I'll inform you when I get a goat.

Within the next month, the decision by the elders was carried out, although enmity between father and son continued. Njiru died in 1974, his hut was destroyed according to custom, and he was buried on his land, which reverted to Ireri along with the old man's beehives and other moveable property. If Njiru had more than one son, he might well have attempted to deprive Ireri of land in favor of another heir. As it stood, however, Ireri had one sibling, a sister, who was never considered a possible heir. Also, recognition of Njiru's shortcomings by the elders made it very unlikely that they would countenance any notion by Njiru to disinherit his son in favor of a classificatory son or brother. Although I suspect but cannot demonstrate that physical violence and cursing between fathers and sons has grown more frequent over time, it is nonetheless clear that the sources of domestic conflict have expanded. At the same time, the elders in this case upheld customary values while recognizing a potential for filial violence in their own sons and a corresponding loss of paternal authority.

147

The major change facing the people of Nguthi is of course land registration, and further alterations in the domestic group, paternal authority, and agnatic kinship will likely follow in its wake. It is still too early to assess fully the outcome of this tenurial transformation and the concomitant effects on domestic social relations of land shortage, cash crops, and agricultural innovation. Similar processes are also reshaping other African agrarian systems, although consequences vary and do not inevitably include diminishing paternal authority.

Among the Nyakyusa, for example, Gulliver argues that land shortage has enhanced the authority of fathers. Customarily, a son, before the onset of puberty, moved from his father's village to join youths of the same age in founding a new village. The new village was independent of those where the youths' fathers resided and was also independent of the age villages of older and younger brothers. The Nyakyusa developmental cycle thus admitted only very short term co-residence of fathers and sons. Because land was freely available for new villages, inheritance played no role in the acquisition of land. But with growing land shortage and increasing population pressure, the authority of fathers over sons has increased along with conflict over inheritance, which is now "the most common way of acquiring land." Gulliver goes on to point out that "sale and purchase of land is disapproved and almost impossible" (1961:17).

This latter feature particularly contrasts with the experience of the Mbeere for whom sale and purchase of land has long been familiar. It could be carried out on an individual basis if lineage land were not at stake, or, in the latter instance, with the cooperation of agnates. Registration of titles, however, will ultimately render superfluous the interests of agnates in one's land, as buying and selling land have already reduced paternal control over the minority with the resources to enter the growing marketplace in land. Acquisition of land thus does not depend solely on inheritance. But founding new land from wilderness is no longer feasible, for extensive land claims have created an artificial shortage. According to the 1969 census, with a population of 205 persons per square mile (Kenya Population Census 1971:24), Nguthi is the second most densely populated sublocation in the three oldest Mbeere locations. By 1979, according to census figures (David Brokensha, personal communication), the population density of Nguthi had dramatically increased to 311 persons per square mile. Individuals with the resources can buy land either to augment holdings they stand to gain from inheritance or to form an estate exclusively on the basis of purchase. The number of people capable of entering such transactions is very limited, but the marketability of land has nonetheless encouraged an impulse to private gain and a concomitant weakening of customary constraints on some individuals. At the same time, the cooperation of agnatic kin remains essential, for most farmers will gain registered title as members of groups which corporately claim particular land parcels. The role of extra-domestic kinship relations as well as the nature of individual action regarding land acquisition will be taken up in the following chapters.

Chapter Four

Clanship, Descent, and Descent Groups

Patriliny represents a fundamental principle of
Mbeere social organization and descent ideology. It
not only underpins clanship and lower level agnatic
groups but also provides the idiom of fictive kinship
created by the age organization and blood brotherhood.
Although patrilineal descent among the Mbeere is not
the encompassing principle it is among the Nuer and
Tallensi, it nonetheless defines the social core of the
domestic group and organizes those descended from the
founder of a landed estate. Until recent years, only
shallow lineages up to three or four generations,
sometimes coterminious with the domestic group itself,
exercised corporate rights in land. The widespread
availability of land set only natural or ecological
limits to the process of hiving off and the founding of
new estates. But in the last two decades, as land
registration became an inevitablility, agnatic kinship
has assumed a new importance as previously independent
shallow lineages coalesced into larger units claiming a
genealogical depth well beyond four generations.
Agnates thus forge themselves together into corporate
bodies larger than those heretofore known and make
collective claims to exceedingly large land parcels
much more extensive than the traditional estates of
domestic groups or shallow lineages. In order to
understand this critical transformation, it is first
necessary to examine patriliny and Mbeere ideas about
it in the context of clans and shallow lineages.

Clanship

Patrilineal descent forms the basis of clanship
and stands in opposition to affinity since marriage in
one's clan is strictly forbidden. Indeed, the
regulation of marriage, even in a negative, non-
prescriptive manner represents the major *raison d'être*
of the clans. A number of men suggested that clans
developed so that men would not marry their "sisters;"
they thought their argument all the more cogent when I
pointed out its tautologous basis. That is, a man

151

without genealogical knowledge cannot identify his "sisters" except through their common possession of a clan name. The arguments my informants offered nonetheless emphasize the importance of common descent, even if not demonstrable.

People of one's clan (*mūvīrīga*) are referred to as "our people," or simply as "ours." *Mūvīrīga* in its derivation refers to the entrance to a homestead and thus connotes something of the primordial qualities of the family. Clanmates are descendants through unknown genealogical links from the same mythic ancestress. They are united by a common clan name and the diffuse expectation of mutual support and a generalized sense of common interest symbolized by the fiction of domestic bonds, although economic realities and attendant conflicts frequently provide a stark counterpoint to ideological unity.

Clanship contrasts most strikingly with affinity, which creates very different expectations connoted by its Kimbeere form, *nthoni*, meaning shyness or shame. Marriage and its prestations are known as *ūthoni*, which also derives from the same ubiquitous Bantu root, *-thoni*. Behavior between affines (*athoni*, sing. *mūthoni*) takes place in the narrow range between extreme respect and complete avoidance. The former pattern characterizes the relationship between a man and his father-in-law, whereas the latter form defines the relationship between a man and his mother-in-law. Additionally, his wife's elder siblings are assimilated to the *athoni* category and similar expectations inform his relationship to them. Extreme respect begins with the onset of bridewealth negotiations between a woman's father and older brothers on the one hand, and her prospective husband and his father and brothers, on the other. Those who call each other *mūthoni* must be highly circumspect and spurn any but the most decorous behavior, which extends to a complete absence of interaction between a man and his mother-in-law. Both patrilineal descent and affinity, compounded by classificatory usages within the clan and by the extension of kinship terms to several fictive relationships, create a system of formally defined behavioral patterns which pervade entire parishes and contiguous neighborhoods. Fear of the stranger, especially from a clan not represented within one's locale, is predicated in part on his absence from the established network of clan, affinal, and fictive relationships, and hence from a ready-made set of guidelines for proper comportment.

From a woman's perspective, patterns of affinity are somewhat different, and within a homestead constituted of any of the family types identified in Chapter Three, affinal relationships, as conceptualized by the Mbeere, are not operative. With her husband, she addresses his parents as father and mother (*baba* and *nyanya*, or *maitu*) and comes to identify herself closely with his clan. I found that a married woman, on being asked her clan, was much more likely to name her husband's rather than her own natal clan, for it is through her husband that she gains use rights in gardens and livestock. Also, this identification is further enhanced by the secondary marriage practices previously identified, which also bond a woman, in her own right and through her children, to her husband's group. She also maintains a formal, distant relationship to her husband's father with whom even the slightest hint of intimacy, such as eating together or engaging in idle conversation, ought to be avoided. But this formality also characterizes the father/daughter relationship, and, more generally, that between people of opposite sex in adjacent generations. This relationship thus derives from categorical differences of age and sex and not specifically from affinity.

The patrilineal clans themselves assume the names of women, who are reputed to be their mythic founders. Each clan may in addition be known by a nickname (*njaū*, literally "calf") which is infrequently used. Occurring most often in songs, which tend to be highly metaphorical in their criticism of indiscretion, the nicknames also make possible ellipsis and indirection. Earlier observers (Lambert 1950) suggested that female names might be evidence of a matrilineal past. Although I have no data to the contrary, the evidence of female clan names alone cannot support the argument for evolutionary transformation in the system of descent. It is instead more pertinent to argue, as Evans-Pritchard did in somewhat paradoxical fashion, that patrilineal descent is passed on through females (1940:247). That argument derives from observations similar to those I have made of Mbeere domestic organization, namely, that a man's children by two wives are differentiated according to matrifiliation. Indeed, some Mbeere who have considered this paradox turn to the domestic group analogy and argue that common interest in property and sharing a more "complete" (biū) descent (that is, from two parents instead of from one) bond full siblings in opposition to half-siblings. In the same vein, they argue that children of each founding ancestress were opposed to each other by interest and descent. Certain clans, however, maintain a special relationship based on the belief that their founders were sisters. These groups, which I term phratries, are made up of only two or three clans. The relationship between clans within a single phratry is reflected in the applicability of the incest taboo and a rule of phratry exogamy.

Mbeere clans are further characterized by their division into two exclusive units, which I designate as "moieties," although this does not accord with general anthropological usage (based particularly on New World ethnography) emphasizing exogamy as a defining feature of moiety organization. Mbeere moieties maintain no such rule as people may marry within a moiety or across moiety lines, as long as other prohibitions, such as clan exogamy and avoidance of marriage with a first degree cross cousin, are observed. The moieties are named divisions--Thagana and Irumbi in Evurore, Mūruri and Ndamata in Mavuria. Other names, Ngua and Gatavi, are also occasionally used, but these appear to be more common designations for the analogous clan division among the Embu. These metaphoric names present allusions to strength and generation and become the symbolic idiom of boastful opposition so characteristic of dual organizations. Thagana is the Kimbeere name for the Tana River. The Tana is formed of numerous smaller rivers and streams flowing down to it from their source on Mt. Kenya, just as the Thagana moiety forms itself from its constituent clans. Irumbi, on the other hand, glosses as "mist," and refers to the

154

clouds which seem to envelop Mt. Kenya to the northwest. Members of Irumbi moiety may thus boast that their division is superior to Thagana, for the Tana exists only because of the Irumbi clouds which replenish it.

Neither clans nor moieties constitute corporate groups, although the bonds of patrilineal descent, even when putative, draw clanmates together through the use of classificatory kin terms linking clanmates with primary kin. Although an idiom of common descent vaguely characterizes the relationship between people of different clans within a single moiety, kin terms are not extended within the moiety, except in cases of intra-moiety phratry relationships. Members of a clan or moiety share a common identity embodied in its name, but they maintain no collective responsibility for control of resources, ritual, or sacred emblems. The extent of membership and its dispersion preclude the exercise of such corporate functions, but in view of land disputes clan and moiety identity have grown important in extending the range of possible alliances so vital in litigation. Any inquiry into moieties without exception provoked animated discussion about land claims, alliances, and legal cases. A similar pattern of moiety opposition activated by land issues developed in Embu Division in the early 1950s when processes now at work in Mbeere were enveloping the Embu (Embu District Annual Report 1951). Relatedly, moiety identity and appeals to moiety solidarity have emerged in the context of local politics. Particular chiefs and subchiefs are often cited by disgruntled constituents as favoring only people of their own moieties. Even in parliamentary elections, numerous informants argued that the two members who represented portions of Mbeere throughout the late 1960s and 1970s played upon moiety affiliation in garnering votes. In Nairobi, moiety organizations were formed during election campaigns (David Brokensha, personal communication).

It is difficult to determine the precise number of Mbeere clans due to their variation in size and distribution. Moreover the location of some Mbeere clans among the Embu, Meru, and Kamba represents one more example of the impossibility of firmly establishing "tribal" boundaries on the basis of discrete, cultural criteria. Clans are not associated with particular territorial segments, although certain clans, such as Mūkera in Evurore, may be heavily concentrated in a particular administrative unit. Table 7 lists Mbeere clans, divided by moiety and grouped into phratries.

It is important to note that the list of clans represents a composite of names provided by informants in northern and southern Mbeere and also drawn from Embu District records. In addition, Mbeere secondary students from various areas provided information in a survey of clan names (Brokensha and Glazier 1973:186). The restricted and variable distribution of clans within Mbeere is reflected in land disputes in Nguthi, where people from only sixteen clans have been engaged as litigants and witnesses. These clans are Gakaara, Ikandi, Kere, Mbutha, Mūrūrī, Mwendia, Nditi, Ngai, Ngithi, Thaara, Gatīrī, Magwi, Mbuya, Mūkera, Ngūgī, and Nyonga. People of some other clans live in Nguthi, but their numbers and their length of occupation have been insufficient to press a claim. I found no single informant able to list more than twenty-eight clans. This latter instance was unusual as the informant was ex-senior Chief Kombo, whose long experience in office enabled him to travel far more extensively than was common. More typically, elders of much more restricted experience would first name clans in their immediate parishes and sublocations, and these names never exceeded twenty-three.

Particular clans are well-known for certain distinguishing traits or capabilities. A segment of Kamūturi clan, for example, assumed an important role in determining the time for *nduiko*, the investiture of a new generation-set with ritual responsibility for sacrifice. While all clans participated in the investiture, some elders of Kamūturi initiated the proceedings.

Gekara clan, on the other hand, is noted for its skills in medicine, magic, sorcery, and *kioni*, a kind of evil eye. One segment of the Gekara clan, living at

Table 7

Mbeere Clans
Arranged by Phratry and Moiety

Thagana/Mūruri	Irumbi/Ndamata
Nditi	Kamūturi
Kere	Gekara
	Gatīrī
Gakaara	
Ngai	Mūgwe
Mūrūrī	Cīīna
	Ngūgī
Ngithi	
	Mbuya
Kiguru	
	Mūthiga
Mwendia	
	Mbandi
Ngui	
	Magwi
Thaara	
	Mūkera
Ikandi	
	Nyonga
Mūruga	
	Kacugu
Rūeru	
	Kamumo
Iguna	
	Iruma
Mbutha	
	Igamūvia
Ikunda	
	Irimba
Kiragua	
	Kathi
Ikambi	
	Rūangondi
Mūthigi	
Mwithia	
Riemi	
Marigu	

Uvariri on the northern slopes of Kiang'ombe hill in Kathera Sublocation, elicits greater fear and respect than any other group of magico-medical specialists in Mbeere. They are said to cause misfortune simply by their utterances, for the "tongue has magic" (*rūrīmī rūrī ciama*), as one deferential elder put it. They are famed for performing such extraordinary feats as driving wooden pegs into solid rock in order to secure animal skins for drying. It is also said that the Uvariri people of Gekara can turn water into milk (hence the name Kiang'ombe, the hill of cattle) and can even protect murderers by causing a kind of collective amnesia within the area where the crime was committed. The latter deed as well as other magico-medical services are rendered for a fee, and it is said that people from throughout Central Kenya seek out the Uvariri practitioners. The latter also travel beyond Mbeere to Nairobi and other towns in order to ply what my Nguthi neighbors considered a lucrative trade. Such experiences brought forth a sophistication I did not expect when I went to Uvariri to learn more about these famous magicians. After a lengthy trek to the slopes of Kiang'ombe, which in 1970 was still a very isolated portion of the Mbeere interior, I met a leader attired in coveralls, and I offered to snap his photograph. On many occasions, such an offer proved a useful device for gaining rapport, but my would-be informant replied with a rather haughty disdain that if he wanted his photograph taken he would go to a studio.

Although their various powers are not restricted to the members of Gekara clan, the Uvariri segment contains the most renowned purveyors of magic and medicine in Mbeere. Indeed, Mbeere, which has a reputation in Central Kenya as a place inhabited by powerful medicine men and sorcerers, derives some of its notoriety from Gekara clan and Uvariri in particular. As early as 1916, the Embu District Commissioner, R. G. Stone, noted:

> Embere [sic] is known as the great home of witch doctors for the majority of tribes on the East and South sides of [Mt.] Kenya, as well as for people from Nairobi, Kiambu, Mwimbi, and Machakos. For years Kichugu [sic],

158

Embu, Chuka, and Kamba in adjacent
districts have gone to Emberre [sic] for their
medicines, but it is only recently that their
fame has grown to the extent that it has now
attained . . . The principal medicine men live
together in a group of villages on the northern
slopes of Kiang'ombe mountain (1916:EBU/45A,
iii).

The skills of the Uvariri medicine men are taken
as evidence of the superiority of Irumbi moiety over
Thagana moiety in arcane matters, although the clans of
the latter are not bereft of practitioners. In the
recent past, people have in turn associated political
skill, particularly in the office of chief, with
Thagana moiety not only because of the lengthy tenure
of Chief Kombo of Mūruga clan but also because of the
successful and extensive land claims of two Thagana
clans of Nguthi during the influential term of a
Thagana chief from one of these clans.

The distinction between clans, and hence clan
identity, is so fundamentally important that a Mbeere
myth expresses clan differentiation in natural terms,
equating its import with the differences between the
sexes (Gorfain and Glazier 1978:927). Yet despite the
centrality of patrilineal descent in determining clan
identity, and the seemingly ascriptive quality of clan
membership, it is nonetheless possible for one to enter
a clan other than his father's. This possibility is
always latent when any child is born, for transfer of
genetricial rights in children depends on complete
payment of bridewealth, which normally remains
incomplete during a woman's reproductive years.
Particularly during circumcision rites, the latent
jural interest which people maintain in children of
their daughters and sisters becomes manifest; prior to
the rite, the initiate must gain permission from his or
her mother's brother. Moreover, this man, supported by
his agnates, takes the occasion to remind his sister's
husband of the latter's continuing obligations to him.
He may also threaten to withhold permission to proceed
with the rite, although I have no recorded cases of
actual refusal. But in addition to these rather formal
verbal expressions of a man's residual rights in his

sister's children, he may assume a father's prerogatives in the event that bridewealth in sufficient amounts has not been paid. In one case, a man betrothed the very young daughter of his sister to an age mate and received livestock in return; as the child's father had paid no bridewealth, he could not legitimately protest the action. In a more far-reaching case, clan identity was determined by uterine links. A woman, Ngūkū of Nditi clan, bore a child fathered by Gatiti of Mūkera clan. Gatiti paid no bridewealth to Njue, brother of Ngūkū, who remained with her brother. The child, Mbiti, was then considered a member of Nditi clan; he became known as Mbiti wa Njue, taking the name of his mother's brother rather than his biological father. Njue became his sociological father, helping Mbiti with his school fees and, later, his bridewealth. Mbiti addressed Njue as "baba," father, and the customary joking relation between mother's brother and sister's son was never realized. Mbiti's children, in turn, belong to Nditi clan.

Blood brotherhood presents a second mode of changing clan identity or creating fictive agnatic bonds in addition to those defined by one's clan affiliation. Known in Kimbeere as *gūciarana*, literally "to be born together," blood brotherhood creates the same expectations as the natural sibling bond. These ties might be formed between a Mbeere and someone from a neighboring group. A number of Kamba people, for example, settled in Nguthi in the late 1940s following food shortages in Kitui. The men were able to forge blood brotherhood links with members of the Cīīna clan, which is said to have historic connections to Ukambani. The Kamba settlers subsequently identified themselves as members of Cīīna, and the rule of clan exogamy has applied with equal force to their children. Between two people of Mbeere, blood brotherhood does not entail a formal change of clan affiliation but rather creates a fictive sibling bond and expectations of fraternal support and a concomitant renunciation of sorcery and other evil intent. These various expectations are mutually affirmed through an oath ritually guaranteeing that one who commits vile acts against his blood brother would himself be grievously harmed through the effects of the oath. Blood brotherhood within Mbeere is especially utilized by people who wish to share the craft secrets of such mystically dangerous practices as forging (ūturi) or medicine and magic (ūgo). Because divulging secrets inevitably makes one vulnerable to those who might abuse a newly acquired power, oaths are taken to reduce this threat.

People within a single clan or in different clans of the same moiety also utilize oaths to affirm solidarity and alliances. Sometimes termed kūnyua makara ("to drink charcoal"), such oaths of unity are believed to bond disparate groups together into a single entity just as a piece of charcoal is unitary despite its various fissures. The land issue particularly has stimulated oath-taking in preparation for legal cases, which, up to 1971, sometimes called for public oaths as an affirmation of truthful testimony. At the same time, such oaths also reiterated the alliances between disputant and witnesses, most of whom were of the same moiety.

Clan History

In precolonial days when clanship organized social relations locally, "Mbeere-ness" was not an issue owing to highly fluid ethnic and geographic boundaries. In addition, between northern and southern Mbeere, practice and belief marking what people call "Kimbeere," that is, Mbeere language and custom, vary, and some of these features came to resemble those of neighboring peoples as much as each other. Moreover, a diffuse precolonial polity, localized in a multiplicity of elders' councils and age-sets unintegrated at a higher level, militated against a strong collective identity. Mbeere history prior to European rule must consequently be seen as a plurality of local histories. Despite the ubiquitous occurrence of such legends as that of Kaviū, pre-colonial Mbeere history as a whole has little significance apart from the history of particular clans, clan segments, and age-sets within the circumscribed area of parish or neighborhood. But since the colonial era, as indicated earlier, ethnic identity has begun to assume significance in various contexts transcending clan identity. In regard to some land disputes, ethnic identity served the Mbeere well in their struggle against the Embu to secure control over the frontier area joining Nguthi and Kyeni Location of Embu. The government supported the Mbeere effort to settle on the frontier and further crystalized ethnic differences between the two peoples whose different responses to the Mau Mau movement conditioned official policy. Ethnicity has thus assumed an economic utility, which I consider in Chapter 5.

Even amidst the competing and interlocking claims to land, the Mbeere do not manifest a particularly energetic concern about clan history, except in its lower reaches where the issue of lineage rights to land based on length of occupation is chronically at issue. The early stages of clan history tend to be very vague and stylized, occurring as they do in a remote past prior to the emergence of age-sets or generation classes. Indeed clan history sometimes takes on a mythic quality as the narratives are set in a world of primordial incest or superhuman endeavors. Because each clan lacks corporate functions, territorial identity, and a publicly recognized leader, clan history has not customarily served to legitimate economic rights, ritual prerogatives, or political succession. The land issue, however, has created a new urgency for the construction of histories which sanction corporate land rights. It is thus the present and the recent past which condition the depiction and interpretation of antecedent events extending into remote time.

Clan histories I have collected parallel the tripartite pattern identified by Richards (1960:177-178). She argues that indigenous historical accounts of clans are preserved because they explain contemporary social arrangements, although the actual events and sequences depicted in these home-made versions of history may in reality be vastly different from actual events. Accordingly, the first stage in the account very briefly and with scant detail posits a place of origin of the clan or perhaps names an ancestor who may possess mythic or demigod attributes. Such qualities, for example, have been attached to the Mbeere hero, Kaviū, whose fame in resisting the Maasai has led several clans to claim him. Certain ancestors may have migrated to Mbeere because they committed incest and had to flee their original homes. Some informants claim that the Embu people descended from the incestuous union of a Mbeere brother and sister who were driven out by their kin. In a version of Gekara clan history, an ancestor of the Uvariri people is said to have dropped from the sky and to have possessed a tail. The second stage of clan histories emphasizes familiar social processes such as lineage fission, yet here may be included telescoped genealogies which compress history. Recurring structural relationships are thus emphasized at the expense of a temporally accurate chronicle of events. Finally, a third phase depicts recent events referrable to actual, uncompressed genealogies.

To illustrate both the relationship between clan history and genealogy and the contemporary concerns which constrain individual versions of local history, I include the following abbreviated account by Mwanīki Mūgendi from Mūkera clan:

Mūkera, a man, had three wives--Ciamūturi, Cianjeru, and Ciangoci. Ciamūturi gave birth to Mūturi; Cianjeru gave birth to Njeru and Nderi; and Ciangoci gave birth to Njage and Ngoci. Mūkera and his wives were from Ūgoti in Meru. The first man of Mūkera to come to Mbeere was Gumba; his son was Nthawi, and Nthawi's son was Muranja. These three men and their families fled from Mbeere when the Magogo arrived. They were called Magogo because their language could not be understood. Gumba, Nthawi, and Muranja fled as far as Tigania, Meru. Ngūkū of Mūkera left Tigania and returned here to dwell at a place near the present home of Nyaga of Gatīrī clan. I don't know the generations between Muranja and Ngūkū. Ngūkū had two sons, Ngoci and Njage, and these began the nyūmba (lineages) of Ngoci and Njage. These

163

two men found the people of Chuka and Embu hostile at that time. Each man produced a very large family. [According to the informant's genealogy, the generations from Njage, the reputed lineage founder, to the informant are: Njage, Mūgwe, Njenga, Iragu, Gīkombe, Mwingi, Thiba, Mūgendi, Mwanīki.]

Several elements in Mwanīki's narrative, diagrammatically represented in Figure 3, allude to migrations and alien peoples mentioned in other clan histories. I would not wish to dismiss such accounts as utterly devoid of historical value, but the historiographic problems of separating fact from fanciful legend are manifold. Nonetheless, suggestions of connections between the Mbeere and their neighbors, as well as their purported relationship to other, earlier inhabitants remain ubiquitous in these histories. For example, Mūkera clan is also found among Meru peoples, notably the Chuka. Moreover, the nickname, or *njaū*, of Mūkera is Igoki, the name of one of two territorial divisions of the Tigania and Imenti peoples of Meru (Bernardi 1959:9-10). The narrative also identifies Gumba as the first Mūkera man in Mbeere, although I never encountered an individual with this personal name. It nonetheless recalls an autochthonous people, called Gumba, whom numerous informants describe as diminutive hunters like the Ndorobo. The Gumba are said to have inhabited the land before ultimately disappearing. The son and grandson of Gumba take the equally unusual names of Muranja and Nthawi, which are normally used to designate two early generation-sets of the Nyangi generation class. Here the scope of Mūkera clan history is further enhanced by connecting it to the emergence of the generation system. This recitation attempts to connect the purported history of the Mūkera clan to the migrations and struggles of the people in Mbeere from what is posited as the beginning of remembered history. Mūkera people thus occupied the land before the Magogo whose antiquity antedates the earliest named age-sets and generation-sets. (The Magogo, who are widely known in other local histories as intruders, are sometimes called Thigagi; they are said to have been a "white" tribe whose language sounded like the squawking of

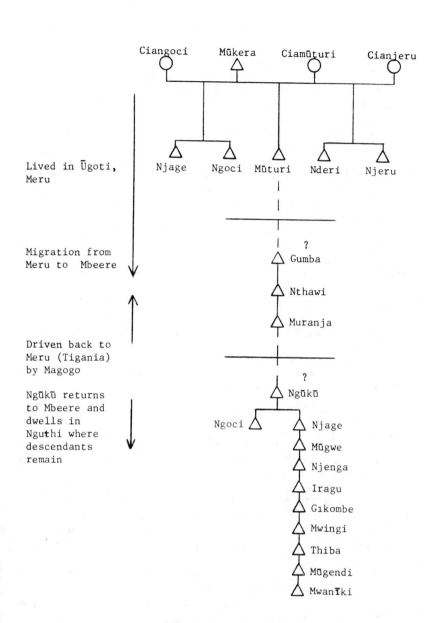

Lived in Ūgoti, Meru

Migration from Meru to Mbeere

Driven back to Meru (Tigania) by Magogo

Ngūkū returns to Mbeere and dwells in Nguthi where descendants remain

Mūkera Clan History

Figure 3

hornbills, *magogo*.) Like other clan founders, moreover, Mūkera is unfettered by collateral or ascending lineal bonds, as if all kinship ties had been previously broken and the social world begun anew with his marriages and the birth of his descendants.

In a Malinowskian vein, Richards has argued that genealogies function as mythic charters. This point is immediately germane in Nguthi, where people for the first time must cast about for genealogies and agnatic histories to legitimate claims to land. Yet the narrative itself begins with an anomaly, for the informant says that Mūkera was a man. The more usual assertion that clans were founded by women is thus contravened. L. Bohannan (1952:309) points out a similar phenomenon among the Tiv for whom the sex of an eponymous ancestor can vary. The significance of both the Mbeere and Tiv examples ought not to be dismissed as simple inconsistency or confusion about a fundamental genealogical feature. Rather, the import of these examples lies in what is communicated about the structural relationships of dependence or superiority between lineage segments. Among the Tiv, such relationships between different segments may be articulated regardless of the sex of the eponymous ancestor. Similarly, in the Mbeere case, the informant in the first phase of the narrative, which notes the origin of the Mūkera clan, presents the relationship between the five maximal lineages of the clan in Nguthi by playing on familiar principles of the house-property complex and matrifiliation. Alternatively, the relationship between these lineages could have been expressed equally well by designating Mūkera a woman with five sons. The informant's version gives greater emphasis to the division within the clan, for three of the segments become manifest immediately on Mūkera's marriages. If Mūkera were presented as a woman, segmentation would not become apparent until the following generation; moreover, in the latter case, the relationship of the eponymous brothers, as sons of one mother, would be structurally closer than the relationship described in the actual account. In either case, the emergent lineages are Njage (the informant's), Ngoci, Mūturi, Nderi, and Njeru. Njage and Ngoci are full brothers who stand in opposition to

Mūkera's other offspring, namely the full brothers Njeru and Nderi, and Mūturi, who is the only son of Ciamūturi. Although the order of wives given in the narrative suggests that Cianjeru and Ciamūturi are senior to Ciangoci, this assumes less significance than the membership of the three separate houses formed by Mūkera's wives.

In the third phase of the narrative, which describes the return of Mbeere people to Nguthi, the association of Ngoci and Njage is reiterated as they are named the immediate founders of their respective lineages. The particular house complexes represented in this account are especially meaningful in relationship to current struggles over land, for genealogies, especially in this highly factionalized area, speak to immediate interests centering on corporate control of land supported by assertions of long-term occupation. Although an indeterminate number of generations typically falls away between the lineage founder and clan founder, the Mbeere are not much troubled by the vagueness of remote history. It is rather the activities of more recently deceased kinsmen which are pivotal in framing a proper land case. Because prolonged occupation of the land, recounted for each generation, is asserted as a matter of course by Nguthi cultivators, the specific activities of fathers and grandfathers corroborated by witnesses become vital in pressing a claim.

The informant's lineage, Njage, has opposed Mūkera clanmates from the lineages of Njeru and Nderi in land cases, and Njage men have served as witnesses on behalf of other non-Mūkera lineages against the claims of Njeru and Nderi. The lineage of Ngoci has been allied to Njage as reflected in their positioning as full brothers at two points in the genealogy. Mūturi and his descendants emerge as somewhat neutral figures in this representation since Njage and Mūturi are not antagonists in land cases nor are they opposed as witnesses in other cases. The order of presentation of Mūkera's offspring also reflects a generally agreed upon view by Mūkera clansmen about the size of the various segments. Mūturi is the largest followed by Nderi, Njeru, Njage, and Ngoci.

If genealogies and clan histories function as mythic charters to explain the configuration of present interests rather than to chronicle the past, then a clan's history and the genealogies embedded within it must be variable. Indeed this is the case as one or another lineage of a large clan like Mūkera offers its own version of clan history. A man of Nderi lineage of Mūkera clan, for example, chose to deny that Nderi and Njeru were full brothers, as claimed by my informant from Njage lineage. From the latter's point of view, Nderi and Njeru people had simply been opposed to those of Njage. But from the perspective of Nderi, a protracted land case involving valuable land surrounding the Kanyuambora market had been contested in a particularly difficult case between Nderi and Njeru. In his version of Mūkera history, my Nderi informant emphasized the full sibling relationship between Nderi and Mūturi, the eponymous ancestor of the largest Mūkera lineage to which Nderi has been allied.

In the absence of writing, such variability is inevitable and provides flexibility in the uses to which genealogies can be put. Political and economic interests change through the course of social life, and genealogies as a fundamental expression of this interest subject the past to continuing scrutiny and reinterpretation without the burden of reconciling inconsistencies. In discussing the legitimating role of genealogies among the Tiv, Bohannan has suggested the possibility that a lineage system may flourish only in an illiterate society (1952:314). Although Chinese examples indisputably undermine her claim, it is nonetheless clear that the growth of literacy in a previously illiterate society, as Bohannan demonstrates, is very germane to the question of how genealogy functions as a mythic charter and indeed how the very quality of social relationships can change. When I sought genealogies or clan histories, I was often referred to lineage secretaries who, in consultation with particular elders, had recorded what were considered the most salient features, often reiterated in litgation, of migration and the line of descent from a clan or lineage founder. Certain informants would not discuss their genealogies until they could consult notebooks where the "official" record had been set down. Literacy has thus militated against the flexibility implicit in oral recall of genealogy and clan history. Moreover, it dramatically narrows the circle of those who now legitimately command this knowledge and is consistent with the continuing development of economic and political differentiation. Names and relationships in the consensual written versions of clan history become static, which effectively removes them from the ebb and flow of social life through which they ordinarily would be shaped. This process of fixing genealogies is also intimately connected to the increasing mediation of social relationships by courts and other legal institutions predicated on conflict resolution through reference to evidence which presumably is immutable.

A written genealogical record lends itself to exclusivity in group membership, yet can be modified as new coalitions form and additional financial contributions are collected from clanmates. Literate leaders or leaders supported by a literate cadre control membership. Although particular clan segments, having just recently migrated to the new area, may well have no historical connection to a given piece of land, the written genealogy can be readjusted by "discovering" a previous ancestor of the line in question and asserting that he lived in the territory to which rights are sought. Of course, such discoveries are usually contingent on financial contributions from the new group and on insider decisions that the newcomers could advantageously extend the range of cultivation in the disputed land.

Literacy is limited to a small proportion of the population, and economic position and conficts over access to productive resources have been influenced by differential mastery of the written word. For the first time, the past is dramatically set apart from the present. Its interpretation is subject to the decisions of lineage leaders who fix history in the image of their own group's narrow exclusionary interests. Accounts of the past are set in writing, subject to disagreement and skepticism, and thus they become the wellspring of continuing factionalism. Certainly the

169

past was at times re-created when non-literacy was universal, but it was re-creation that was highly fluid, readjusting relationships between non-hierarchical groups without creating distinct classes of landless outsiders. Of course, literacy and non-literacy co-exist in Mbeere, leading to two strata within the population defined by access to the written word. Moreover, writing sensitizes people to inconsistencies in oral transmission resulting in "the notion that the cultural inheritance as a whole is composed of two very different kinds of material; fiction, error and superstition on the one hand; and, on the other, elements of truth which can provide the basis for some more reliable and coherent explanation of the gods, the human past and the physical world" (Goody and Watt 1971:49). The Mbeere, like so many other people to whom literacy has been spreading, perceive in the written word a particular force, not so much derived from an intrinsic quality of the sign but more from a perception of the power accruing to those, such as blacksmiths, medicine men, and sorcerers, who own specialized knowledge. Like the secret which derives its power from highly restricted social access to it, the written word, which is mastered by Europeans, the local political elite, lineage secretaries, and some other controllers of material and non-material goods, is surrounded by an aura of authority. Something of this attitude toward literacy inspired several old men who regularly carried small notebooks and pencils tucked into their pockets. With great difficulty, they would write their names for my inspection, implicitly declaring that they too had access to the fixed truths of the written word and the changing world it has come to symbolize. Set against the spoken word, writing, as Goody and Watt note, is the source of "reliable and coherent explanation."

Where literacy is a growing but relatively new phenomenon, the status of the written word can take some ironic twists. When I was investigating the age organization and its generational aspect in particular, I was eager to collect generation-set chronologies and descriptions of the defunct succession rituals. One of the few published sources on this topic was Lambert's *Kikuyu Social and Political Institutions*, which

170

contains sections on the age organization among the various Kikuyu-related peoples. It is a study well-known to any anthropologist or historian who has worked in Central Kenya. As I collected various chronologies and accounts of rituals from men in their sixties and seventies, I heard from some of them that I should also consult two men, considerably younger than themselves, who would provide me with very rich and detailed information. I found it unusual that older men, some of whom had participated in the no longer viable generation-sets, would defer to their juniors, who had no comparable experience. The younger men nonetheless proved to be very knowledgable. But in closely studying their accounts, collected in Kimbeere and Kiswahili, I noted a more than passing similarity to the descriptions of Mbeere and Embu generations in Michuki's *Būrūrī wa Embu (The Country of Embu)*, written in Kikuyu and available as a local history for secondary students. Coming full circle to Lambert, who extensively interviewed Mbeere elders, I found that my informants had indeed read the Michuki pamphlet, which itself faithfully follows descriptions contained in *Kikuyu Social and Political Institutions*.

Control over people, once sufficient in itself to create "big man" status, currently depends on the strict control of land now facilitated by written records. When land was a free and virtually unlimited good, genealogical manipulation was superfluous, especially as an arbiter of land access. At the same time, migrants would be absorbed by local descent groups and their parent clans through rites of blood brotherhood and adoption. Similarly, warriors could marry captured women or could sell them to other men, but in either case the pattern of absorbing strangers continued, thereby enhancing the human resources of the various groups. But as land has become both scarce and valuable, the older pattern of absorption and inclusiveness has been reshaped into one of exclusiveness. Money, literacy, and land scarcity have now combined to alter Mbeere society along lines that anthropologists have identified as traditional in many Asian societies, where the political economy was more severely constrained by population and land shortage.

Recently, Watson (1980:11-12), following up on Goody's arguments (1971), has compared African and Asian (particularly Chinese) forms of slavery in terms of open and closed models. African forms, predicated on the control of people as the means to power, absorbed slaves and other outsiders into local groups with relative ease, consistent with the easy availability of land. Asian systems, in contrast, were very exclusive owing to limited land. It was highly unlikely that a slave or other outsider would be absorbed into a local lineage unless great outlays of wealth went into the coffers of the host group. Chinese lineages made every effort to control closely their landed estates, and this control included severe restrictions on rights of access to lineage land.

Ancestral Shades and the Range of Effective Agnation

I have been arguing that Meere social organization was historically predicated on mobile domestic groups and shallow lineages reaching three or four generations in depth and that the emergence of larger descent groups claiming greater depth is a recent development coming in the wake of national land policy. The larger question here concerns effective agnation, that is, the range of agnatic kinship in which social relations are frequent and functionally significant. Here I emphasize the exercise of corporate responsibilities as an index of functional significance, for collective rights and duties load agnatic relations with a content that is otherwise missing in the relationship between more distant clanmates bound together only by an ideology of shared descent and common proscriptive marriage rules. An examination of the Mbeere conception of spirits of the dead can shed additional light on the scope of patrilineal relations. I do not assume that a people's view of its ancestors perfectly mirrors the social order, for noteworthy exceptions to this simple view spring immediately to mind (e.g., Evans-Pritchard 1956; Lienhardt 1961). On the other hand, neither do I assume that beliefs and practices surrounding the ancestors develop *ex nihilo*, as it is clear that ancestral cults often reveal a refracted "structural matrix" (Fortes 1965) and a segmentary division of labor, so to speak, among the ancestors.

172

The Mbeere data, in this vein, suggest that the scope of agnatic kinship coincides with the range of ancestral power, which diminished in its specificity beyond two generations from ego.

The Mbeere refer to spirits of the dead as *ngoma*. I shall follow Wilson's usage (1957) in calling these spirits "shades" since this term also conveys part of the Mbeere conception of ancestors. People thus liken a shade to a shadow (*kīruru*), which is visible but beyond reach. A shade in its physical manifestation takes on a distinct form yet is completely insubstantial.

Ancestral shades are associated with various places including hilltops, forests, pools of water, and other natural formations or areas beyond human habitation. Shades reveal their presence primarily through their singing, although Christians and non-Christians alike claim that such singing has been less often heard since the coming of Europeans, and the missionaries in particular. It is believed that in some areas the shades have completely disappeared. Indeed, I encountered few cases of shade affliction. In seeking mystical explanations for specific misfortune and suffering, people more readily turn to their beliefs in sorcery. They are generally much more concerned with the human agents of evil, who may well operate through mystical means, than they are about the effect of the dead on the living.

People believe that the shades do not inhabit cultivated areas because they wish to remain hidden in a nether world. But at night, they might well venture into open country, well-trodden paths, or fields, where their singing can also be heard. Although songs are generally associated with celebration, singing by the shades is no cause for levity. But as these songs evoke apprehension in the living, they presage celebration for the shades, who will augment their own numbers if they can visit death on the human community. Thus people regard the shades as a dangerous force whose intrusion into human affairs always brings illness, misfortune, or death. The living seek to keep the shades at bay and never attempt to gain their active assistance as they might attempt to do with elders. If one is fortunate, the shades will remain at a distance, but should they make themselves known, people must placate them to avoid misfortune.

The relationship between people and shades is asymetrical, for people regard shades as powerful, often arbitrary forces which may strike a devastating blow against the living or even against their livestock. In placating the shades with beer, people conceive of their libations or sacrifices, which they term *mbako*, as a coerced offering rather than as a gift or a token exchanged for something of equal value. Sacrifice to the shades, while it certainly possesses the trappings of exchange, is performed in order to suspend this quasi-social bond rather than to create or to renew one. Ironically, the welcome disappearance of the shades from particular areas is intimately connected to the suspension of sacrifices by those who have begun to doubt shade efficacy. Sacrifice itself thus gives symbolic recognition to the continuing connection between the living and dead despite the ostensible purpose of severing the relationship.

The term *ngoma* also describes consistent abnormal behavior which people associate with mental illness. In this instance, it is said *ngoma* have gotten inside the head of an afflicted person causing him to flaunt convention. One man, for example, often appeared at elders' councils where he might unexpectedly break into a case with a completely irrelevant discourse sometimes punctuated by singing and dancing. Such individuals, whose sensibilities had been distorted by shades, were consistently treated with a kind of amused tolerance; they were not regarded as conduits of instruction from demanding spirits. Possession is considered a more or or less continuing state which explains the unconventional behavior of victims. Yet there has not developed among the Mbeere any extensive spirit medium cults of the sort described for numerous other African peoples (Beattie and Middleton 1969).

The shades bring about misfortune in order to punish kin who have violated their wishes, or, alternatively, they may simply cause suffering capriciously. In the first instance, a shade may afflict a kinsman abrogating an injunction issued prior to the shade's decease. Known in Kimbeere as a curse (*kīrumi*),this injunction acts to insure that an elder's wishes, particularly regarding his estate, are observed. In its operation, an ancestor's curse is very similar to the curse (also known as *kīrumi*) of the elders' assembly. Both types of curse are phrased in contingent terms; that is, if one acts in a particular manner such as abusing kinsmen, he will fall victim to the pains and infirmities articulated by the curse. A Mūkera clansman, for example, has long been afflicted by a palsied condition causing his hands to tremble and his speech to slur. He explained that as a youth he was very disobedient, and his father threatened to curse him should he persist in his bad conduct. He remained insolent and uncontrite and now suffers his physical condition, which he attributes to his father's wrath. His malady represents a particularly serious form of the curse because the condition is regarded as permanent owing to the shade's refusal to withdraw its power.

In other instances, libations of beer poured out around the home are believed to placate an angry shade, and a victim may thereby return to health. Most often beer is poured out from the entrance of the hut, where a sick individual resides, to the periphery of the homestead where the cleared area gives way either to bush or to a path which will lead the shade away. It is believed that the shade is then escorted from the world of the living, including habitations and cultivated areas, back to the wilderness. Sometimes beer is deposited in hollow tubes set about the homestead in order to induce the shades underground where they are also presumed to reside. I found no restrictions on rights to approach a shade, although a father will do so should his minor child's illness be divined as shade affliction. In no sense does the senior male in a homestead exercise exclusive prerogatives to placate shades.

The capriciousness of shades most often occurs through their collective action. Like their human counterparts, the Mbeere explain, the shades live in families which carry on familiar activities; they herd animals and even perform circumcisions. The various families of shades are in turn grouped into clans. But more interested as they are in the effects of the dead on the living, the Mbeere maintain very vague notions about the habitation of the shades and their organization. Although they are said to live in families and clans, conventional loyalties, especially to agnates, constraining human social relationships have little place among the shades, who regularly contravene normal human expectations about kinship. They thus exercise their greatest threat collectively, as they cooperate to strike at kinsmen or others indiscriminately and with little warning. An elderly informant, for example, gave the following account:

> Don't you know that the shades beat people?
> They might also hold celebrations for
> circumcision. We were even chased by them.
> They threw sticks at people. There was a man
> called Nyaga Mate of Mbandi clan. He lived at
> Ciangai. He migrated to a place near the Uya
> stream. People helped him build a house in
> one day. During the night, he heard this:
> "Drive the cows away. Who has built his
> house here? It is Nyaga Mate." It was the
> shades. They said: "Tell him that he has
> built on the path our cattle take to the
> river. Tell him that we should not find him
> here tomorrow. If we find him here again, we
> shall kill him. Tell him to return where he
> came from." Nyaga returned to his old home
> the next day.

In other cases, one who merely reports that he has heard the shades singing may be asked to sacrifice a goat to keep the shades outside of human settlement.

The generalized association of shades with the wilderness rather than with particular grave sites is consistent with Mbeere mortuary practice in precolonial times. At death, disposal of the corpse only in rare instances entailed burial. Normally, the dead were set out in the bush for scavengers such as jackals and hyenas to carry away. Popular fear and loathing of the

176

hyena (*mbiti*) derive in part from its association with death, and indeed those who disposed of corpses were protected from pollution by special techniques termed "magic of the hyena" (*kīama kīa mbiti*). People sought to remove the dead quickly and expeditiously without resort to elaborate ritual. They also spurned the creation of shrines or other commemorative acts. If a person died within a dwelling, that structure was promptly destroyed to purge the taint of death from human habitation. The recently dead then joined the other shades at some indeterminate place, and the living sought to reaffirm that separation whenever shade intrusion into human affairs occurred. Under colonial edict, burial of corpses was instituted in 1930. People now prefer to be buried on land they have cultivated, and this very different means of disposal of the dead has created rather more enduring links between the deceased's descendants and the land. As a consequence, people have begun to assert that particular territories have come to be associated in a tangible way with individual forbears they consider to be founders of the land. By pointing out grave sites of such people and enumerating their kin buried in the same locale, individuals and lineages attempt to demonstrate continuity in a line of descent within a circumscribed but often disputed territory.

In the precolonial period, individuals of particularly noteworthy achievement might be buried. These persons may have been rich in cattle or particularly old at the time of their deaths. It is said that burial occurred in order to preserve these auspicious attributes which might otherwise be dissipated by the more usual procedure of exposure. These burial sites known as *iri* were not subject to any special attention but, like other natural formations, they harbored shades whose singing could be heard within. As people cut down bush to begin cultivations, they sometimes encounter groves of trees where someone has heard the shades. These groves are then left intact, for it is believed that they may be burial places, although the identity of the dead person has likely been forgotten. Cutting such groves constitutes a taboo, which in itself risks community misfortune, for it threatens to bring down the wrath of the shades,

177

who wish such forests preserved as their own abode.

The few cases of shade affliction by specific spirits which I recorded centered on fathers or grandfathers. I am unable to discern if shade affliction has in fact declined in recent years as people uniformly contend, but the interest in genealogically closer patrilineal kin as the source of specific suffering suggests that beyond this level agnatic kin are submerged in the generic category of "shade." In cases of specific affliction, corporate action to placate the shade does not occur as the afflicted person, except minor children, takes responsibility for imploring the shade to desist from causing harm. In those instances when people hear shades singing or cut a tree from an *iri* grove, there is little concern about the identity of specific shades. Rather, they wish to avert the collective wrath of the shades, and they may sacrifice a goat in an *iri* grove to this end. Otherwise, drought, human or animal disease, or other catastrophes may strike the inhabitants of a parish. Unlike the sacrifice to a particular shade by an afflicted kinsman, this form of sacrifice is directed to the shades as a potent but internally undifferentiated threat to the community at large without regard to kinship relations between the living and the dead.

Mbeere ritual addressed to the shades does not reflect corporate lineage unity at any level. One either sacrifices on behalf of himself or his children or as part of a wider multi-lineage community defined by residential association. Unlike the Tallensi cult of the ancestors which is predicated on an intimate relationship between particular lineages and local areas (Fortes 1945:197), Mbeere social organization does not derive from a coincidence of community and lineage groups. Lineage and locality must be regarded independently as neither principle can be explained in terms of the other. Exposure of corpses in Mbeere funerary custom did not create an enduring association between lineage and locale; on the contrary, it dissolved any tangible connection, in the form of shrines or graves, between lineage and territory. In no sense, then, can Mbeere lineages be regarded as religious congregations defined either by common veneration of specific ancestors at particular structural nodes in the genealogy or by common territorial bonds which could be genealogically mapped in segmentary fashion.

Several years ago, Kopytoff (1971) suggested that anthropologists consider African ancestors in the same context as African elders. Relations of authority between elders and juniors, he argued, continue after the elders die, thus preserving the essential jural relation between generations. He preferred to talk of elders, whether living or dead, rather than to differentiate elders from ancestors. Kopytoff asserted that his formulation is more consistent with African conceptions and thus avoids the ethnocentric pitfall created by such English terms as "ancestor," which stresses the break rather than the continuity between the living and dead. While he demonstrates the relevance of his thesis to the Suku, they are probably exceptional in the uniformity of their linguistic and conceptual formulation regarding living elders and those deceased. Brain's contribution (1973) to the brief debate Kopytoff's article stimulated makes precisely this point. Although the Mbeere conceive of the effects of certain activities of living elders (such as cursing) as closely akin to the effects of a specific shade on the living, the term *ngoma* is linguistically quite distinct from the terms for elder (*mūkūrū* or *mūthuri*). Moreover, the noun classes subsuming "shade" and "elder" are different, as only the latter term falls into the person class in Kimbeere.

Illness and misfortune follow from anti-social or immoral actions explicitly prescribed by elders who, at death, can act as shades directly afflicting miscreants. In the case of living elders as embodiments of the moral community and capable of punishing non-kinsmen, violation of their collective curse invites a just doom much in the manner of the "breath of men" among the Nyakyusa, whom Wilson explicitly compares to the Kikuyu, Embu, and Meru in this regard (1951:168). Yet for the Mbeere, capricious affliction by shades acting in concert significantly

179

departs from notions which invest elderhood with moral authority. Thus Kopytoff's argument cannot be sustained in this context, for although the Mbeere conception of the shades is in part tied to their ideas about elderhood and its moral authority, it is not wholly explicable in terms of elderhood. What is especially significant here is the comparative unconcern of the Mbeere about the identity of shades beyond father or grandfather. Outside of one's specific connection to these lineal kin, relations to the dead are more categorical than structural and may perhaps represent a projection of the generic authority of elderhood, without an avowedly moral component, onto the spirit world. Thus an elder who dies may potentially afflict his sons and grandsons should they flaunt his moral authority just as he might have cursed them in life. But ultimately his identity as a shade will be submerged in subsequent generations as he joins other shades of his shadowy world in unprovoked assaults on non-kinsmen and the wider community.

Despite the use of lengthy genealogies to support land claims, fabricated tradition does not extend to the attribution of misfortune to remote ancestors, as one might initially surmise. The separation of recent forbears from genealogically more distant ancestors has been maintained, which can be explained in light of other varieties of legal evidence. Such evidence, including land improvements and loans secured prior to land reform, has proven extremely important, and successful litigation often follows from its presentation. Since the public record documenting this evidence has been set down only in the past two generations, it reinforces the identity of specific recent forbears as the parties responsible for key land transactions and, potentially, for affliction. These forbears, in turn, were among those first buried after the colonial authority banned corpse exposure.

Currently, burial represents a refiguration of the relationship between lineages and the land since graves establish a visible emblem linking territory to the individuals buried within it. By citing individuals buried in the land and pointing out their graves, a lineage emphasizes both its continuity and its territorial representation. This effort to reclaim the dead from their customary place in the untamed wilderness I have called the "domestication of death," for ancestors are now interred in contested land, which their descendants hope will be titled and the site of permanent residences and farms. The domestication of death is thus intimately connected to the social uses of tradition, which is constructed to serve pressing economic interests (Glazier 1984: 142-146).

*Maximal Lineages
and the Emergence of Descent Coalitions*

In discussing the Mbeere lineage, it is important to keep in mind its relationship to the clan, on the one hand, and the patrilineal core of the domestic unit, on the other. As I have noted, the Kimbeere terms *mūvīrīga*, *nyūmba*, and *mūcii* help to distinguish three levels of Mbeere society. Of course, living in a society is rather more complex than neat social anthropological models would imply. Although close to the actual experience of people and built up out of indigenous categorizations, these models attempt to make sense out of an empirical reality inevitably elusive and ambiguous wherein the clear distinctions of the anthropologist's models do not obtain. Thus the Mbeere usage of the above terms is fluid as people will designate various levels of descent as the clan. They may apply the term to a narrow range of people sharing a common grandfather or to the more inclusive descent group traced from a remoter ancestor. Clanship itself has become the main context in which people discuss corporate land holding, but the actual collective control of rights to land is vested either in a lineage segment of a clan or in genealogically unconnected segments (descent coalitions) purporting to be maximal lineages. The entire clan never serves as a corporate body in any context, although the inclusive nature of the term is used to designate descent-based groups at any segmentary level. At the same time, the usually more restrictive designation, *mūcii*, referring either to a domestic group or to a shallow lineage constituted of residentially proximate homesteads whose senior males are brothers, may sometimes be applied to a broader grouping. Similarly, the term *nyūmba* has several meanings; it may refer to a married woman's hut within the homestead cluster or to her children, especially her sons, as distinct from those of a co-wife. Moreover, the term also designates a maximal lineage, that is, a group of people claiming descent from an ancestor, sometimes genealogically traceable, whose antecedents remain unknown.

Despite frequent informant references to collective action by the clan, extended explanations of the distribution of various rights make clear that lower order agnatic segments form the locus of corporate responsibilities. In precolonial days, the rights to seek revenge or compensation after a homicide extended only minimally beyond the homestead of the victim; angered kin of the deceased would look immediately to the culprit's closest agnates for redress. Moreover, customary punishment of an unregenerate or chronic sorcerer was meted out by people of the parish led by close agnates (described by informants as people of the *mūciī*). Although particular punishments for persistent sorcerers varied, all were capital in nature. For example, a sorcerer might be bound hand and foot and then thrown into a river to drown. Some informants said that death by fire or stoning was also inflicted on sorcerers whose actions had been directly linked to recent deaths. In initiating the punishment, close agnates could remove any taint of suspicion that they too were sorcerers. At the same time, their active role also proclaimed the public nature of the punishment and their renunciation of any claims for compensation. Of course since the early colonial period, the government has assumed responsibility for the prosecution and trial of murderers and has suspended the customary right of local communities to execute sorcerers. In cases of outright homicide, informant testimony suggests that states of continuing feud, when compensation had not yet been paid, did not expand the range of antagonism. Rather, these matters remained the concern of a highly circumscribed body of agnates in the respective homesteads of the murderer and his victim. That is, the *mūciī* (domestic group or shallow lineage) in its

182

more restrictive referents was the socially significant group in this context. Indeed, agnatic relations were essentially played out in this narrow framework, and collective action or corporate responsibility was not characteristic of wider agnatic categories such as the maximal lineage.

With the beginning of intense competition for sizeable acreages of land, the maximal lineage and the descent coalition (also termed *nyūmba* and not distinguished from the maximal lineage by the Mbeere) have developed into kin-based corporations whose major *raison d'être* is the control of land. Each corporate group, comprised of a set of shallow lineages of the same clan, collectively presses land claims requiring money for the cost of litigation, labor for the demarcation of boundaries (according to official directive), and sufficient membership to demonstrate extensive use of the land being claimed. Accordingly, the labor and financial imperatives facing these larger lineages and coalitions overlay the values implicit in common descent. Although descent or the fiction thereof informs the membership of these groups and rationalizes their existence, it alone will not guarantee to an individual member an award of land following successful litigation. Rather, a member's contributions of money and labor are essential if he is to secure land from the corporate group at the conclusion of the land reform program. I consider in detail in Chapter Five the land policies which have stimulated the coalescence of shallow agnatic groups into larger units, but at this point I turn to the organization of these units--the maximal lineage and the descent coalition.

The general weakness of the maximal lineage prior to land reform stems from the diminished intensity of social interaction and common interest as well as the sense of attenuated obligation in the wider circle of agnates beyond full and half siblings and first degree patrilateral parallel cousins. Moreover, geographic proximity affects the extent of mutual support and assistance. One is more likely to turn for assistance to lineage mates in nearby homesteads than to those who live miles away, and the latter are more likely to be

genealogically distant as well. Without a corporate
identity in regard to land, vengeance, ancestral
veneration, care of shrines and the like, the maximal
lineage could not cohere with any more than a modicum
of solidarity. Compared to the shallow lineage, the
greater size and dispersion of the maximal lineage
further inhibited collective action, which was more
effectively and manageably undertaken by the smaller
descent group. But it is precisely the factors of size
and dispersion which make the maximal lineage
particularly well-suited to establishing claims to
parcels of land larger than any held heretofore by the
shallow lineage, for proof of extensive cultivations
in claimed territory, which the maximal lineage makes
possible, figures importantly in litigation. In
addition, descent coalitions may form out of shallow
lineages uniting with an established maximal lineage,
although assertions of common descent cannot be mapped
onto a unitary genealogy. Nonetheless, these
coalitions function like maximal lineages and are
identified with them, and the contemporary role of both
groups can be understood only in relationship to the
changing system of land tenure.

Maximal lineages and descent coalitions also
differ from smaller scale agnatic units in the nature
of their leadership. Seniority and the hierarchy of
age figure prominently in the organization of domestic
groups and shallow lineages, but in the larger agnatic
groups, other criteria for leadership obtain. Of
course, one must be rhetorically adept in the manner of
the skilled elders who regularly hear cases in council,
for leadership demands not only a capacity for the
organization of legal strategies but also the skill to
utilize them before legal bodies. But in addition,
one's position as a present or former chief, subchief,
policeman, or teacher can be turned to great advantage.
Thus some former chiefs and subchiefs, with the support
of the colonial authority, led the early settlement of
upper Nguthi and staked out claims for themselves and
their agnates, and they now plan the tactics for the
defense of these claims. As examplars of official
policy, their initial migration to upper Nguthi
provided important evidence in subsequent litigation.
At the same time, assertions about their forbears'

activities on the land, articulated in the idiom of tradition, continue to embellish their claims. Teachers, who command English, often serve as secretaries for their maximal lineages or coalitions and draft letters to court or to the land officers overseeing land reform.

In other instances, individuals who have been involved in significant transactions with the government, such as obtaining an agricultural loan prior to land reform or ceding land for public use, are called on by their kin to plan testimony relevant to those transactions and in support of additional claims. The current site of the Kanyuambora Market, for example, was ceded to the County Council in the early 1940s by a leader of the Njeru maximal lineage of Mūkera clan, and his transaction figures importantly as evidence supporting claims to surrounding territory. In another transaction, a member of the Kigamba lineage of Nditi clan who served in the home guard during the Mau Mau Emergency secured a grant of land from the government in recognition of his services, and he has utilized his initial grant to expand his claim well beyond its original limits. Leadership within a maximal lineage or descent coalition thus devolves to individuals capable of extending an initial advantage to encompass larger territories, but these individuals are also dependent on the cooperation of a coterie of literate kinsmen and the willingness of other agnates to contribute money to the cost of litigation.

Normally, agnates recognize a group of men, perhaps as many as half a dozen, who constitute a leadership *kamiti* (committee), although only one man can represent the group in litigation. He can nonetheless call on other committee members to support him as witnesses. Committees discuss legal strategies and will often set up mock hearings in which the *mūciri*, or litigant, representing the committee and agnatic group, is systematically challenged on the major points he will present. Although different litigants may represent a maximal lineage in disputes involving each of several contested parcels of land, it is much more common for a single individual to represent his group in all cases.

185

The organization of people identifying themselves as members of the Kigamba lineage of Nditi clan aptly illustrates the contemporary role of the maximal lineage and descent coalition in Nguthi. This group has successfully litigated over most of the land in Kavengero parish, and should their claims stand, several hundred people of Kavengero will lose the right to cultivate in that fertile area. They will either be forced off the land or will necessarily strike tenancy or purchase agreements with the Kigamba group. By early 1979, this vitally important case pitting Kigamba against numerous other groups it had defeated in litigation had been appealed to the highest level--the Ministry of Lands and Settlements, which oversees land reform throughout Kenya. The Kigamba cases have been more frequent and its claims more extensive than those of any other lineage, and should its legal successes be upheld, more than one thousand acres of rich land will remain under its control.

The Kigamba lineage proper is part of a larger group of agnates, a descent coalition, constituted of Kigamba and one additional segment of the Nditi clan. In not distinguishing the lineage, or *nyūmba*, from coalitions of genealogically unconnected clanmates, and indeed in the fluid usage of terms referring to descent-based groups, the Mbeere can readily justify the variable range of inclusiveness of intra-clan alliances. Figure 4 represents a skeletal genealogy of the Kigamba coalition, but it is important to bear in mind that this "official version" has been arrived at by the leadership committee solely for purposes of land litigation. What is immediately striking here is the alleged genealogical depth of the two coalition segments. I collected genealogies from forty-four male informants, and the recall of direct patrilineal forbears ranged from two to twenty-two. Those of greatest depth (sixteen and twenty-two) came from men of the two component segments of the Kigamba coalition. One of the leaders, Ndwiga, when he is engaged in litigation, recounts the generations and claims that a Nditi clansman, Kigamba, first cultivated Kavengero. Yet the genealogy reveals a distinct lack of collateral extension in any generation beyond that of the fathers

186

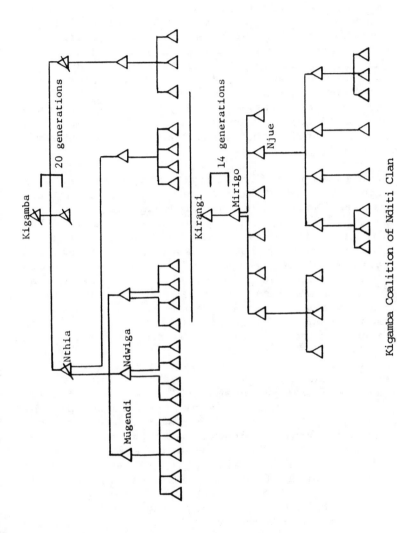

Kigamba Coalition of Ndiiti Clan

Figure 4

187

of the present leaders, who are the men of Ndwiga's and
Njue's generation. Popular opinion, including that of
other Nditi clansmen not immediately implicated in the
Kavengero litigation, asserts that only within the last
fifty years has the parish been settled by Mbeere
people. Yet Ndwiga and his agnates predicate their
numerous land cases on adamant assertions of their
ancestors' occupation of Kavengero many generations
before the appearance of those they consider recent
interlopers. In contrast to the more usual pattern of
telescoping genealogies embedded in clan history, the
Kigamba leadership audaciously stretches the line of
descent from the putative founder of Kavengero to the
present generation and further asserts that the allied
segment of Kirangi also descended through unknown links
from Kigamba.

Leadership within Kigamba has devolved to a
committee composed of Mūgendi and Ndwiga, eldest sons
of Nthia, and Njue and his sons. Ndwiga has emerged as
the public spokesman of Kigamba and represents the
group in land litigation. In addition to planning legal
strategies, the committee also organizes boundary
demarcation, which has required the labor of Kigamba
men. By threatening to deprive them of land, the
committee can mobilize agnatic kinsmen to plant sisal
along Kigamba's boundaries. Moreover, the committee
assesses members for the cost of litigation. Failure
to contribute money is also penalized by cancellation
of a member's right to land. Such a monetary
contribution, known as mūvothi, is distinguished from
payments amounting to hundreds of shillings each by
outsiders who have purchased land from the coalition.
Much wrangling among Kigamba people about the
disposition of the proceeds has resulted. Contributions
come primarily from within the coalition and from other
Nditi clansmen, but the committee has also taken money
from others, who seek compensation in land following
successful Kigamba litigation. Affines may also give
money to the coalition, although they must provide a
greater sum than that given by an agnate in order to
receive an equivalent amount of land. Whether through
purchase or contribution, the coalition by the mid-
1970s has agreed to cede land to approximately sixty
men outside of Kigamba pending the outcome of appeals

and the establishment of the final adjudication record. Included here were seven Nditi men from other lineages and seven affines of coalition members. But the vast majority of men outside of the coalition who stand to gain from its successes bore no ostensible kinship relationship to coalition members. These outsiders included men from ten different Mbeere clans of both moieties as well as men from Embu Division and from Meru. It is fundamentally a monetary transaction which transfers rights to Kigamba land from the coalition to non-agnates and thus provides a stark counterpoint to often-stated principles of customary law. That is, informants assert that land claimed by an agnatic group ought to remain under the control of members of that group and the same clan.

Amidst a seeming speculation in land by those able to purchase land from coalitions likely to win at litigation, pressure has built up within some groups, most notably Kigamba, against the leadership, which allegedly sacrifices the rights of members for financial gain from outside purchasers. Widespread complaints charge that male children will be deprived of land, and that some adults will receive less than fifteen acres, which they consider inadequate in light of the size of the coalition and the amount of land successfully contested. Sale of land has been spurred on by the steadily increasing value of Kavengero land, which sold for approximately 400 shillings per acre in 1973 and rose to approximately 1500 shillings in 1979. The impact of money and the financial cost of waging litigation, without which no one can gain the most valued land, also affect the organization of lineages and coalitions. Thus, although the principle of descent ostensibly underpins this organization and confers on members a right to a portion of corporately held land, these rights have also become contingent on one's labor and monetary contributions to the agnatic group. Despite its frequent invocation as the basis of land rights, the principle of descent enshrined in customary law competes with a growing monetization of land transactions, which also creates schisms among agnates increasingly pressed to balance their need for cooperation against a growing sense of self-interest.

189

In the Mbeere agricultural context, the fundamental constraint ordering personal choice is a land policy explicitly designed to enhance already well-developed entrepreneurial tendencies among local farmers. To enter the game, so to speak, one must gain title to land not only to achieve what will soon be the sole means of secure tenure but also to gain collateral for agricultural loans. Maximal lineages and descent coalitions arise in response to these needs, but they exist essentially as single issue interest groups quite unlike small scale shallow lineages and domestic groups wherein social bonds are much more diffuse and multifaceted. Hence a segment of one descent coalition may be allied, for purposes of alternate litigation, with other agnates, thus comprising another coalition. Of the Kigamba coalition, organized solely for litigation over the parcel of land in Kavengero, the segment headed by Njue is allied to a Kanyuambora segment of the Nditi clan descended from the famous prophet Mbogo Kirangi. Although limited in their success in opposing people of the Mbutha clan, this second Nditi coalition has contested land independently of the remainder of Kigamba; their ties to the latter (as represented by Mūgendi and Ndwiga, primarily) developed at a time when Njue lost his claim to land in Kanyuambora.

Leadership within the larger groups (coalitions and maximal lineages) falls to those who are best able to serve as brokers between official bodies administering land reform and their own supporters. Such leaders may be former chiefs and functionaries or allies and kin of these individuals. It is also widely believed that lineage and coalition leaders, such as those from Kigamba, especially, have attempted to bribe land officers to alter adjudication records.

While shallow lineages cooperate to protect their common interests in land, and may themselves form coalitions, they are increasingly drawn into alliances with more distant agnates as the scale of legal conflict and the size of contested land parcels increase. Large groups, whether they represent a single descent unit or simply use the fiction of descent to define themselves in a customary idiom, can mobilize more resources and manpower for the task of settlement, demarcation, and litigation, and thus gain a decided advantage in competition with smaller units. Within maximal lineages and descent coalitions, economic interest, apart from the diffuse bonds of kinship, activates agnation at its outer reaches, where clanship and a belief in shared descent are invoked to support a common struggle for land. In this respect, the wider range of agnation begins to make sense only in relationship to the transformation of customary land tenure and the unabashed self-interest it explicitly promotes. Accordingly, customary law, which has been the arbiter of land tenure through the entire process of land adjudication, is manipulated by the leadership, and evidence of both lineal succession and the concomitant passage of rights to a given land parcel is grossly exaggerated.

Chapter Five

Land Tenure and Government Policy

Until the period of land reform beginning in Mbeere in the 1960s, land for herding or cultivation was not a scarce resource. A mobile population migrated within Mbeere and beyond owing both to the quest for food during frequent famines and less severe shortages and to the less dramatic exigencies of shifting cultivation and pastoralism. Population did not press on a limited territory but rather expanded freely into previously unsettled land or into areas reclaimed from fallow. Small family groups could clear wilderness, claiming the newly cultivated land as their own, unfettered by extra-familial kinship bonds. Genealogical reckoning played little role in defining and limiting access to land, which was a free, uncontested resource. But a new drive has arisen by larger groups of kinsmen to maximize their claims to land and to gain a government-awarded title which will provide the security of tenure that only recently has become an issue. Claims must in large measure be based on customary rules as these have been interpreted by the government, at the levels of court and adjudication bodies, and by local contenders. In this chapter, I will examine customary land tenure as it is locally conceived, and the shifting official policies which are reshaping it. The melding together of small agnatic groups into larger coalitions, examined in the last chapter, is one index of these changes, which are rooted in the colonial past. It is thus necessary to consider both "tradition and change," but not in ways which identify an unchanging, insulated people suddenly plunged headlong into a modern world at the beginning of the colonial era. Although it is certainly true that events after 1906 have profoundly affected Mbeere society, it is necessary to examine the active role that people have played in using and at times in helping to shape these changes. Alterations in Mbeere custom must then be regarded not merely as a passive index of change but rather as a set of purposeful strategies for coping with economic and social

193

realities. These realities are best understood in the broad context of historical developments in central Kenya.

Land Tenure Prior to the Reform

Principles of land tenure are complex in any society and are usually understandable only in relationship to other social principles. In Mbeere, land tenure must be considered in the context of patrilineal kinship emphasizing seniority based on age and the organization of shallow descent groups in the politico-jural domain. At the outset, it is important to add a cautionary note about the familiar anthropological problem of translation, which seems especially acute in the present context. In regard to land tenure, terms such as "ownship," "sale," and the like applied to African systems may connote inappropriate meanings in light of Western conventions about private property, its disposition, and control. Ownership in a Western setting, for example, normally denotes certain individual prerogatives which are more comprehensive than one might likely find in kin-embedded forms of customary land tenure where, as in the Mbeere case, agnates limit a kinsman's prerogatives to alienate land outside the lineage. It is therefore preferable to discuss land tenure in terms of various categories of rights including those of use, sale, and tenancy. In thus discriminating between usufruct and transfer, the relationship between individual action and descent group constraint can be more finely charted.

Near each homestead are located gardens cultivated by various members of the domestic group. The senior male in the homestead allocates gardens to his wife or wives as well as to his married sons and their wives. Uncircumcised boys do not garden in their own plots but rather may assist parents in their cultivations. Commonly, people also maintain gardens beyond the immediate homestead area in other parts of the parish or sometimes in other parishes. Fragmentation of individual holdings forms a common pattern, reinforced in every generation by a mode of inheritance enjoining

194

a man to divide his own and his wives' gardens among his sons. Moreover, cultivators understand the variable requirements of different crops for particular soil types and minimal moisture levels, and thus value the prevailing pattern of fragmentation. Three separate surveys carried out by Glazier, Brokensha, and Heyer, Ireri, and Moris (1969) document this pattern of multiple holdings (Brokensha and Glazier 1973:190). Distances between gardens range from less than a mile to more than two miles. Individuals claiming more than four gardens do not cultivate these lands simultaneously but rather they permit some of these gardens to revert to fallow or allocate them to other people as the domestic group expands.

Cultivated land normally exists as part of a larger parcel known in Kimbeere as *kīthaka* (pl. *ithaka*). *Kīthaka*, as distinct from the cultivated garden (*mūgunda*), refers to a number of different conditions regarding the land. It can refer to unclaimed, uncultivated wilderness, and indeed the term can be used to designate anything which is untamed. Thus a wild animal is *nyamū ya kīthaka*, an animal of the bush, as opposed to a domestic animal (*nyamū ya mūciī*). The term may also designate uncultivated but claimed wilderness as well as claimed land containing both cultivations, gardens gone to fallow, and uncultivated bush.

All men tracing descent to the original claimant of a *kīthaka*, which I am glossing as "land parcel", are ideally entitled to gardens within that land. In reality, pressures on a particular parcel of land mount in each generation and spur the hiving off process whereby new wilderness areas are brought under cultivation. The particular land parcel claimed by an initial cultivator and his descendants is referred to as "founded land" (*runo* or *rūtego*).

Normally, one man within the lineage, the *mūtongoria wa kīthaka*, leader of the lineage, serves the group as a kind of trustee in matters concerning the land. He represents his agnates, although they assist him as witnesses in disputes concerning the land parcel. Such conflicts, however, were virtually non-existent prior to the 1960s; more commonly in this earlier period, land disputes centered on boundaries between gardens rather than on entire parcels of lineage land. Disputes over garden boundaries were generally easily settled and might bring about an adjustment of the boundary without questioning the very right to cultivate in a land parcel, which is a recent issue. With a marked increase in the frequency of litigation and a shift toward larger scale disputes coming in the wake of the land reform program, the role of lineage leader has accordingly expanded in those directions noted in Chapter 4.

Once an individual has inherited land from his father or begun cultivation of land gained from his lineage, his agnates do not interfere in these use rights. That is, a person freely uses the land as he wishes, determining what sort of crops to plant, including cash crops. Further, the lineage exercises no rights to any part of the harvest nor to money gained from the sale of tobacco, cotton, or food crops. Use rights gained from inheritance within the domestic group or from acquisition of lineage land (assigned by the trustee on behalf of the group) are indissoluble and provide the cultivator with wide latitude in the ways he will exploit the land.

Lineage control of land (whether a shallow lineage or one of greater depth) begins to assume special significance when a cultivator wishes to transfer use rights to another individual. Here ultimate "ownership" by the descent group asserts itself. Such transfers might entail either the granting of use rights to tenants or affines, or more seriously, outright sale of the land. I emphasize that such transfers were only occasional before the 1950s when pressure on land was developing, and when the land itself became a marketable good.

In transferring rights to land, either through tenancy or sale, special consideration is given to the disposition of useful trees. Valuable hardwood trees, such as *Mūkau (melia volkensii)*, which can be hollowed out to make beehives, may be sold or retained independently of the land itself. A purchaser must

196

explicitly provide for the transfer of tree rights
which usually requires extra payment; otherwise rights
to use trees do not, as a matter of course, accompany
the transfer of other rights in the land. The issue of
trees is especially acute in granting temporary use
rights to affines or tenants. Trees are not only an
economic good; once they have been used, such evidence
of exploitation of the land can be turned to advantage
in litigation.

A tenant (*mūvoi*, pl. *avoi*) may secure use rights
in gardens controlled by a particular individual
through the latter's membership in a lineage, or he may
gain rights to clear bush land controlled outright by
the lineage. In either case, representatives of the
descent group must grant permission. Although the
prospective tenant is expected to provide beer for
those whose permission he seeks, his tenancy rights do
not depend on providing either cash or livestock, as if
he were renting the land. Nor is he required to give
his patrons any portion of subsequent harvests. Once
permission is granted, however, a tenant cannot
transfer his cultivation rights to another individual,
nor can he bequeath the land to his heirs, although
tenancy rights are renewable by his sons. In cases of
long-term tenancy, informants argue, the possibility of
land disputes between tenants and hosts increases as
tenants grow to feel vulnerable at the prospect of
having to relinquish the land once written titles are
provided. Recognizing the potential for conflict
between tenants and their hosts, the latter attempt to
restrict tenants to the growing of seasonal crops only
(*irio cia mbura imwe*, literally "foods of one rain"),
such as maize or millet. Perennials, including such
familiar crops as bananas, mango, and *miraa (Catha
edulis*, the leaves of this tree are chewed as a
stimulant) should not be grown by a tenant. Since
these trees require years to mature, they may be cited
as evidence of long-term occupation of the land.
Tenants could then argue that they would not have made
such improvements to the land had their rights been
only temporary. Preventing tenants from growing
perennials thus undermines their ability to wrest
control of the land from their hosts; the latter can
more easily ask tenants to depart at the end of a

growing season. Such requests to leave have been rare until recent years.

Men seeking gardens from affines are in somewhat the same position as tenants. They control production, including planting and disposition of the harvest, but their usufruct rights are not transferrable, even through inheritance. As in the case of tenants, children of men who gain cultivation rights through affinity can renew these rights with their mother's agnates, and, until the issue of land shortage arose, cultivation through tenancy or affinal agreement was little practiced. Although a woman cultivates land by virtue of grants from her husband and husband's father, and thus gains usufruct rights through affinity, her position is rather different from that of a man whose affines provide him with land. She comes to identify herself with her husband's descent group, and her gardens are heritable by her sons according to the house-property principles discussed in Chapter Two.

While the descent group intrudes itself very little in the exercise of usufruct rights by any of its members, it takes a special interest in any procedure which may effect the transfer of use rights outside of the descent group. Such transfers occur not only in cases of tenancy but also through sale, where independent action by a lineage member is, at least in principle, opposed. If a man wishes to sell any of his gardens which fall within the boundaries of a larger lineage parcel, he ought to convene the men of the lineage to inform them of his plan. They in turn attempt to provide him with the cash or livestock he requires. Those agnates who assist their kinsman can then assume usufruct rights to the land in question. If members of the lineage are, on the other hand, unable to provide money, they may grant permission to their kinsman to dispose of the land outside of the group, although they only relunctantly do so. Customary efforts to maintain land within the descent group are rationalized by a few elders through vague reference to the curse of the founder of the land, who is said to have enjoined subsequent generations not to relinquish land outside the lineage. I found, however, no recollection of actual shade affliction which had been thus divined. Nonetheless, the numerous instances of land sale to non-agnates as noted in Chapter 4, are very much at odds with the ideal, presented as "traditional".

Men who have claimed bush land and brought it into cultivation independently of their kin are not bound by the usual constraints attendant to membership in a descent group. Such founders maintain more than simple usufruct rights, for they also control the disposition of the land and the transfer of various rights. At the death of the founder, and in subsequent generations, his land will become the joint property of his descendants whose interests will thus necessarily mutually constrain the sorts of individual transactions the founder alone might enjoy.

At the same time that one holds an exclusive interest in land which he has founded or purchased, he may also exercise rights in land controlled by his descent group. This extremely important distinction between individual and corporate control of land was misinterpreted by a succession of European observers during the colonial period, when the officials tended to see only the corporate aspects of land tenure in central Kenya. Often land tenure was simply seen as "tribal" without regard to either lineages or individuals. Individual claims, especially, were redefined in "tribal" terms; accordingly, the grievances of individuals were met by the addition of land, although agriculturally marginal, to the Reserves (Sorrenson 1967:22-24). Nevertheless, some European observers, such as Beech, a District Officer in Kiambu, emphasized individual aspects of customary land tenure extending beyond usufruct rights to include the right of sale. He identified these features in Kiambu, where he was convinced of the accuracy of Kikuyu claims that they purchased land from the Ndorobo prior to European rule. Beech also cites R. G. Stone, an early District Commissioner of Embu, who argued that cultivated land among the Embu could be individually owned (Beech 1917).

The transfer of usufruct through sale raises the issue of residual rights. These may be held not only by a descent group, which must give its permission to any member attempting to sell land, but also by an individual. Although evidence on this point is not consistent, some informants argue that the sale of land was redeemable; that is, the seller could reassume his use rights in land by returning the original amount of livestock or money to the purchaser, who in turn was obligated to relinquish the land. Redeemable sale thus approximated a loan against collateral rather than an outright sale suspending all subsequent rights of the seller. The division of opinion about the existence of redeemable sale must be seen in the context of a growing cash economy in which land itself has become a commodity. Contemporary opinion about the past is of course shaped by a current economic interest best served by denying the existence of redeemable sale, especially among those who have acquired choice holdings through purchase and wish to loosen any constraints on their gains. Indeed, what was held up by chiefs and other members of the Local Native Council may simply have been a rationale for land acquisitions made possible by their participation in the civil administration. Nonetheless, in the representation of land as ultimately inalienable outside of the descent group, the principle of redeemability balances self-seeking action against the common interest. The repudiation of this principle further evidences the growing imbalance between individualistic economic endeavor and agnatic constraint.

Colonial Land Policy

Until the post-independence period, Embu District stretched beyond its present boundaries to include Ndia and Gicugu. These areas joined Kikuyuland and, together with the rest of Embu District and Meru District, formed the old Central Province. This large area was also known as the Kikuyu Land Unit, thus designated by the Native Lands Trust Ordinance of 1938, and within that Unit colonial land policy took shape. Land alienation, its relationship to official policy, and the politicization of the Kikuyu have been the subject of a number of excellent studies (e.g. Rosberg and Nottingham 1966; Sorrenson 1967), and there is no need to review in detail what is now a familiar story.

But what is of special concern here is the effect on Mbeere of an official program aimed fundamentally at the Kikuyu. Promoting European settler interest by legitimating the alienation of African land, colonial land policy also sought to contain Kikuyu political and economic aspirations. It is thus necessary to examine both the aspects of policy impinging on the Mbeere and the conditions which prevailed in Mbeere society and in Embu District more generally.

Of fundamental significance in distinguishing Mbeere from Kikuyuland to the west is agricultural potential. Although portions of Mbeere that I have designated as Zone I support cash crops as well as a range of staples, vast areas of Mbeere are considerably drier and economically less promising. Indeed, even the richer areas of Zone I have been vulnerable to a highly erratic pattern of rainfall and have then yielded only fitful harvests. Colonial officials from the very beginning of European rule in Embu District emphasized the marginal features of the Mbeere ecosystem. The succession of Mbeere famines and shortages also captured the attention of the Local Native Council which not only allocated funds for famine relief but also sought to relocate some Mbeere at the higher elevations. Owing to the wide perception of Mbeere as agriculturally unpromising, it was never designated a "Scheduled" area to be alienated to European settlers, who sought instead the more temperate highlands occupied by the Kikuyu. Moreover, available evidence indicates that the Mbeere population remained stable up through the decade of the 1930s and that pressure on land, characteristic among the Kikuyu, was not a problem in Mbeere. The Embu District Annual Report of 1930 lists the Mbeere population as 22,876; the Annual Report of 1939 notes the population as 23,314. The recurrence of famine and disease as well as the absence of systematic efforts to transform Mbeere agricultural practices held the population in check during the first four decades of European rule, and, with the absence of land alienation, inhibited the population congestion characteristic of the Kikuyu Reserves (Sorrenson 1967:35). Unlike the Kikuyu setting, Mbeere geography kept European interlopers at bay, thus leaving the Mbeere people very much outside of the mainstream of agricultural developments in Central Kenya during the colonial period.

The land policy developing in Embu District was in the main conditioned by events in Kikuyuland, where overcrowding on the Reserves, as well as a desire for security of tenure, drove Kikuyu migrants into the District. This migration soon created a number of problems including the unauthorized sale of land and the growth of tenancy. But the Local Native Council (LNC) delayed acting on these matters. In 1936, Chief Kombo joined four other chiefs on the LNC in opposing registration of sales, although the Provincial Commissioner had suggested registration. Kombo stated that land was easily available in Mbeere; the chiefs from Embu, Ndia, and Gicugu argued that few disputes had been brought to the elders' councils, and these few cases concerned only land boundaries. Since land transactions were always supposed to be witnessed by elders, they also argued against registration on the grounds that it would be redundant with custom. But by 1938, the LNC began to deal with the effects, including the growth of tenancy, of Kikuyu migration into Embu District. It formally established the rights and duties of lease holders. The LNC also concerned itself with a spate of land sales coming in the wake of the Kikuyu migration. These sales drew the attention of the LNC owing to reports that individuals, acting solely for themselves, were illegitimately selling portions of lineage land. Nonetheless, the LNC resisted instituting a system of registration of sales. Instead, it reluctantly created vigilance committees in 1945 in each location "to smooth the way for desired changes in land custom" and "to prevent secret sales and undesirable transactions" (Embu Local Native Council 1945:108). The pressure on land and the growth of monetization in land transactions could no longer be ignored by the administration working through the LNC.

The new agrarian problems impinging on Embu District beginning in the late 1930s were not yet felt in Mbeere proper where indigenous people were themselves increasingly on the move owing to a particularly devastating confluence of environmental crises. The failure of the short rains of 1933, a severe rinderpest epidemic that year, and the failure of the long rains of 1934 set in motion a major migration, encouraged by the government, from the lower zones of Evurore and Mavuria up to the sparsely populated areas adjacent to Embu Division. The Embu District Annual Report of 1934 documents these events and sounds the theme of famine and shortage so often repeated in District records:

> The Mbeere have had poor harvests since 1932. The short rains of 1933 failed except in a few areas and the food shortage that was produced assumed the character of famine when the long rains of 1934 also failed. The areas affected were Njamburi's location [Evurore] and about one third of Kombo's. Food shortage is common in Mbeere and the Mbeere people are accustomed to exist mainly on their stock. Many have done so this year but it has become increasingly impossible on account of the diminution of the numbers of Mbeere stock due firstly to deaths from disease and secondly to enforced sale of stock at the prevailing low prices to realize tax money. The abundance of food available in Embu was most important of the alleviants [sic] of distress but under government supervision many Mbeere were brought to uninhabited areas between Embu and Mbeere to cultivate areas less liable to failure of rainfall than Mbeere proper.

Migration to this erstwhile frontier area has continued until the present. Although some Mbeere cultivated this area for generations prior to 1933, the fear of raids from neighboring peoples effectively checked large scale migration from the lowlands until the government intervened.

It should be emphasized that LNC activity was very much subject to the control of the civil administration at the district level since the District Commissioner served as President of the LNC and ultimately controlled LNC membership. Indirect rule appears as a

203

convenient fiction, for although the preservation of custom consistent with Western morality was much vaunted, its arbiters on the LNC held positions inconsonant with customary leadership roles. At the same time, LNC members, particularly the chiefs, were in the best position to understand policy and to take advantage of it through the system of rewards in land which was to reach its pinnacle during the Emergency.

The LNC minutes do not clarify the sort of "desired changes in land custom" which the government was trying to effect. This is not surprising in view of the sometimes inconsistent policies which were promulgated by different departments of the government (Sorrenson 1967:69). Even the Embu District Annual Reports, prepared by the District Commissioner, begin in the 1940s to sound a note of equivocation in regard to land issues, which were rapidly creating serious conflicts. In reference to the newly established Land Vigilance Committees, for example, the Annual Report of 1945 states:

> In view of a number of instances in which land had been sold secretly to Kikuyu of other districts . . . and the possibilities that large buying of land might be going on by prominent persons without control it was decided that something should be done a) to strengthen public opinion with regard to retaining old customs until better ones could be found and b) arranging for a liaison between those with modern views and ruling age grades so that amiable agreements might be reached during transition stages.

Here the District Commissioner voices the government's growing concern over unregulated individual transactions yet betrays a naive, even desperate faith in the effectiveness of custom in constraining them. Administrators typically were not cognizant of the customary basis for individual action and how the flexible, indigenous structures of age-sets and generation classes preadapted the Mbeere and their neighbors to the individualism of a growing cash economy.

Although the Mbeere evidence strongly suggests that such transactions could occur, the question of whether the peoples of central Kenya maintained a customary system of land transfers between individuals has been clouded by political considerations, most notably the conflict between European settlers and Kikuyu farmers. On the one hand, opinions of such individuals as Lord Hailey indicate that "it is not surprising that some of the Kenya tribes who have come most closely in contact with Europeans have now substantially modified their traditional procedure of land holding, more especially in admitting the validity of the transfer of land rights, whether by sale or otherwise" (1957:784). Similarly, Lambert believed that Kikuyu versions of customary land tenure rules were conditioned by European contact and were fit to contemporary politics so that claims of a traditional precedent for outright irredeemable sale, especially by the autochthonous Ndorobo to the Kikuyu of Kiambu, were used to justify Kikuyu demands for titles in the face of European claims to the land (1950:79). The Kenya Land Commission 1933, also known as the Carter Commission, followed this reasoning in investigating African land grievances stemming from alienation of land to Europeans. As a result, the Commission dismissed Kikuyu arguments that they had gained land through purchase. Although sanctioning individual freehold tenure as an ultimate goal, the Commission found that its origin lay in European contact and not in tradition. Thus, instead of adjudicating claims of individual Kikuyu, the Commission operated on the premise that "tribal tenure" characterized the traditional system; it could thus add land, although of questionable quality, to the Reserves as compensation for individual holdings alienated to Europeans and incorporated into the "White Highlands" (Sorrenson 1967:23-32). On the other hand, European observers such as Leakey, in agreement with Beech and Stone, found within the Kikuyu system of land tenure ample precedent for irredeemable individual transaction distinct from the joint control of land which could be exercised by a descent group (1952:4-6 1977:105-108).

In either case, land policy in Central Kenya separated individualized European from corporate African agricultural development. The Scheduled Areas had been reserved for Europeans following the alienation of this land from Africans. Europeans gained freehold tenure in these highland areas beginning early in the century under the provisions of several registration statutes (Jackson 1970:222-232). The Trust Lands, on the other hand, initially known as "Native Reserves," were held in trust by the government for the African population under the assumption that communal tenure defined the indigenous system of land-holding under customary law. Various African efforts to secure individual titles, thereby providing the security enjoyed by European farmers, failed until the momentous change of the 1950s. Up to the era of Mau Mau, government policy sought to control the individual aspirations of African farmers by supporting indigenous authority, which was consistently seen in corporate terms.

However sale of land between individuals came about, the government attempted to regulate it. The emphasis on "traditional authority," "old custom," and the like, which recurs in LNC minutes and Annual Reports of Embu District, follows from a belief that custom would hold in check the various excesses of individualism while still permitting controlled transactions in land. Attributing untrammeled individualism and a decline in cooperation to European contact, the government through the LNC gave much lip service to strengthening indigenous controls variously designated as "ruling age grades," "elders," and "clan heads." It was hoped that such community controls would restrain land acquisition and sale while at the same time inhibiting what some people in the government considered the disastrous agricultural effects of unsupervised individual land tenure (Sorrenson 1967:56).

An important question arises about the influence of European administrators on the interpretation of custom. Administrators controlled membership on tribunals and on the LNC; additionally, they exercised authority over chiefs, who were themselves influential on both bodies. Moreover, after 1930, District Commissioners gained the authority to hear appeals from tribunals. Administrative influence in the determination of custom thus cannot be discounted and indeed the attempt to justify the ban on female circumcision in these terms is an extreme example of the influence of these European arbiters of tradition. Of course chiefs and other notables on the LNC or tribunals could effectively "interpret" custom for the Europeans while at the same time taking advantage of opportunities afforded by their position. But critically important in Embu District and indeed throughout Kenya was the alien institution of chiefship itself. Although Africans were appointed to these new positions, they were office holders as novel and intrusive as the European District Commissioner to whom they were answerable. When Mair remarks that the District Commission was "a new kind of territorial chief" (1962:253), she was referring to colonial control of the interlacustrine area where a political hierarchy of chiefs was a well-established indigenous feature. But in Kenya the political transformation through colonial rule over acephalous societies was more profound and far-reaching than in those areas where central authority had long existed. By fundamentally altering the shape of political relations and the structure through which custom worked itself out, the administration unwittingly defeated its own efforts to control the pace of change by upholding allegedly fixed customs and increasingly ineffective elders. The regular invocation of custom by the government thus appears as a convenient metaphor for the ultimate administrative value on control and stability. At the same time, the varied local interpretation and use of custom would enjoy official sanction while masking self-interested land acquisition by chiefs and other functionaries.

The LNC sought to use custom, in the form of a ritual oath, to constrain excessive individualism and to control the activities of increasing numbers of Kikuyu and Kamba tenants in Embu. Through the oath, newcomers could enter ties of blood brotherhood, or fictive kinship, with local people. In 1947, the LNC resolved that 1) all immigrants into Embu District should take an oath in order "to be born again" into a local clan, 2) such adoptees would then be considered local inhabitants with the same rights and duties, and 3) immigrants in the District should undergo the ceremony within the following ten months or otherwise answer to the LNC (Local Native Council 1947:Minute 99). By August 1948, the LNC found that very few tenants had refused the required ceremony and that few clans had rejected the immigrants. Believing as they did that the bonds of descent, even if artificially created, were necessary to insure right action, the LNC unanimously agreed that the government should evict those who resisted the blood brotherhood rites. In addition, the LNC reiterated an earlier resolution that adoptees could be ejected from the land if they broke the terms of the oath or refused to conform to local custom. It was also agreed that no new tenants should be allowed to settle anywhere in Embu or to be "born again" into any of the Embu tribes without the approval of the chief and the locational committee composed of various parish elders and members of a host clan.

By 1955, the Embu African District Council concluded that earlier efforts to control tenancy had failed. Finding that most tenants had entered the District between 1933 and 1947 at the invitation of chiefs but against the will of local people, the ADC stated that few tenants had been properly absorbed into local clans. The ADC did not make clear what a failure of "proper absorption" entailed, but it nonetheless appears that earlier problems of improper sale of land and disputes between tenants and locals had continued unabated. Furthermore, the ADC pointed out that the government did not return any tenants to their previous districts because of land shortages in the Kikuyu areas, despite the earlier resolution (1948) that tenants ought to be expelled for improper dealings in land.

By 1948, the government proposed to deal with the twin concerns of growing individualism and what was regarded as improper land use by encouraging "progressive farmers" to utilize mixed farming and crop rotation and to avoid fragmentation of holdings.

Although the Carter Commission had noted the desirability of land consolidation, the idea was not seriously considered until the late 1940s. Through a process of consolidation of scattered fragments of land, it was believed that efficient, modern farming could be carried out. The progressive farmers, after their land had been consolidated, would then be awarded title, which they could then use to secure agricultural credit. Land consolidation was to become the keystone of both improved farming and agrarian reform.

Sorrenson suggests that the government, prior to the period of Mau Mau, remained equivocal about consolidation, in part because it feared the opposition of Kikuyu political leaders, who were beginning to oppose any plan because of the government's support of land alienation to Europeans. Further, he argues that there was some official apprehension about the possibility of creating landed and landless classes as wealthier individuals would build up their holdings through purchase (1967:32). Of course, the process of class formation had been proceeding all along as land transactions and secret sales throughout Central Kenya, including Mbeere, were occurring independently of any official policy on land consolidation.

By 1952, with the declaration of the Emergency in response to Mau Mau, the government detained much of the Kikuyu leadership and thus could proceed to consolidate land without overt opposition. Consolidation was then carried out not only as part of a program of agrarian reform but also as a political measure to create a stable, progressive agrarian class immune to the enticements of Mau Mau. It was hoped that this group of progressive farmers, whose consolidated farms would be secured by title, would see their interests outside of the context of a revolutionary movement bent on altering the very system at the source of their prosperity. Moreover, as a political measure, the alteration of land tenure would reward those who did not participate in Mau Mau with larger, choicer pieces of land. As consolidation proceeded, the government undertook a policy of "villagization" whereby the coerced resettlement of Kikuyu into nucleated villages was effected and the customary pattern of dispersed homesteads was overturned. "Villagization" occurred throughout Kikuyuland and in some parts of Embu and Meru where Mau Mau activity had been intense; it was officially believed that nucleated villages would enable the government to exercise greater control over the populace and to curb Mau Mau access to settled areas. This measure represented a counterinsurgency measure to check guerrilla support among local people (Sorrenson 1967:107, 111, 113).

During the Emergency (1952-60), Mbeere, unlike Kikuyuland and portions of Embu and Meru, was not subject to forced resettlement in nucleated villages. Moreover, land consolidation, developing in conjunction with forced resettlement in villages, did not proceed in Mbeere during the waning years of the colonial period. Although some Mbeere did swear the Mau Mau oath of unity, they did so in Kikuyuland or in Nairobi or in other towns where they were labor migrants as Mau Mau proved ineffectual in penetrating Mbeere proper.

As early as 1932, Lambert, District Commissioner of Embu, reported that Mbeere was the area of the District least affected by politics, and no branch of the "Association" [Kikuyu Central Association] had appeared in Mbeere (Embu District Annual Report 1932). The KCA was subsequently proscribed in 1940. The assessment of the Mbeere as essentially indifferent to political as well as missionary activity was a popular view among European observers during the colonial period.

Throughout the 1950s, Embu District reports reiterated Lambert's theme and also emphasized Mbeere loyalty to the government in the face of Mau Mau efforts to make inroads. The Embu District Annual Report of 1953, for example, states:

> These difficulties, in building up an effective campaign against the terrorists, were experienced in all Divisions except Mbeere, where intense hostility to the Mau Mau was evident. Their feelings were exacerbated by terrorists' atrocities, which

produced no intimidating effect on these tribesmen.

A year later the District Commissioner attributed without further explanation Mbeere rejection of Mau Mau to "the influential position maintained by Chief Kombo who has been in government service since before the First World War" (Embu District Annual Report 1954). A later report also stated that "the government's policy was one of supporting and rewarding the tribe," which was "impervious to Mau Mau indoctrination" (Embu District Annual Report 1955). The report is not explicit about how the government rewarded the Mbeere, but opportunities included service for Mbeere men in the home guard and police during the Emergency. A large detention camp for accused Mau Mau activists was set up at Ishiara in lower Mbeere; home guard duty, including service at this camp, not only provided employment but also led to officially-supported settlement of former home guardsmen in Nguthi, especially near the Embu/Mbeere border. The Evurore chief and two former chiefs also gained extensive holdings in this area.

Although the government utilized rewards for chiefs and tribal police during the Emergency, widespread if passive acceptance of the government had characterized the Mbeere response to administration throughout the colonial period. The government, on the whole, devoted little attention to Mbeere, especially in comparison to the other divisions of Embu District. Sporadic efforts to introduce new crops and other agricultural innovations into Mbeere failed outright or met with only limited success (Watt 1969).

Minimal interest of the government was matched by the indifference of other Europeans, especially settlers. The Mbeere thus suffered no land alienation to Europeans and, in this respect, differed significantly form the Kikuyu. As a result, the Mbeere never developed the intense land grievances against an administration more concerned with the development of European farming on alienated African land to the west. By contrast, the most consequential example of the government's interest in Mbeere occurred as various

211

administrative officers encouraged the Mbeere to expand their territory through migration to upper Nguthi and other upland areas on the border with Embu Division. Maher's recommendation (1938) was the most far-reaching, for he suggested that the entire population of the eroded lowlands of Evurore migrate to the Mbeere/Embu border. Although this migration began in the 1930s, it proved smaller in scale than Maher originally had hoped. It was in no sense a systematic and directed resettlement scheme. Most Mbeere remained in their lowland homes owing to a continued preference for a more pastoral way of life. But for those who entered the upper zone, they discovered that the land was not uncontested as Embu people were equally interested in claiming what had once been a periodically dangerous frontier. This conflict between the Embu and Mbeere grew more intense as they divided over participation in Mau Mau at the time that the government supported the continuing migration of the Mbeere.

A second, more equivocal land conflict articulated in ethnic terms challenged the government to reconcile competing claims of Kikuyu, Ndia, Kamba, and Mbeere. Centering on Mwea, an area of about 215 square miles, these peoples laid claim to what had been a sparsely occupied land, most suited to stockeeping. By the 1930s when population pressures on land were being felt for the first time and dispossessed peoples, particularly the Kikuyu, were seeking land, Mwea became highly coveted. Kikuyu and Kamba migrants were streaming onto the land which the Ndia and Mbeere were each asserting belonged to them. The Kenya Land Commission in 1933 heard evidence from Chief Njega of Ndia and Chief Kombo of Mbeere in regard to the respective claims of their people (phrased in collective, ethnic terms, not in the context of individual claims). The government wanted Mwea to remain open to Kikuyu migrants as a way of defusing pressures from landless people. Meanwhile, Mwea became the focus for an irrigation scheme which by 1967 was supporting 1700 rice-producing farmers and their families. Following independence when the Central Province was reorganized, the site of the irrigation scheme in upper Mwea was ceded to Ndia, which became part of the new Kirinyaga District of the Central Province. Lower Mwea became part of Mbeere land which, along with that of the Embu and Kamba, was ceded by the Central Province and became part of the reorganized Eastern Province (Chambers 1969:43-46; 103-105). Older claims by Kombo that lower Mwea had been a pastoral zone for the Mbeere were finally vindicated.

Sorrenson argues that the distinction between Mau Mau participants and those who spurned the movement was complicated by a division between landed and landless classes. He interprets the famous Lari massacre in this light. At Lari, landless Kikuyu slew ex-Chief Luka, members of his family, and other loyalists numbering ninety-seven in all. Luka and the others, regarded by the former land holders (who themselves supported the Kikuyu Central Association) as beneficiaries of European favor at their expense, accepted land at Lari in exchange for the Tigoni block contiguous to the European farms near Limuru. Those who refused the exchange were removed by force from Tigoni; they became labor migrants or squatters in Maasailand. In suggesting that it may well have been this new landless class which perpetrated the Lari massacre, Sorrenson also notes that it was officially interpreted as Mau Mau activity despite a dearth of firm evidence (1967:100-101).

This argument is instructive about the schism between the Mbeere and Embu during the Emergency. Unlike the Mbeere, the Embu suffered colonial counter-insurgency methods as a result of alleged Mau Mau activity in Embu Division. Moreover, efforts to suppress Mau Mau also included the aerial bombardment of the Mt. Kenya forests, extending from upper Embu Division, in order to eliminate guerrillas using these forests as bases. Skirmishes between Mau Mau from Embu and the Mbeere occurred at least once in 1953 and twice in 1954. Fazan, who had been secretary of the 1933 Kenya Land Commission, noted the following:

> The tribesmen of the Emberre [sic] division set their faces against Mau Mau from the start. At the end of October [1953] five Embu guards in that division surprised an

oath ceremony being conducted by a party of some fifteen or twenty mixed Embu and Kikuyu. The guards raised the alarm; within a short space of time 150 tribesmen assembled, armed with spears and bows and arrows. On their own initiative they organized a sweep assisted by a large number of guards (1956:82).

In February and April of 1954, fighting broke out between Embu and Mbeere people, and in the latter encounter fifteen Mbeere were killed in the vicinity of the Mbeere/Embu border in upper Nguthi. The Kanyuambora market and school were also burned. The District Commissioner's report of the earlier engagement hints that tensions over land between the Mbeere and Embu played some role in Mbeere opposition to Mau Mau:

It is cheering to relate that in February some Embu attempted to oath the Wa-mbere[sic] and this led to a civil commotion and the routing of the administrators. The Wa-mbere [sic] remained staunchly on Government's side, and are to be most sincerely congratulated on their loyalty. The Wa-mbere [sic] apart from long standing animosity regarding their boundary with Embu Division, considered the inhabitants of the latter to be Mau Mau (Embu District Annual Report 1954).

Informants also pointed out that jealousies over the land were contributory to Embu incursions. Repeated land disputes between the Mbeere and Embu, the relatively greater success of the Mbeere in pressing their claims, and early and continuing government support of the Mbeere expansion thus mark the land issue as a major point of schism which turned violent during Mau Mau.

As a result of Mau Mau activity, various peoples of Embu District, excluding the Mbeere, became subject to the program of land consolidation during the Emergency. Known as the Swynnerton Plan, the land consolidation effort aimed at eliminating the established pattern of land fragmentation and issuing registered titles to individual holders of newly consolidated farmsteads. The Swynnerton Plan set in motion a series of agricultural changes under consideration two decades before and at other times in the interim but which were not implemented until the crisis of the Emergency. No longer concerned about the creation of a landless class nor about the activities of increasingly active entrepreneurs operating independently of kinsmen, the government quite to the contrary supported these tendencies in the Swynnerton Plan. This document makes very explicit the impending about-face in government policy:

> In the past Government policy has been to maintain the tribal system of tenure so that all the people have had bits of land and to prevent the African from borrowing money against the security of his land. The result is that there is no agricultural indebtedness by Africans . . . In future . . . former Government policy will be reversed and able, energetic or rich Africans will be able to acquire more land and bad or poor farmers less, creating a landed and a landless class. This is a normal step in the evolution of a country (Swynnerton 1954:10).

Through this policy, it was believed that frictions which had ignited the Mau Mau movement--insecurity of tenure, rural congestion, and the frustrations of an achievement-oriented people--could be eliminated. At the same time, new provisions for land title and agricultural credit would reward rural entrepreneurs, enabling them to increase productivity through various methods of improved farming.

Since the original proposal for land consolidation and registration set forth in the Swynnerton Plan, similar policies have continued into the period of independence. Since the 1950s, rural development in the agricultural areas of Kenya has been predicated on divesting agnatic groups of their corporate interests in land and on awarding registered titles to individuals. Mbeere remained relatively untouched by the registration and consolidation provisions of the Swynnerton Plan as originally set forth, but by the late 1960s, it became a target area for a series of agrarian transformations governed by post-independence land reform legislation. These changes, including land demarcation, adjudication, and registration of title, were foreshadowed in the Swynnerton Plan.

Prior to the onset of land reform in Mbeere in 1968, the provision for loans, underwritten by the Swynnerton Plan, tangibly affected people in Nguthi. Although a relatively small number of farmers actually availed themselves of the opportunity, those who did take out loans gained a decided advantage in the subsequent land adjudication, for evidence of loans weighed heavily as proof of uncontested control over land. In a 1966 circular to agricultural officers in Mbeere, the District Agricultural Officer explained the nature of the loans and made explicit the requirement that the land not be subject to dispute:

> It is Government policy to encourage . . . many farmers in the district to acquire . . . loans. Therefore it is your duty to encourage farmers with . . . acreage [of] more than fifteen acres to apply . . . In non-consolidated areas, individuals or registered clans may apply for these loans [and] the land should be free of disputes and have well-defined boundaries. Large scale loans can be used for . . . erection and maintenance of permanent improvements, purchase of dairy cattle, purchase of beef cattle and agricultural machinery, [or] the establishment of any other agricultural or rural industries.

The Agricultural Finance Corporation, which provides rural development loans for farmers putting up land as collateral, defined the "large scale" farmer in a 1966 memo to Agricultural Officers. Such a farmer would have "fifteen acres of land [and] be able to produce five hundred pounds income after the loan." In response to the new loan opportunities, a few

216

coalitions of agnates collectively awarded land to particular members seeking assistance. In one case, ten men of Mūkera clan representing all maximal lineages of Mūkera resident in Nguthi conveyed thirty-five acres of land to a community development worker of the Mūturi lineage:

> We [of] Mūkera clan certify that we have given thirty-five acres to Mr._____ of Mūkera clan for . . . development and that he [can] make any development concerning agricultural progress and that the land given him can serve as his security.

This transaction gained the support of seven witnesses, representing four different clans, who stated that the boundary of the ceded land was correct as designated by the Mūkera clansmen. Their testimony later corroborated Mūkera litigants during land adjudication. In a similar case with equally important repercussions during land adjudication, Chief Samson and his agnates of the Mbutha clan received over 80 pounds from the British American Tobacco Company; this payment was given for land later used as a tobacco nursery. At about the same time in the early 1960s, Chief Samson secured an agricultural loan by putting up land as collateral without the objection of other farmers. These endeavors served as crucial evidence of "ownership" during land adjudication and enhanced such customary forms of evidence as genealogical recitation. In the award of loans on the eve of land reform, the government perpetuated a pattern established in the early years of the colonial regime. The immediate beneficiaries of this new mode of financing agricultural improvements were chiefs and other functionaries. By virtue of their positions, they were able to reap rewards of collaborative service to an administration which hoped that these same individuals might serve as exemplars of progress (in this case progressive farming) built on a nascent system of private ownership of land and rural stratification.

217

Land reform refers variously to land adjudication, consolidation of dispersed gardens into a single farmstead, and registration of individual title. These various aspects do not necessarily co-occur as they did in Kikuyuland. In Mbeere, land adjudication and title registration have proceeded without concomitant consolidation, although where it seems feasible consolidation can be effected; but it has not been a central feature of land reform in Mbeere. From its inception in the Swynnerton Plan, land reform has been enshrined in the various Kenya Development Plans. The 1970-74 Plan, for example, states:

> It has long been Government Policy that the land tenure system in traditional Kenya should be changed so that farmers can be provided with the title deeds to their land and, where necessary, so that scattered fragments of land can be consolidated into one holding. This change has manifold benefits. Time and money no longer need be spent on land litigation, nor is it necessary for farmers to waste time travelling between numerous scattered plots of land. The reform acts as a powerful stimulus to agricultural development. Farmers are willing to make long-term improvements to their land; and they can obtain agricultural credit more easily to help them effect these improvements, for the land title deeds provide good security for agricultural loans. Because agricultural development proceeds more rapidly after land rights have been adjudicated, the reform also tends to encourage a much higher level of employment in rural areas (1969:210).

This rationale continues to be an important feature of rural development strategies. Indeed, the most recent development plan reiterates this rationale for land reform, which also seeks to establish the family farm as the basic rural productive unit. The 1979-83 plan also seeks to discourage the ownership of large holdings, tenancy, and land speculation as it calls for the family to own, manage, and work its own land. Nonetheless, land adjudication and registration have brought about an increase in land transactions among small farmers; at the same time, "the incidence of concentration in land ownership among the better-off small-scale farmers has increased" (1979:53) despite the existence of District Land Control Boards, which were established to prevent excessive concentration of land holdings. In Mbeere, an unequal distribution of land begins in the very process of adjudication itself as the subsequent discussion of case outcomes will indicate.

The intricate procedures of land reform have been legitimated through a series of statutory laws encoding the key changes in official thinking regarding African land tenure. These various statutes evolved from the conventional view that African land holding has customarily been corporate or communal to the recognition of the rights of individuals unmediated by kinship or community ties. The most important laws underwriting land reform in Mbeere date from the 1960s and govern in turn land adjudication under the Land Adjudication Act of 1968 and land title registration through the Registered Land Act of 1963. The 1968 Act governing adjudication of claims, which has been an essential step prior to registration, represents an important point of departure from the procedures in Kikuyuland and Embu. The Land Adjudication Act of 1968 emphasizes the adjucation of claims, under customary law, in the Trust Lands but does not provide for land consolidation. Once disputes are adjudicated--a complex, difficult process--those who have successfully justified their claims receive title through the provisions of the Registered Land Act. At the same time, control of land tenure through customary law becomes inoperative.

The decision to separate in law the distinct processes of land adjudication and land consolidation derived in part from recommendations of the Commission on Land Consolidation and Registration. Appointed by the government and chaired by J.C.D. Lawrance, the Commission noted that consolidation is beneficial only if "fragmentation is positively harmful" (1965:19). While strongly supporting yet distinguishing the separate processes of land reform (including consolidation, enclosure, distribution and registration), the Commission proposed a law (the Land Adjudication Act of 1968) which would deal with adjudication independently of consolidation. At the same time, the Commission suggested that the name of the existing Land Adjudication Act, which had governed both consolidation and adjudication, be changed to the Land Consolidation Act. The single most important general recommendation of the Commission was for "a realistic acceleration of the program of land consolidation and registration with the aim of establishing the most important precondition for a rise in productivity in peasant farming areas" (1965:2). Within Mbeere, the government has expected the greatest output following land reform to derive from the high potential areas defined by the 35-inch isohyet. Other, drier portions of Mbeere have been designated for group ranches since the time of the Lawrance Commission (1965:189-190). Although collective control of land, following land reform, is centered in the drier sublocations of Evurore, corporate tenure can persist in the high potential areas under the provisions of the Land (Group Representatives) Act of 1968. Few groups in Nguthi have taken advantage of this option; thus by the mid-1970s when approximately 8400 acres of land had been registered, including individual plots, County Council land, and group holdings, the latter comprised only about 440 acres. Most of these group holdings were located in the lower portions of Nguthi. By 1973, Brokensha and Glazier had found a correlation between high potential land and the preference of farmers for individual ownership; moreover, farmers felt that group holdings would be more vulnerable to appropriation by the County Council for public purposes (1973:200). Livingstone has recently pointed out that where the Land Adjudication Department held out the prospect of registering individual titles, residents were resistant to plans of the Range Management Division to organize group ranches. Aside from the obvious problem of uncoordinated plans by two departments of the government, this evidence further indicates that if land tenure changes must occur, the Mbeere are

220

considerably more disposed to individual rather than group forms of title. Since most of Mbeere will support at least some subsistence food crops as well as livestock, local resistance to group ranching schemes is hardly surprising owing to the fact that such collective efforts require the abandonment of individual gardens (1979:372,376).

Although land reform has held out the promise of economic development, it also has presented a more immediate threat to the security of a considerable number of people. People fear that they may lose the land they are cultivating in the proliferation of suits and countersuits which have engulfed the area since 1968, when Mbeere was formally declared a land adjudication area subject to the provisions of the then newly instituted Land Adjudication Act. It is a supreme irony that land reform, which aims to eliminate costly expenditures of both time and money for litigation, precipitated a surge of litigation before elders, the Mbeere Divisional Court, and the judicial and arbitration bodies expressly created by the Land Adjudication Act. Informants often expressed the wish that they would not find themselves with less land after land reform was concluded. They insisted that Mbeere cultivators were never without sufficient land and that land reform should not alter what has always been a fair distribution of the land. Ex-Chief Kombo emphatically stated on several occasions that until recently every person utilized his own gardens (here Kombo uses the term *ngamba*, which can also include fallow lands) without dependency. He continued:

Nobody would prevent me from building a home in his *ngamba*, or even from cultivating there. The only improper action was in selling the land. But now hatred has taken a firm root. You cannot even come to my *ngamba*. You cannot graze your animals there. You cannot do anything in my land. It is enmity which has crept in. Long ago my cow could graze anywhere, even in land claimed by somebody. I could cut trees for building anywhere I saw a good one, but now no.

Aside from a not uncommon Mbeere proclivity to idealize the past and to attribute to malevolent European influence such diverse problems as chiggers and the ineffectiveness of animal sacrifice (all condensed in the term *comba*), Kombo's remarks are nonetheless apt. Marketable land, the independence of action of administrative functionaries and others with regular cash incomes, and the prospect of definitive freehold title have created a self-seeking spirit not possible in Kombo's youth. In the brief period between 1970 and 1973, for example, barbed wire fences and signs in Swahili reading *mbwa kali* (fierce dog) and *hakuna ruhusa kuingia* (no trespassing) sprang up around several homesteads in Nguthi. Moreover, people have grown suspicious not only of their neighbors' intensions but also of clanmates' motives which they fear may bring about the loss of land during the final registration. A work song of the 1970s encapsulates these sentiments; it laments both land reform and the inability of farmers effectively to register their complaints. The song disparages the reform as having spoiled the land, but when people enter a vehicle to carry their grievances to the President, they find that the chain (as on a bicycle) has broken.

Despite numerous reservations but with no choice other then compliance, the Mbeere of Nguthi and other high potential areas of the Division have cooperated with officers of the government in effecting the various steps of land reform as mandated by national statute. The Land Adjudication Act of 1968 giving impetus to Mbeere land reform replaces the earlier Land Consolidation Act which itself has undergone various changes. The Native Land Tenure Rules of 1956, created under the auspices of the Native Lands Trust Ordinance of 1930, legitimated land consolidation in Kikuyuland without providing for individual registration. Through the Native Lands Registration Ordinance of 1959, individual registration gained legal status. This Ordinance became the Land Adjudication Act of 1963 (later renamed the Land Consolidation Act) after the passage that year of the Registered Land Act which governed registration in consolidation and adjudication areas. The 1968 Land Adjudication Act applied to areas where consolidation was considered undesirable. Moreover, the new Act simplified land reform procedures since the task of consolidation, also carried out by local committees, was eliminated. The government's reliance on local committees provides an important procedural continuity between the Land Consolidation Act and the current Land Adjudication Act.

Under the auspices of the Land Adjudication Act of 1968, land reform proceeds through the Ministry of Lands and Settlement and the direction of Four Officers. In spite of the critical legal responsibility of the local Adjudication Committee, administrative control pervades each stage of the land reform plan. Among the four officers for demarcation, survey, recording, and adjudication, the adjudication officer exercises most authority. According to the Land Adjudication Act, the Minister is authorized to

> appoint a public officer to be the adjudication officer for the adjudication area, and the adjudication officer may in writing appoint such demarcation officers, survey officers, and recording officers . . . as may be necessary for demarcating, surveying and recording interests within the adjudication area, and they shall be subordinate to him (cited in Glazier 1976b:43).

These various officers were from outside Mbeere, but this did not quell complaints about official bias. In addition, the adjudication officer defines the adjudication section and advises people of their rights to make a claim within a section, one of which was coterminous with Nguthi. Further the adjudication officer

> after consultation with the District Commissioner of the district within which the adjudication section lies, shall appoint not less than ten persons resident within the adjudication section to be the adjudication committee for that adjudication section (cited in Glazier 1976 b:43).

This Committee, composed of elders of clans resident in Nguthi, began in 1971 to settle claims, both corporate and individual, under customary law.

Prior to adjudication, the demarcation officer, beginning in 1969, ordered the demarcation of boundaries within the officially declared Adjudication Section. Lineages and coalitions organized members into labor parties for planting sisal between gardens and land parcels. In addition to ordering the demarcation of land, this officer is also empowered to mark out new boundaries if old ones are irregularly drawn. He is also required to prevent the demarcation of uneconomical plots defined as less than .50 acres in area. No Nguthi garden falls below this size and only a very few are this small. Although the Land Consolidation Act is not formally applicable to Mbeere, the demarcation officer can on request readjust claims so that a cultivator may consolidate several dispersed gardens. Consolidation, usually requiring individuals to exchange one or more gardens, has not been frequent in Nguthi.

Disputes following boundary demarcation fall within the purview of the recording officer. If a plot of land is contested, the recording officer can attempt to arbitrate the dispute informally. Should his efforts fail, he then refers the case to the Adjudication Committee for settlement. After the Committee makes its decision, the recording officer amends, if necessary, the adjudication record and establishes the owners of each demarcated parcel and garden in the adjudication section. Most efforts at informal arbitration proved ineffectual because of the complexity of the cases. The Adjudication Committee thus heard the vast majority of disputes. Litigants dissatisfied with the decision of the Committee had the option of appealing the decision to the District Arbitration Board. Beyond that level, a few appeals were filed with the Minister, although the probability of overturning Committee decisions at the top level remained marginal. Some successful appeals were made to the District Arbitration Board, but these cases were a small minority of the total number taken to that body. At this point, I turn to land litigation and its consequences for the people of Nguthi.

Chapter Six

Law and Litigation

The examination of land tenure in Chapter Five
laid out the rules which govern land use, tenancy,
sale, and control, and the relationship between these
rules and official policy from the colonial era into
the years of independence. In this chapter, I continue
the investigation of Mbeere land tenure but from the
vantage point of what actually occurs when rights and
claims are in conflict. It will be necessary to
consider again the ideal rules concerning land, for
claimants regularly invoke these standards in their
cases. But the fundamental task here is to discover
what kinds of evidence in the various loci of dispute
settlement bring about favorable outcomes in the
struggle to control land and to exclude others from it.
At the same time, it is necessary to be cognizant of
extra-evidential factors such as payments to officials
and political influence in shaping legal outcomes.
Most of these data are necessarily difficult to acquire
and to verify; yet the ubiquity of charges of corrupt
practice cannot be ignored, and indeed conflict of
interest in court proceedings is apparent in some
important cases from the 1960s. These in turn set the
stage for litigation before the Land Adjudication
Committee and for appeals up to the ministerial level.

Claims to land are regularly cast into the
framework of kinship and genealogy, for genealogical
recitation reiterates the fundamental principle of
customary law governing land. That is, a man gains
rights in his father's land which in turn may derive
from the latter's father. The idiom of descent gives
an immutable, timeless quality to one's claim, which an
individual can thus consider as constant and as
irreproachable as the fact of descent itself. Yet the
effort to legitimate economic interest through
reference to the ideology of descent is complemented by
a second level of legal discourse. That is, claims are
justified initially by reference to the putative facts
of genealogy and patrilineal history, but in substance

227

the most consequential legal battle lines are drawn in terms of loans granted, recent and unchallenged improvements to the land, and numbers of credible witnesses attesting to these pieces of evidence, which lie beyond the primordial value of descent ideology. The latter is manifested in the identification of a particular lineage with a land parcel, yet this assertion is insufficient by itself to win title to the land. As land grows scarce, people exaggerate their genealogies or rework patrilineal history, thus manipulating tradition to limit competition from non-kin. But they also exploit new criteria of "ownership" reflecting the changing realities of economic life.

Legal Institutions Over Time

Writing in 1944, Phillips stated that "it is probably true . . . that in no other branch of public affairs in Kenya has there been such an extreme devolution of responsibility to Africans as in the administration of justice" (1944:5). Customary law in substance and, to a lesser extent, in procedure gained official recognition in the earliest years of British rule. Administered by divisional tribunals, government-sanctioned customary law related in the main to civil matters. Yet tribunals could also deal with criminal offenses in restricted ways, as the tribunals were authorized to administer statutory rather than customary criminal law (Phillips 1944:6). Various aspects of the legal system of colonial and independent Kenya have been referred to in previous chapters, but it will be helpful to review briefly the major developments which have shaped the legal institutions of the country before proceeding to an examination of Mbeere land disputes in relationship to customary and statutory law.

From the first days of administration at the end of the nineteenth century until approximately 1902, the government had little understanding of the nature of traditional acephalous authority throughout Kenya, but it nonetheless permitted a continued exercise of the legal prerogatives of elders in council. By 1902, the role of headman was created, and these new office holders came to participate in the previously recognized councils, which were also designated "tribunals." Despite the radical departure from custom represented by these appointments, headmen exercised great influence in the traditional councils by virtue of the official support they enjoyed. Phillips remarks that although

> the jurisdiction of a "council of elders" was recognized, the influence of the chief seems usually to have been dominant. The elders who were traditionally qualified to exercise judicial functions were driven into an attitude of apathy, of sulky acquiescence or even hostility (1944:14).

After 1910 and in full recognition of the influence of the new chiefs on the elders' councils, the government attempted to return power and judicial prerogative to the elders' councils, but the "authority and self-confidence of those bodies had been badly shaken and chiefs continued to dominate the councils" (Phillips 1944:14). In the years between 1920 and 1930, administrative reports on native tribunals regularly complained of corruption and inefficiency, owing to a lack of supervision. As a result, administrative officers scrutinized the tribunals more closely and, in some districts, including Embu, appeal tribunals were established (1944:15). Yet "progress" in formalizing procedure was variable. Regarding Embu District, Phillips lamented that the tribunals

> are still of a somewhat primitive character, and there has not so far been any spontaneous movement toward the modernization of procedure. Tribunal halls are provided, but the elders invariably prefer to sit outside under a tree (1944:80).

After 1930, efforts at tribunal reform continued. The 1930 Native Tribunals Ordinance and the 1942 amendments streamlined the tribunal system by reducing the number of elders in each body. The new rules also set Native Tribunals even more squarely within the context of the Provincial and District Administration by severing the one remaining link--African appeal to European courts--connecting such tribunals to the colonial judiciary. A dual system of justice had been developing in colonial Kenya whereby British courts were integrated into a hierarchy of judicial bodies overseen by British magistrates, who administered English statutory law in both civil and criminal matters. Ultimate appeal lay in the High Court. In contrast, the policy of indirect rule sanctioned the utilization of African councils or tribunals in the administration of customary law by "tribal" area in "so far as it is not repugnant to justice or morality" (Phillips 1944:336). Indigenous law was thus largely preserved, and its administration depended on African legal bodies, which existed independently of the judicial department. African tribunal members served at the discretion of the civil administration which controlled appointments and dismissals (Cotran 1971:129-130). By virtue of the 1930 Act and its amendments, Africans could no longer file appeals to the High Court but rather had recourse only in appeals to the District Commissioner and Provincial Commissioner, whose control was further enhanced by explicit prohibition against advocates representing litigants before tribunals or administrative officers (Phillips 1944:6).

The African Courts Ordinance of 1951 further modified the tribunals in the direction of European courts by attempting to professionalize court members through training in court business and record-keeping, which had been poorly developed in the tribunals. Through this Act, the Mbeere tribunal evolved into the Mbeere African Court centered in Divisional Headquarters at Siakago. It was composed of a presiding elder, a second court member, and a recordkeeper. But the African court, like its forerunner, remained "tribal" in that membership consisted of people from the area under jurisdiction (Cotran 1971:131). The African court also remained under the control of the civil administration.

In 1967, the Magistrates' Courts Act terminated the dual system of law. By eliminating African courts, the Act unified the entire court system of the country through the creation of a single hierarchy of Magistrates' Courts. Moreover, a single structure of appeal now governs all cases from the lowest level magistrates' courts (third class) to the Resident Magistrates' Courts, to the High Court. At Siakago in place of the Mbeere African Court, there is now a District Magistrate's Court Third Class which is headed by a trained appointee, who is not from Mbeere. Local elders have now been eclipsed as court officers. No longer divided into "tribal" and European courts, the unified legal system of Kenya subjects everyone to the jurisdiction of all courts, and advocates can now appear at every level of the court system (Jackson 1970:20), whereas before, customary law was the exclusive concern of the administrative official. Despite colonial efforts to build a legal system on the basis of indigenous institutions, it proved an impossible task in the long run as the basic institutions themselves were increasingly transformed into Western models. *Ad hoc* arbitrating elders' councils with shifting personnel and nebulous jurisdiction gave way to judicial bodies with consistent membership and a well-defined range of authority.

In the course of the various changes in legal institutions, customary law regarding land and civil matters remained very much in force under the administration of councils, tribunals, and the African court. Customary law in part continues to be administered by the Third Class Magistrates' Courts, which succeeded the African courts. Throughout the colonial history of Embu District, administrators regarded customary law as a kind of immutable index of tribal mores. It was not considered a continuously evolving code, neither anachronistic nor inappropriate, owing to its unwritten character and integral relationship to very aspect of social life. Administrators emphasized the fixity of custom except when it was exposed to the perceived disintegrating influence of European culture. Hence District records repeatedly voice expressions of commitment to revitalizing or strengthening custom in order to check what was perceived as the breakdown of authority signaled by a growing individualism. This administrative interpretation was in part the result of a rural policy subordinating African to European agricultural development in which the latter would proceed with a readily available pool of African labor. By considering custom as timeless, conservative, and efficacious in restraining departures from itself, administrators at once found a rationale for, as well as the supposed means of maintaining an African rural status quo. In the 1950s, the government reversed this policy in the face of its inevitable failure to quell African aspirations. In committing itself to official recognition of individual rights, the government utilized customary land law to ascertain existing claims and then supplanted it with national statutory law now regulating all rights in land.

Land Cases: From Council to Court

From the late 1950s, litigation over land greatly increased, and informants' testimony that chronic land disputes were not common in the past can be verified from the records of the Mbeere African Court and its successor, the Mbeere Divisional Court. Prior to 1959, the Mbeere court recorded land disputes, almost exclusively over boundaries, in the general civil registry, which also included such civil disputes as suits over debt, divorce, and adultery. Land cases reaching the court numbered only four or five per year. From 1959 through 1970, land disputes proliferated and were entered into a separate land registry, distinct from the general civil registry. During this period, an average of 24 cases per year was filed. In 1970, the peak year of land cases at court, 69 cases were registered. Most of these cases concerned disputes in the high potential areas, especially Nguthi, which accounted for more disputes than any other Mbeere sublocation.

The relative ineffectiveness of local elders' councils in settling the new variety of land disputes was demonstrated by the official closing of the court to land cases during 1969. In that year, it was hoped that local settlement might head off an inundation of cases at court during the period of land reform. That goal was not achieved, for when the court once again admitted land cases in 1970, a flood of cases engulfed the registry. Disputants believed that their rights to land could be pressed most advantageously before official bodies whereas elders' councils lacked the capacity to enforce decisions. It is impossible to determine the number of land cases heard by local councils, for records are not kept at this level. But this locus of settlement is probably little utilized. Recent land disputes concern outright ownership of land parcels and concomitant exclusion of other claimants from the land, and these more absolute definitions of rights are not consistent with the usual council attempts at compromise. District Records, moreover, give some indication that traditional remedy agents have been ineffective in dealing with the new variety of land cases. As early as 1945, the Embu District Annual Report commented on Lambert's suggestion that clan elders be called to assist Native Tribunals in cases of an "indigenous nature:"

> It [is] successful in matrimonial cases, of considerable value in cases with regard to inheritance, sale of cattle in accordance with ancient customs and in land matters where both parties belong to the same clan; but in land cases between two different clans it has little, if any value (1945:17).

Although this comment probably refers primarily to cases in the divisions of Embu, Ndia, and Gicugu where conflicts over land first began in the District, the same processes eventually occurred in Mbeere.

Land purchase and sale between unrelated people began to capture official attention as disgruntled individuals complained to chiefs about secret transactions depriving them of agnatically-based rights to land. Land transactions between agnates were no longer the dominant form of land transfer, and the customary moral constraints of kinship, so often invoked in elders' councils, were not operative in a rapidly changing social and economic climate. Moreover, as the 1945 report notes, the informal legal institutions geared to agnatically controlled land-holding were also proving impotent. Disputants were

233

beginning to find in officially constituted legal bodies the necessary authority to enforce decisions, although these could prove irksome. Thus, legal procedures not sanctioned by the government are now superfluous to the task of protecting one's interest in any kind of land.

In the land cases of the 1960s, two coalitions dominated the proceedings, both in terms of the number of their cases and in their nearly unbroken record of successes. These two coalitions engaged in more than twenty land cases. One coalition, Kigamba of Nditi clan, regularly litigated over much of Kavengero parish. Its counterpart in Kanyuambora, the Mwake coalition of Mbutha clan, claimed with equal success most of the parish while two Mbutha clansmen served in the Mbeere African Court constituted of three elders. Furthermore, the Evurore chief during the 1950s and early 1960s was a member of the Mwake coalition.

Much of the antagonism between Thagana and Irumbi moieties, informants point out, stems from the repeated and allegedly corrupt legal victories of these two Thagana coalitions in a sublocation where the Mūkera clan is the most populous clan of Irumbi, which is the numerically dominant moiety. Of eleven court cases from Nguthi between 1959 and 1970, none occurred between Irumbi clans. (Here I exclude those land cases between Mbeere and Embu over land in Nguthi.) Of the four intra-Thagana conflicts, Mwake coalition appeared in each one. The remaining cases occurred between groups of different moieties. Moreover, information on moiety affiliation of witnesses is available for five of those cases indicating that only three out of a total of forty-six witnesses crossed moiety lines to support, through testimony and oath-taking, groups of the opposite moiety. Although moiety affiliation has served as a basis for alliance formation, moiety identity is by no means definitive in shaping legal cases. Nonetheless, the opposition inherent in moiety identity has become emblematic of all rifts over land.

Many land cases have become closely inter-related, for witnesses in any one case bring to bear evidence from past cases, held either at court or before an elders' council. The same groups of people can repeatedly be found as witnesses and litigants in cases over different pieces of land. Often the same segment of land or parts of it are disputed in case after case, with different groups laying claims to the same territory. As there is necessarily reference to prior cases and events, a premium is placed on consistency in testimony from litigants and witnesses. If a man is inconsistent, as litigant or witness, from one case to another, his credibility is seriously impaired, and this fact becomes relevant in the determination of claims. The outcome of one case sometimes immediately initiated another, as case results influence subsequent legal strategies of lineages or coalitions attempting to wrest control of land from groups previously successful at court. Litigation nonetheless socially defined the contending groups as legitimate claimants to the land and thereby served to exclude other potentially serious interlopers.

Successful land litigation thus functioned as a kind of interim title of record during the difficult transition from customary tenure to tenure legitimated by registration. Indeed, court rulings became binding on the Adjudication Committee of the 1970s despite the ubiquitous hope that the local Committee, backed by land reform officers, would better serve local interests than the socially and geographically distant Divisional Court. Section 7 of the Civil Procedure Act thus states:

> No court shall try any suit or issue in which the matter directly and substantially in issue has been directly and substantially in issue in a former suit between the same parties, or between parties under whom they or any of them claim, litigating under the same title, in a Court competent to try such subsequent suit or the suit in which such issue has been subsequently raised and has been heard and finally decided by such Court.

The principle of law expounded here, known as *res judicata*, upholds court decisions in order to curb litigation and to prevent duplication of previous cases.

Despite reliance on customary law to settle land claims at court, specific features of procedure began to fall into disuse in the 1960s and eventually were formally proscribed before the Adjudication Committee. I refer here particularly to the ritual oath, which the Mbeere Divisional Court Magistrate in 1970 described as a "nasty" procedure. Although once in common use before elders' councils, the ritual oath has declined as a significant procedural step in land cases as well as in other civil disputes. Yet elders have continued to praise oath-taking as an effective and impartial way to resolve disputes, although they also lament a now ubiquitous scepticism threatening the power of the oath.

By consuming goat's blood and soil from the contested land--a mixture ritually cursed by elders in the manner depicted in the case record in the Appendix--litigants and their witnesses, it is believed, will testify truthfully for fear of the oath's capacity to destroy liars. Oath-takers also renounce mutual retaliation in consuming the blood and soil. By closely watching the demeanor of the oath-takers, elders in council or officers at the Mbeere court look for evidence of equivocation or stammering which they interpret as incriminating. That is, they reason that fear of the oath's lethal power is so disturbing to would-be liars that their mode of testifying will reveal dishonest intentions. But some cases may not be so easily concluded, and these would remain in abeyance for the next seven months. It is believed that during this time, the undetected liar, or perhaps one of his close agnates, will perish, thereby revealing the truth of the matter under litigation and resolving the case.

The allegedly fatal consequences of dishonesty under oath could be subject to more than one interpretation. A noted elder, for example, from the Kigamba coalition, died in 1972, and his agnates attributed his demise to sorcerers from defeated groups who were said to have avenged themselves on this man, owing to his role as a key legal strategist of Kigamba. Members of opposing groups, on the other hand, insisted that the dead man succumbed to the ritual oath he swore before an elders' council hearing a land case. Despite his death more than seven months after taking the oath, people nonetheless cited that event as directly instrumental in causing death, thus revealing the allegedly duplicitous nature of his testimony under oath. Controversy over the cause of death has continued, but it has not been subject to public, divinatory interpretation.

Although discrepant interpretations of oath-taking outcomes were certainly a feature of Mbeere customary law prior to land reform, such controversies in the last decade and a half are very likely less consequential as oath-taking has been eclipsed by exclusively rational means of dispute settlement. Durand has explicitly argued against the continued use of customary oath-taking in legal procedure because it can operate independently of evidence, thus subverting written law which guarantees evidential assessment in all cases. Moreover, oaths which are used to settle disputes rather than to swear witnesses lack legal authority as they are beyond a court's power to invoke (Durand 1970:24). Currently, the Oaths and Statutory Declaration Act guarantees the right of litigants and witnesses to refuse the customary oath while affirming the truth of their testimony by other means. The decline of oath-taking in legal disputes is attributable to official disapproval without outright legal proscription, the effects of Christian teaching against oath-taking, and what Durand calls the "increased sophistication of the populace" (1970:1970:17). In Mbeere, this latter point finds expression in common complaints about the cleverness (*ūūgī*) of litigants, who are said to lie so skillfully that the oath itself has proven inadequate for its intended purpose. Consequently, ubiquitous doubt now characterizes popular attitudes about the oath, and the association of oath-taking both with the Mau Mau movement and with more recent efforts of GEMA to forge political unity among Central Kenya Bantu has further estranged some individuals from this once vital legal procedure.

237

One of the final court cases utilizing the oath occurred in the latter part of 1966 when Mbiti, representing a coalition of Gatīrī clansmen sued Njiru, who represented the Mwake coalition of Mbutha clan. This protracted case also exemplifies the uses of evidence by litigants, the relative value of particular facts in the final decision, and the power of chiefly office and court influence in effecting legal success. Thus, ex-Chief Samson of Mbutha clan figures importantly in this case as does his classificatory brother, who served as a court elder together with a presiding elder not connected to the case. Despite the obvious conflict of interest (the former court elder and Samson are also classificatory brothers to Njiru) and a complaint from Mbiti to the presiding elder, the Mbutha elder participated in the hearing of this case. Mbiti also objected to the presence of Samson's son, who also served as a court elder. Without explanation, the case record indicates that this objection met with success as the Chief's son did not hear the case. The transcript of the case appears in English, although all testimony is given in the vernacular. The presiding elder also served as the recording member and provided the English translation. Procedurally, the plaintiff testifies and then is questioned in turn by the defendant and the court. Then follows the testimony of each of the plaintiff's witnesses, who in turn are questioned by the defendant and the court. The procedure is repeated when the defendant testifies. As the entire case record runs to nearly twenty pages, I will summarize the salient points of this important case after presenting the verbatim opening statement by the plaintiff and the defendant. The key issues are by no means unique in the litigation record of Nguthi land cases.

The case began with the plaintiff's statement:

I [Mbiti] am a resident of Kanyuambora and a member of Gatīrī clan. I am representing the clan of Gatīrī in this case because the land is the property of the clan.

238

I am claiming land called Ngoro. Njiru took part of this land when my case with Mbaka over this same land was taking place. He started using the land.

The defendant sued my brother for burning charcoal in that land. This land was founded by Mbogo who produced twelve generations.

[Plaintiff names natural features forming the boundary.]

I had a case over this land against a man of Mbutha clan; actually it was my father who had complained. This case was heard before local elders at home, and my father continued using the land.

I was sued by a man of Mbutha clan for preventing him from cultivating this land, and I won the case. Another Mbutha clan member got annoyed about it, and he complained to the chief; we had a land case before local elders, and they decided the land was mine. I had a case against a man of Ngugi clan over this same land before the local elders, and I lost the case. I filed the same case in court against him, but he died before it was heard. I remained on the land.

I stopped Ngarī of Mbutha clan from cultivating the land, because it belongs to my clan. My father planted nine *miraa* trees in this land. I have used four *mīkau* trees on this land and no one questioned me. I used a big *mūruruku* tree in the same land and no one said a word. Mwarania used a tree in this land without my permission, and I took a beehive from him. In June of this year, I used four *mīruruku* trees in this land, and no one asked me about it.

Jeremiah used a tree in the land, and I took away a beehive because he did not get my permission. I gave several people trees to use in this land.

There is a *murrum* (gravel) pit in this land, and I was paid 450 shillings compensation for *murrum*. Actually, 900 shillings was paid, and it was shared with the defendant. Samson of his clan was then the chief in my location, and he pressed me, and even caused me to be remanded so that Njiru got half the money. We agreed that later we would have a case over the land.

In this land, Ngoro, there was a place where my father killed a goat for the customary blessing of the stock.

On the day that Njoka was giving out land for a school area, my father was called to protect the land so that Njoka would not give ours away. Over fifty members of my clan live here.

In 1963, I sold part of this land to Mūvaniki, and Mūkera and Magwi clan elders were present when I sold it. I cultivate this land and live on it. There is an *itiri* (sacred grove) called Ngimari in this land, and my clan elder killed a goat there.

There is *iganda* (blacksmith's forge) in this land which belongs to Njuki of my clan.

When Samson was chief, he called people of our location together and asked them to accept loans and to cultivate in these lands. We agreed, and his son got a loan to cultivate in my land. After some time, Kenda of my clan complained about his use of our land, and he was arrested.

I have given permission to cultivate to about 67 people.

240

I expelled Gatiti from a garden he had cultivated in this land without my permission. I also expelled Igūna of Mbutha clan from a garden in this land.

I have no more to say.

Following questions from the court and the defendant as well as the testimony of six witnesses, the defendant testified:

I am a resident of Kanyuambora. I am a representative of Mbutha clan in this case.

This land is called Karangana and it is the property of Mbutha clan. [He indicates what the boundary is, reciting the trees, stones, and streams which form it.]

This land was founded by Mūgwe, who produced the following generations. [He names six.] When Mbiti had a case with Mbaka, Mbaka won the case. I sued Mbaka and won the case from the first instance through all appeals. This is the same land over which the plaintiff lost his case against Mbaka.

I have used a *mūruruku* tree, which the plaintiff saw, but he didn't say a word. About 1962 a tree was uprooted by the road and the plaintiff made beehives from it without my permission, and I took them from him.

Gaconi, wife of Kivoi of the plaintiff's family, came to Mūtinda of my clan with a gourd of beer and asked to be given a place to cultivate for two Gatīrī people. Nyaga and Mūturi were present, and they saw the beer and drank it. Mbuko came to me to secure a place to cultivate, and I gave it to him; he is a member of Gatīrī clan. Samson of my clan gave a man of Mūkera clan a

241

beehive from a tree in this land.

Kariuki and Mirongo had a case over a garden, and Ngarī of Mbutha clan came to court to say that he had given Mirongo the place to cultivate. This enabled Mirongo to win the case.

In this same land, Samson of my clan was paid 1666 shillings as compensation for land given over as a tobacco nursery [belonging to British-American Tobacco], and the nursery was in this same land. Ezekiel, who will give evidence in this case, was given permission by my clan to cut and burn charcoal for sale in this land. We gave him permission to do so.

Igūna [of Mbutha clan] has had a business of pit sawing in this land for a long time. He has used trees in this land, and no one has said a word.

Ngimari is a place in the land where my clan people used to slaughter goats. Ngurungu is another place where Mbutha clan people used to pray for bees to swarm in the area. Mbutha clan people who own the land established these sites.

During the time when compensation was paid for the *murrum*, Mwigi objected to my getting the money. We were advised to share the money and to have a case later to determine ownership of the land. I was registered as the land owner, but owing to the plaintiff's troubles, we shared the money. The land is ours.

[After brief questioning from the plaintiff, the defendant responded and also answered the court's questions. He then called seven witnesses including both clanmates and others, to corroborate the various parts of his testimony.]

In the ensuing month, the court visited the land in
dispute to examine boundaries and to witness the
swearing of the customary oath. Approximately six
weeks after the case began, the following judgment was
rendered [transcript edited]:

The plaintiff claims land called Ngoro
from Njiru. He represents Gatīrī clan in
this case. He claims that the defendant has
taken this land in this case against Mbaka
over the same land.

Mbiti claims to have acquired this land
through his ancestor Mbui. He claims that he
has been using the land over a long time and
has had two cases over it before local elders
and that he won the cases. He has cut and
used trees; he has chased people out of the
land when they used it without permission.
He has also received a half share of *murrum*
compensation for the stone dug out of the
land.

He produced several witnesses. Some of
these are border witnesses from Magwi and
Mūkera clans, who affirm that their land
shares a boundary with that of the plaintiff.

In answer to the claim, the defendant
says the land is his and that it has a
different name. He represents Mbutha clan in
the case and says that the land was founded
by Mūgwe many generations ago. He also
claims that they have used this land over a
long time and in many ways. They have
permitted people to live and to cultivate in
this land; they have chased away those who
have cultivated against their will, and they
have gotten money from this land.

It is found that this same land has been
in dispute between Mbaka and Mbiti in the
Mbeere African Court. Plaintiff lost his
case over this land and then filed a case

243

over this land against Njenga. Njiru won the
case over this land, even on appeals. Now,
Mbiti, who lost the case against Mbaka, over
this same land claims it from Njiru.

At present, Mbiti's application to
submit the case to the Court of Review (in
the case against Mbaka) is pending. This
Court must therefore consider this case fully
according to the evidence given, as if Mbiti
did not lose his case against Mbaka.

When the Court visited this land, the
boundaries shown by the plaintiff and one of
his witnesses did not at all agree. Each of
the two claim to have known his clan land
well. In this Court's opinion, it is not by
mistake that the boundaries do not agree;
each of the two is trying his luck.

Both Mbiti and Njiru claim to have done
many things in this land and so the Court has
taken into consideration those outstanding
deeds by each clan which could not escape
notice by the members of other clans in the
area.

It is found that this land is to a
larger extend occupied and cultivated by the
Mbutha clan people. It is a fertile and
developed land, and this has brought on many
cases.

Both Gatīrī and Mbutha got 450 shillings
in compensation for the *murrum* because both
claimed the land. Mbutha clan has received
1666 shillings as compensation for the
tobacco nursery in this land. This is a
remarkable deed, and no land owner could let
it pass to someone else.

Samson of Mbutha clan put up a piece of
this land as security in order to get an
agricultural loan. He could not be allowed
to do this by another clan if the land were

theirs. He was given the piece of land by his clan and this piece is part of the land in dispute.

Cases heard before local elders cannot be considered here because no sufficient evidence has been given about them. This Court does not believe that Samson of Mbutha clan, when he was chief could do the many things in this land without anyone [the rightful owner] asking him about what he was doing. No land owner could agree to give out a piece of land to Samson which he could then use as security.

It is also found that although the plaintiff claimed to have sold part of this land to Mwanīki, he has failed to produce this man as a witness. During the customary oath-taking, this man, Mwanīki, was present but he never took the oath. The Court believes the story was untrue.

On the northeastern border of the land in dispute, Mūkera clan people have supported both parties. On the northern side, the plaintiff is supported by Mbuya clan, yet that land involves a dispute between that clan and Nditi clan. Until a decision is made in that case, the rightful owner is unknown. The plaintiff's support over the boundaries is therefore doubtful and despite the fact that the defendant also has little support over the boundaries he claims, his clan's deeds in this land and his knowledge of them support his sole claim.

For all these reasons, this land does not belong to the plaintiff's clan, and this court finds that it belongs to the defendant's clan.

The weight of evidence shaping the court's decision in this case as well as in others falls heavily on the side of non-traditional criteria for demonstrating "ownership." Although litigants continue to utilize traditional canons of proof and techniques of disputation, including reference to sacrifices in the land, genealogies, and remote historical fact, such evidence diminishes in significance when compared to recent observable activity such as building, extensive cultivation, grants of permission to cultivate, and offering land as collateral for securing loans. Testimony about boundaries remained significant in this and other court cases, yet the proliferation of disputes called into question evidence on boundaries provided by those individuals whose claims remain unsettled. By the same token, a single court victory confers a certain advantage in pressing or defending subsequent claims, as Njiru demonstrated in recalling his court success against Mbaka. Of course, a court record existed to verify his version of the case. But for those, such as Mbiti, who attempt to found their claims on the outcome of cases before the local elders, disappointment will likely result for the uncertain or conflicting recall of witnesses pales in importance beside the unambiguous written record of the court.

Although Njiru and his coalition of Mbutha clansmen won this extremely important land case against the Gatīrī people, his victory seemed little more than nominal during the ensuing years (up to the period of land adjudication) because Mbiti and his kinsmen continued to occupy the land and to utilize its timber. In 1968, Njiru sent a letter to the court requesting that Mbiti and his people be enjoined from using the land. Njiru accused Mbiti of bringing new areas into cultivation and planting banana trees.

When summoned to court, Mbiti stated that he had cut timber for building huts, but denied planting banana trees or cultivating new areas. The reference by Njiru to banana trees and his concern about Mbiti's alleged planting is not explained in the court record, but informants indicated that setting out perennials can cause disputes as they provide evidence of long-term occupation and hence another proof of "ownership." This tactic proved useful for Mbiti when Njiru's request for an injunction against Mbiti was struck down by the court. That is, Mbiti's *miraa* trees adjacent to

246

his home established, to the satisfaction of the court magistrate (this series of events occurred after the reorganization of the courts in 1968), Mbiti's long-term occupancy of the land. When the magistrate visited the land to investigate Mbiti's continued occupation and activity on the land, he found that Mbiti's actions were confined to the area he had utilized preceding his case with Njiru. Furthermore, the magistrate found that since *miraa* trees planted by his father were growing around Mbiti's gardens and that since Mbiti's home lay within the land while Njiru's was a half mile away, Mbiti had a right to remain on the land. Finally, the magistrate cited Mbiti's establishment of a home on the land years before the suit began. He thus determined that Mbiti was using the land in the same manner as he did prior to the suit, and since Mbiti had appealed the results of the case to the higher court (and that appeal was pending), he should be permitted to continue using the land in the same manner. The magistrate further warned Njiru not to interfere with Mbiti and his occupation of the land.

Mbiti's appeal of his case with Njiru was filed in 1968 in the Nyeri High Court, just as were many other Mbeere land cases. Because the appeal related to unregistered land, the appeal was allowed under the provisions of Section 30(1) of the Land Adjudication Act No. 25 of 1968 which reads as follows:

> Except with the consent in writing of the Adjudication Officer no person shall institute and no court shall entertain any civil proceedings concerning an interest in land in an adjudication section until the adjudication register for that adjudication section has become final in all respects . .

> No written consent having been filed at the commencement of this suit and the Appellant not having satisfied the Court that his cause is entertainable despite the mandatory provisions of the . . . Act the proceedings before the District Magistrate's Court were a nullity.

The effect of this ruling, repeatedly issued by the Nyeri Court to Mbeere appellants of the 1960s, was to continue the adversarial relationship between Mbiti and Njiru and their respective agnatic coalitions. The process of appeal and the ultimate declaration of nullity by the Nyeri court prolonged the period of indeterminacy surrounding customary ownership and, in effect, consigned responsibility for dispute settlement to the local adjudication committees formed in 1971. Yet despite the hope of Mbiti, his coalition, and others defeated in court that they would succeed in pressing their claims before the Adjudication Committee, the principle of *res judicata* discussed earlier insured that the court decisions would be binding on the Adjudication Committee.

Mbiti's bitterness over the outcome of his case with the Mbutha clansmen expressed itself in two ways. He was particularly unhappy that a member of Mbutha had been a court elder and had testified in this case. It mattered little that this court elder was married to Mbiti's sister, for in matters relating to land and the political relations between lineages, affinity provides no countervailing pressure for settlement. Mbiti's sister supported the Mbutha clansmen, as all women are expected to identify themselves with the clan and lineage into which they marry. Equally troublesome for Mbiti was the influence he claimed Chief Samson exercised during his tenure in office, for Mbiti argued that Samson insisted that the *murrum* money be shared between Gatīrī and Mbutha people. Mbiti believed that the money *in toto* rightfully was due Gatīrī but that he had little recourse, under threats from the Chief, other than to share the money.

A second source of Mbiti's disappointment lay in the divided position of the Mūkera clan. One segment supported him, but a second lineage provided two witnesses for Njiru and the Mbutha position. It had been rumored, at least by people in Irumbi moiety, that Njiru's two Mūkera witnesses and some of their lineage mates had been promised land by the Mbutha clansmen in the event of a legal victory, which appeared likely in view of their repeated court successes. Although other breaches of moiety solidarity had occurred, Mbiti spoke most angrily about this example as the two witnesses of the Nderi lineage of Mūkera testified against the Gatīrī litigants. Mbiti's dismay with the Nderi lineage spilled over into his relations with the Subchief, a member of Nderi, whom Mbiti believed was victimizing him. I offer from my field notes the following edited description of an encounter between Mbiti and the Subchief which Mbiti believed was shaped by the land issue. The following events occurred in the Kanyuambora market in May, 1970:

> Passing through the market today, I saw an old man asleep on the grass next to the tannery. No one paid any special attention to him. A few minutes later, however, returning to the market after having gone home, I found the Subchief and the son of Mbiti, the latter in handcuffs; both were standing beside the old man, still unconscious. The old man is the father-in-law of Mbiti's son.

> The Subchief accused the handcuffed man, Mbiti's son, of having beaten the old man, but Mbiti's son denied it all. At one point, he said it was shameful to be seen in handcuffs before everyone on the market. He was embarrassed and angry about the charge. The Subchief tried to keep him quiet and at one point attempted to close his mouth physically. Mbiti's son protested his innocence, saying that he had been drinking with the old man but had not beaten him.

> From half-way across the market, Mbiti began shouting angrily. As he came near the Subchief, the latter told Mbiti to come closer. Mbiti refused, and then the Subchief grabbed his shirt at the shoulder and then held him by the collar. But Mbiti squirmed away. The Subchief and his assistant went behind some market buildings with their prisoner.

Mbiti then began to claim publicly that the Subchief's lineage was stealing land from Mbiti's lineage. That, he argued, was the reason the Subchief was arresting his son, who he claimed was innocent of the charge. Mbiti maintained the innocence of his son to me later, claiming that the charge against him was unreasonable because he insisted that no one in Mbeere could think of assaulting anyone from the group providing him a wife.

At that point, Mbiti entered a shouting argument with Mūgo. Mūgo had seated himself outside the tannery, and, as the two men exchanged epithets, the entire market was attentive to their argument. Mūgo called Mbiti a dog and criticized him for never cultivating and for always drinking beer. Mbiti argued that he did cultivate and that the beer he drank came from people who gave it to him out of great respect. Mbiti responded on a number of occasions by saying that Mūgo was a fool, "Like your mother," *ta njūkwe*. Mbiti said he had chased members of Mūgo's lineage away from the land in question, and that he forced them to remove their beehives from trees on that land; he also charged that in a case with that Mūkera lineage over the land, one of their number had died as a result of falsely swearing the oath. Mbiti claimed that only the clans of Gatīrī and Mbutha have an interest in the land, and the Nderi lineage of Mūkera had no just claim.

Mbiti was obviously very disturbed during the whole proceeding, both with the Subchief and with Mūgo. Mbiti walked around in front of the shops reiterating his claims about the land and his son's innocence. Toward the end of the confrontation, a popular shop owner, and a member of the Subchief's and Mūgo's lineage, approached Mbiti and told him that he had said enough.

Mbiti did not appear hostile to the shop owner and began to walk off. At the conclusion of his shouting, Mbiti summed up his feelings with a proverb: "When the buffalo cannot be killed, the calf is killed instead." By this he tried to make the significance of the incident confirm his claims and status, for by the proverb he meant that the Subchief's fight [actually over land] was with him, but fearing to arrest him (the buffalo), the Subchief instead took his son (the calf).

This scene in the market is one of the more graphic instances I recorded of how the land issue spills over into other domains of social life. Motives and actions are frequently viewed in the context of conflict over land as the present case illustrates. Visiting patterns have altered as people express increasing fear about the possibility of poisoning and sorcery if they eat or drink freely with those who maintain an interest in the same land. Accordingly, deaths in the community are likely to be interpreted in terms of the existing conflicts over land. Some will argue that the deceased has fallen victim to the sorcerer of an antagonistic lineage or, as Mbiti claimed in the market, through the just action of the ritual oath. Other deaths, such as those of children or agnates who did not swear the oath, are attributable to the oath's retribution, although such assertions serve mainly to reiterate one's claims without effecting a rehearing of the case. Mbiti frequently made reference to the death by drowning of two Mbutha children, who had fallen into the *murrum* pit in the rainy season. He argued that the oath sworn by Mbutha clansmen was working its way by consuming the children, thus vindicating his land claims. But such references to the putative effects of ritual oaths in past litigation are little more than desperate efforts to forestall legal outcomes based on recorded transaction and events.

By 1971, adjudication committees began to form in previously designated adjudication sections. Some of the latter, such as the Nguthi section, were coterminous with the administrative sublocation. Modelled on the "Unity Committees" earlier charged with the task of land consolidation and adjudication in Kikuyuland, Embu, and Meru, the Mbeere committees undertook the sole responsibility of settling disputes prior to title registration. Formal authority to appoint elders to the Adjudication Committee lay with the adjudication officer, but his designations were little more than confirmations of individuals who gained the nomination of their clans. The Adjudication Committee was composed of two men from each clan resident in the adjudication section. In Nguthi, thirty-two men sat on the Committee and represented the sixteen resident clans. Underlying this mode of Committee formation is the assumption that the clan represents the fundamental interest group in matters pertaining to land. The clans are relatively few in number when compared to lineages, and, notwithstanding the tendency for people to forge genealogically undemonstrable agnatic bonds into extra-lineage coalitions, the clan as a unit has never represented a land-holding corporation. The Committee members tend to be men of experience as major disputants, witnesses, councilors, and local political leaders. Thus two former chiefs and two former subchiefs, representing their respective clans, served on the Committee as did Mbiti, Njiru, and Ndwiga.

Because Committee members live within their adjudication section, they necessarily maintained extensive ties of kinship in the community and possible interests in the range of cases which came before them. Legally, the potential problem of conflicting interest is formally recognized in Section 8 of the Land Adjudication Act of 1968 which requires the withdrawal of Committee members from those cases in which they had an interest. Adjudication case records do not identify which Committee members do not take part in hearings because they maintain an interest in the claim, but the records do note the occasional peremptory challenges from litigants against Committee members they believe have prejudged the case.

Like the court proceedings antedating the Committee cases, the adjudication process contains its own channel of appeal. That is, appeals from the Adjudication Committee lie outside the judiciary and are taken up instead by an Arbitration Board composed of men appointed by the Provincial Commissioner under provisions of the Land Adjudication Act. The adjudication section coterminous with Nguthi is one of several sections comprising the Embu adjudication area served by the Embu Arbitration Board. It is composed of six members from throughout the District, and their authority is exercised when litigants appeal Committee decisions or, in a very few instances, when the Adjudication Committee refers to the Board a case it cannot resolve. Such referrals occurred in those cases where the Committee was unable to achieve a three-fourths majority, as mandated by law. Direct appeals from litigants, on the other hand, occurred frequently despite their relatively slim chance of success. Shortly after the Committee began to hear cases until mid-1973, 138 cases were heard and nearly half (68) were appealed to the Arbitration Board. When these data were gathered, 40 of the 68 appeals had been heard and only five of these resulted in the Board's reversing the Committee's decision (Glazier 1976b:46). Committee decisions have thus proven definitive in most cases. Although the prospects for successful appeal beyond the local level to the District level remain slight, defeated litigants readily look about for ways to achieve a satisfactory outcome. Thus recourse beyond the Arbitration Board is available through appeals to the Minister of Lands and Settlement, although no such appeals had met with success up to the mid-1970s. By early 1979, a series of objections to Committee and Board decisions had been filed with the Ministry, and these were under review. The most celebrated of these cases involved the Kigamba coalition's successful claim to the land in Kavengero parish and a challenge to that claim by a coalition of Mūkera clansmen, as well as by disaffected members of

Kigamba. I will turn to the Kavengero litigation momentarily, but first I wish to examine the litigation between Mbiti and Njiru in the appeal process.

In April, 1971, some five years after the original court hearing, Mbiti filed a case against Njiru before the Land Adjudication Committee of Nguthi. Contesting the same parcel of land he and his agnates lost at court in 1966, Mbiti sought to gain title to the land through this new means of dispute settlement. Supported by three witnesses, two of whom were not participants in the original case, his arguments covered much the same ground as the original dispute. His two new witnesses, representing clans which provided witnesses in the first case, testified about boundaries which their respective groups shared with people of Gatīrī clan. Mbiti's main witness testified that he had given the land for the Kanyuambora market in 1942, and that people of Gatīrī clan shared a boundary with him at that time. Moreover, he said that one man from Gatīrī formally served as a witness to the transaction. When he ceded more land in 1959, he claimed that a man of the Mbutha clan asked him to affirm that Mbutha people held land adjacent to his, but he refused. As a result, he stated that he was arrested since at that time Chief Samson of Mbutha was able to proclaim that it had ceded land to the County Council by bribing a Mūkera clansman (a witness for Mbutha in the original case) to testify that Mbutha clan held the land. During this case before the Committee, there is no record of written evidence having been submitted in support of these alleged transactions.

On the opposite side, Njiru reiterated the evidence from his court case and enlisted the support of three witnesses. Two were his clanmates who participated at court, and an additional witness, Mūgendi of the Kigamba coalition of Nditi clan, supported Njiru's contentions regarding a boundary (the Ruiria stream) separating Njiru's claim on behalf of Mbutha people from the Kavengero land held by the Kigamba coalition. The Nditi clansman also supported Njiru's contention that he provided land for the B.A.T. nursery, and that this was done publicly and without objection from the appellant and his agnates. In addition, he testified that Mbutha people had received loans using the land as collateral and that again no objections were forthcoming. Finally, the witness stated that a former chief of Nyonga clan, who had long cultivated in Kanyuambora and had earlier pressed an unsuccessful suit against Mbutha, failed to procure a loan because he was unable to gain the assent of Mbutha people that he had a legitimate claim to an enclave of Mbutha territory he was cultivating. They feared that had they supported him in his efforts to procure a loan, he would have gained grounds for later seeking registered title and that a default on his part would moreover have endangered their holdings because the control of land pledged as collateral would devolve to the government.

The decision of the Committee was remarkably brief in light of the diverse and conflicting evidence presented. As in numerous other adjudication cases growing directly out of disputes heard at court, the Committee was constrained by the *res judicata* principle. Despite the Committee's long acquaintance with both disputants and thorough familiarity with the case details, they stated their findings as follows:

> We, the Land Adjudication Committee of Nguthi, have seen that although Mbiti was defeated at Siakago Court . . . he has land where he is [now] disputing with Njiru; if we are given the power, we could get him his land as it is. The reason he has [just claim] is that both [men] shared 900 shillings compensation for *murrum* dug in the land.

Having no alternative but to uphold *res judicata* as directed by the land adjudication officers, the Committee could not adjust what it regarded as past inequity, if such a decision contravened a court ruling. While not preventing appeals, *res judicata* inhibits duplication of previous litigation by upholding earlier case results, thereby limiting the judicial prerogatives of the Land Adjudication Committee.

Nearly two years after the Committee's decision, Mbiti appealed the case to the Embu Arbitration Board composed of six men from the District; none was from Nguthi. In a relatively short hearing in which Mbiti and Njiru repeated their earlier arguments with the support of one witness each, the Board upheld the earlier Committee decision, thus giving Njiru and his Mbutha kinsmen another seemingly definitive legal victory. Although each litigant provided the customary testimony about his forbears on the land, the most telling evidence again related to recent developments, namely loans granted to Mbutha people, and the allegedly undisputed ceding of land by the Mbutha group to the B.A.T. for a tobacco nursery, and to the government for the secondary school. Yet up to 1979, the Mbutha claims were still subject to questions, as objections were filed with the Ministry of Lands and Settlement.

Mbiti's primary witness had come forth with a document in support of his claim that his lineage of Mūkera clan had indeed provided the land for the Kanyuambora market in 1942; and in the only successful suit against Mbutha clan before the Committee, this witness and his agnates succeeded in gaining rights to a portion of the Mbutha claim by proving his cession of the market plot and primary school grounds to the County Council. He insisted that his boundary lay along land legitimately held by Gatīrī, not Mbutha people. Thus, in giving demonstrable proof of his original claim to the market land, his support of Mbiti and the Gatīrī group gave new credence to their contentions. In the balance lay several hundred choice acres which would be registered to members of one or the other group, although the likelihood that Mbutha people would lose any land beyond the portion given over to the lineage of Mūkera clan was very small.

The outcome of the protracted litigation between Mbiti and Njiru extended well-beyond the people of their respective coalitions. Because the acreage contested in this case exceeded that disputed over by the Mbutha group and their other antagonists, the latter found their claims ultimately circumscribed by

the contested land in the case at hand. As a result,
Njiru's victories over Mbiti at various levels of
dispute settlement effectively coopted those groups
which attempted to claim holdings which Njiru could
show were enclaves of the larger territory his group
won from Mbiti's coalition. Thus approximately fifty
people comprising the Mwake coalition of Mbutha clan
have benefited from land reform. Using political
influence at the court and in the chiefship, in
effectively presenting evidence alleging long-term
occupation and use of "founded" land, and in
documenting undisputed loans together with the cession
of land for public purposes, the people of Mbutha will
gain title to land contested for nearly two decades.

In light of the official value placed on
"customary" law in the resolution of land disputes, the
emphasis on "non-traditional" criteria of ownership in
the successful cases involving the Mbutha clan has
created a certain irony. Evidence that is wholly
"traditional," including genealogies deriving from the
alleged founder, activities on the land by various
forbears, and rituals performed, inevitably presented a
weak case, especially because such evidence could not
be corroborated to the satisfaction of the court or
Committee. By contrast, referring to or producing
written documentation of recent activities on the land
did much to sway legal opinion favorably. An elaborate
but wholly ineffectual effort to sue the Mbutha clan
for land was made by a Nyonga clansman who enjoyed a
brief tenure as chief in the late 1940s. Although in
other Committee cases Nyonga people acted in concert,
the former chief in the case at hand acted only for
himself (he sought only the control over his garden and
not over a larger land parcel); this lack of support in
part insured his defeat. The following testimony
emphasizes "traditional" criteria.

The land in dispute with Njiru is mine;
those who began in this land follow from
Mūtua-Nene, and he came from Mbeti. He came
and lived at Thangwe; from Thangwe he went to
Kanyonga. At Kanyonga his descendants were
Namu followed by Ngondi; Ngondi came to
Kīthendu and fathered Mūgo. Mūgo fathered

Kīthendu who fathered Mbogo. There then came invaders known as Magogo, and Mbogo went east where he fathered Ithagu; Ithagu fathered Mūgo, who fathered Nyaga; Nyaga fathered Watene, then Watene fathered Ireri who was my father.

The forebears said that if all went well we should go back to where they had come from beginning with Kīthendu. I came here in 1942, and I asked permission from no one. I went up to where my fathers had been living.

Then the loans began, and I tried to get one but was unable to do so because I had no money.

Then the wife of Mūkunguu died on the land. I went to call him to collect the dead woman for burial. When he buried his wife, I asked him to bring me a sheep. He said he would not re-enter the home where his wife had died; but he asked me to kill a sheep on the boundary. Mūkinguu belonged to Mbutha clan, and he would not have given me a sheep had the land been his. That is why I am demanding this land from Njiru.

I have had cases with two people in this land; both were from Mūkera clan. I asked Njiru if the land was his why he didn't tell me not to litigate with the two men since he claims the right to grant permission. I have accused him because he entered my garden. I am not demanding the entire land parcel, and I don't know his land. I only know that the land I am occupying belongs to me. My boundary is shared with Magwi clan on one side and Gatīrī clan on the other.

The Committee dismissed the case by tersely stating that it was not satisfied with the evidence presented by the plaintiff. The defendant, Njiru, claimed to have been instrumental in insuring that the former chief did not get a loan and additionally argued that the latter's testimony about the slaughtered sheep had nothing to do with ownership of the land. Rather, it was performed only as part of funerary custom. Moreover, Njiru argued that the land the former chief sought was simply a small portion of a larger territory which had been subject to litigation between Mbutha and nine other clan groups. Moreover, Njiru asserted that control of the land had been determined by these other cases. The former chief, despite open threats to use sorcery against anyone who would deprive him of land, will likely return to a home maintained by one of his wives in lower Evurore near the Ishiara market.

The legal conflict between lineages, coalitions, and individuals played out on several stages of litigation during the past twenty years tends to overshadow internal conflicts between agnates. Agnatic solidarity has sometimes been problematic, often expressed by those who lament that "now even brothers are fighting over land." No land disputes between brothers ever reached the level of Court or Committee (indeed only one intra-clan conflict, that between different lineages of Mūkera clan, appeared before the Committee), for these could be settled within the delimited and private context of an elders' council composed exclusively of agnates.

Yet the absence of formal legal suits among brothers or close agnates should not obscure the serious disagreements sometimes reaching public notice through complaints to land adjudication officers and the Ministry itself. Such an internal dispute occurred within the Kigamba coalition of Nditi clan and centered on widespread disaffection with the leadership. The membership has severely criticized the coalition leader whom it charges with pursuing personal profit at the expense of the entire coalition excepting his own children. The leader, Ndwiga, is charged by his agnates with selling land without their permission and taking the very best and most extensive portions of the Kavengero land for himself. Estimates of the amount of money he has secured through private sale are substantial and range upward from thirty thousand shillings, which allegedly lies in a bank account in the town of Embu. The members also complain about the allocation of land within the group and claim that the typical share of ten to fifteen acres is meager in relationship to the relatively small size of the coalition (less than fifty males) and its successful law suits over nearly 1000 acres of land. In 1973, twenty members of the coalition mounted a protest, articulated in a letter to the assistant land adjudication officer, complaining about the self-seeking decisions Ndwiga was making at their expense:

We nominated Ndwiga to deal with cases. From there Ndwiga went on with all cases supported by the Nditi clan which contributed whatever was wanted. All court cases ended, and [then] cases were sent to the Land Adjudication Committee. From this time, clans were ordered to make their boundaries, and we made boundaries for the above land [Kavengero]. We were to contribute enough money for all cases as requested. The Nditi clan won the cases and the land of Kavengero became ours. The . . . Committee told the Nditi clan to . . . demarcate their land. This is . . . when we . . . nominated a demarcating committee from the clan. This committee [carried on] for four days. Ndwiga refused [to accept the decisions of] the committee and went on for two days demarcating the land without the clan's authority.

Ndwiga was called by the demarcating committee, and he refused to attend the meeting. After he refused . . . Nditi clan wrote a letter to the Demarcating Officer . . . informing him . . . how Ndwiga has [sold] plots without any authority from any members of the clan and how he left some Nditi clan people and some children without plots.

The reply from the Adjudicating Officer . . . said that we [should] wait until the Board cases end in Kavengero. When the Board cases ended . . . the land was ours.

This time, we called Ndwiga and told him
that . . . we want to deal with matters . . .
as follows . . . we want to know how he had
demarcated the land [although] he has refused
[to tell us] how land is given to some people
we don't know.

After all this, Ndwiga told the clan
that the land belongs to him and not to the
clan. Now sir, we want you to call us in
your office with Ndwiga and tell us whether
the land belongs to Ndwiga or to the clan.

This letter was signed by Mūgendi and twenty Kigamba
coalition members.

By 1979, the final adjudication record for
Kavengero remained unfinished and the complaints of
Nditi clansmen against Ndwiga were unresolved. Mūgendi
complained about Ndwiga's duplicity and hatred for his
kinsmen, manifested in 1978 by the death of Mūgendi's
daughter through what he believed was Ndwiga's sorcery.
Unable to gain adjustment of their claims up to 1979,
Nditi clansmen, through Mūgendi, were repeating charges
first voiced in 1973 that Ndwiga was using his
substantial gains from the unauthorized sale of land to
influence land reform officers, who might support him
at the expense of his clanmates. Although officially
enjoined to desist from entering land transactions in
the adjudication sections where they worked, at least
one officer secured some land registered in the name of
a kinsman, and it is said that Ndwiga had assisted him.

At the same time the Nditi clansmen were
complaining about Ndwiga, objections to the large Nditi
claim to Kavengero, sanctioned by its succession of
successful suits, were pending in the Ministry. The
main objection was filed by a coalition of Mūkera
clansmen from each of the five maximal lineages whose
members had staked out gardens in Kavengero. Their
disaffection is summed up in a complaint to the
Ministry prepared by a young Mūkera clansman supported
by more than three hundred men (mostly of Mūkera but

261

also representing other clans, such as Nyonga, in danger of dispossession):

> We have lived here with harmony for over thirty years and no dispute over the land has arisen . . . mixed clans as we are. [It was] not until the land was declared under the Land Adjudication [Act] that differences have arisen where one individual person claims the ownership of this settlement . . . This is where the objection comes in, in that we fail to understand how and why the Land Adjudication [Committee] has awarded this land to one person, or say one clan, and we have proof that the land has never been owned by any clan.

In criticizing the Land Adjudication Committee's repeated rulings favoring the Nditi clan, this complaint asserts that upper Nguthi was settled only in the relatively recent past by people from a number of different clans all of whom were searching for an agriculturally more hospitable setting than that provided by the lowland areas. This argument, corroborated by colonial records and generally attested to by upland inhabitants outside the context of litigation, has been regularly contradicted in suits exaggerating length of occupation of various parcels of founded territory in Nguthi. But despite the various manipulations of genealogies to accord with claims of continuous cultivation over many generations, the disaffected voice their sharpest complaints against alleged bribery at various levels, ranging from the Court to the officers of the land reform program. Whether through cash payment or promises of land, individuals such as Ndwiga, together with kinsmen, and coalitions such as the Mbutha group are said to have gained their ascendant positions through wealth and influence. Somewhat more benignly, it is also said that such individuals and groups exercised a certain foresight in understanding that the land tenure changes occurring in Embu Division in the 1950s and 1960s would ultimately reach Mbeere and that evidence of improvements to the land supported by agricultural loans for which the land was pledged as collateral would prove pivotal in gaining legal title.

The trend in land law, and indeed in civil law generally, has been toward a formalization of both substance and procedure. A complex body of statutory land law defines rights of ownership and dictates procedures for settling conflicts over these rights. Formal legal bodies hand down judicial decisions constrained by written law, and thus depart from customary patterns of collective mediation and arbitration by non-judicial elders. At the same time, the procedures in customary law laid great value on reconciling antagonists, who were enjoined to spurn all efforts at self-help or revenge. Whether conciliatory values were promulgated through the ubiquitous oath or through the concerted influence of persuasive and articulate elders, customary procedure made provision for a reweaving of the social fabric rent by litigious conflict. Modern legal procedure is little-concerned with the ramifications of a serious breach in social relationships and does not attend to their repair. The examples of customary procedures recounted in Chapter Three and in the Appendix detail the value on reconciliation characteristic of council efforts under customary law. Springing from pre-colonial Mbeere society, compromise and arbitration were eminently suited to a polity lacking central authority and dependent for order on a multiplicity of elders' councils. The local Adjudication Committee, modelled on the customary council (but approximating the latter more in official rhetoric than in fact), has no choice but to follow the dictates of modern procedural and substantive law. Although Committee members deal with land cases in their immediate neighborhoods, thus bringing to bear intimate knowledge of each case and its litigants, they are unable to negotiate settlements or compromises between antagonists if such efforts contravene the tenets of modern law. Believing that both litigants had just claims to disputed territory, the Committee of Nguthi would thus have awarded land to both Njiru and Mbiti in accordance with the customary values they, as elders in council, were ironically constituted at least partially to uphold. But since this case lay within the purview of the Court and had been subject to judicial decision, the Committee was powerless to take any action other than ratification of the court outcome, despite the Committee's outright skepticism about the earlier decision.

Customary law has continuously evolved, no less so during the era of European penetration than in pre-colonial days. By ignoring the inherent flexibility of customary law and by denying the non-corporate aspects of African society, the district administration of Embu, until the formal recognition of individual rights in the late 1950s, conceived of local law with little regard for the steady stream of changes accruing to it. Individualism, stemming from European contact and what I have argued to be indigenous cultural proclivities toward it, became part of the fabric of society and hence customary. But the government upheld its own static view of custom, attempting in various ways to strengthen it as a bulwark against individual initiative and entrepreneurship. The government was in the somewhat paradoxical position of defending custom, however inaccurately conceived, as staunchly as the most conservative elders. Yet those farmers who, with the aid of kin or with political influence, sought loans or began cash crop production--in short acted outside the bounds of a narrowly defined European notion of custom--were in the best positions to gain registered titles once the government came around to the recognition of individual rights. They could, then, effectively articulate their interests on both levels of legal discourse mentioned at the beginning of this chapter. In other words, they could use tradition toward the goal of gaining registered land at the same time they were exploiting with the same intent opportunities officially and popularly regarded as inimical to tradition.

Chapter Seven

Conclusion

Emerging Stratification

Over the past eighty years in Mbeere an egalitarian mixed economy and a gerontocratic but diffuse polity have been transformed into an increasingly stratified social order. The rise of the chief and subchief, as officers in a hierarchical civil administration, effectively diminished the influence of elders at the same time that the new officials came to rely on authoritarian measures to insure tax collection and the maintenance of order. With their new power, chiefs conscripted labor for the administration and cooperated at least passively in colonial efforts to reduce the age of male circumcision, thus expanding the pool of "adult" male laborers and further undercutting the age organization. Joined by a coterie of retainers, the chiefs were among the first salaried functionaries, who could also aggrandize themselves through gratuities exacted from their constituents. The most successful chiefs insured themselves lengthy tenure by efficiently serving the district administration through prompt compliance with directives, steady tax payments, and orderly supervision of their locations. Chiefs were also joined by other functionaries in the various departments of administration, and the regular non-agricultural incomes gained by this emerging rural elite became a key early source of economic differentiation. As members of the Local Native Council, chiefs were also in the best position to benefit from loan programs, extension services, and agricultural schemes; their agnatic kin often gained accordingly. Political office and government employment at the lower eschelons thus sketched in the first outline of significant political and economic differentiation of the rural scene.

The official establishment of freehold tenure has created yet another mode of economic stratification

265

which will affect rural social patterns as profoundly
as any change to date. Beginning in Kikuyuland in the
1950s and extending to Mbeere in the 1960s,
registration of individual land titles ratified
tendencies toward the individualization of land-
holding, which had its roots both in customary tenurial
rules, and in the steady monetization of land
transactions in the colonial period. The growth of
money transactions, besides creating a spirit of self-
interested individualism far beyond the customary
limits of individual action, made possible private
economic exchanges hardly possible when the transfer of
land rights was most often legitimated by the very
public act of driving livestock from the home of one
individual to another. By the 1960s, the incorporation
of land into the market economy, which had been in
process since the 1930s amidst great official concern,
was fully accepted by the government through land
reform legislation and development policy. Perhaps
more than any other factor, freehold tenure epitomizes
the growth of contractual social relationships whereby
various transactions can occur without regard to the
constraints of agnatic kinship or the diffuse and now
declining influence of elderhood.

The pattern of rural stratification based on
regular cash income gained from employment or from
entrepreneurial activities including cash crop
production or business enterprise is now well-
established, and land reform can only entrench the
pattern further. Indeed, the most recent development
plan, referred to in Chapter Five, states that land
reform has increased land transactions and resulted in
a concentration of land among "better-off small-scale
farmers." If the various objections to the land
adjudication case results still pending in the early
1980s fail to bring redress, then the widespread hope
among Nguthi farmers that people will at least maintain
the land they farmed at the inception of land reform
will not be realized. For the first time, then, free
access to available land such as bush areas will have
been officially proscribed, and the losers either will
remain landless in Nguthi, where opportunities in the
rural non-farm sector are very limited, or will retreat
to the lowland areas from where some of their families

migrated. By the late 1970s, drier sublocations, such as Iriaune, were beginning to witness a much reduced version of the maneuvering for land which has been occurring in the high potential areas of Nguthi (David Brokensha, personal communication). Bernard and Thom have also recently observed that the population pressure among the Kamba of Machakos District is pushing people into lower Mbeere:

> To the north in Mbere [sic] and eastward in Kitui lie areas that are not now experiencing population pressure. It seems likely that as pressure in western Machakos becomes more acute, movement into these adjacent lands of relatively sparse settlement will increase. Already Wakamba have migrated across the Tana River and settled in Mwea and Mavuria Locations in [Mbeere] Embu (1981:405).

The dislocations of land reform in the high potential areas of Mbeere will likely combine with the already established pattern of Kamba migration into the lower zones to create population pressures where none has ever existed.

For the majority of those remaining in Nguthi, it appears that the familiar mode of labor intensive subsistence agriculture will continue. The average size of a registered piece of land, according to land registry records in the mid-1970s, was approximately four acres, but this majority of small-holders is limited in its access to capital. Some individuals will maintain multiple holdings of good agricultural land in excess of fifteen acres, and this minority will be able both to devote more acreage to cash crops and to secure larger agricultural loans.

These latter beneficiaries of land reform include not only those who gained a portion of agnatically-claimed land successfully defended in litigation but also those in regular employment who can purchase land independently of the particular legal fortunes of their close kin. These latter two modes of land acquisition are not unrelated since access to cash enabled

267

individuals to contribute more to the cost of litigation and to demand, in turn, larger shares of lineage land. Larger land owners also have the resources to engage in continuing land transactions whereby they will further increase their holdings. Although land boards have been established in Kenya for the ostensible purpose of controlling transactions that would prevent inefficient land use and unproductive accumulation, a study based on data from two land boards and an assessment of similar research in other areas suggests that economic considerations are only infrequently relevant to board decisions, which rarely reject proposed transactions in any case. Moreover, such boards are powerless to control land dealings occurring independently of the official register (Coldham 1978).

At the onset of land reform, the capitalization of agriculture, which the program was to encourage, was not taking hold extensively. Few people had the money to hire animal-drawn plows or tractors so that the usual patterns of labor-intensive, subsistence horticulture using hand implements remained very much in evidence through the 1970s. In addition, relatively few Nguthi farmers were growing tobacco, the major cash crop. Tobacco production, undertaken by only 110 Nguthi farmers in the early 1970s, is a complex endeavor requiring both shrewd planning and financial outlays. A careful balance must be struck between the labor requirement for food crops on the one hand, and tobacco production, on the other. If one relies only on himself, then it will be impossible successfully to raise a tobacco crop as well as a food crop, for a single person cannot produce sufficient labor for both tasks. Even if one is assisted by a spouse and children, the goal of bringing in both crops remains formidable. Some tobacco growers thus find it necessary to hire local labor--at the rate of about four shillings per day in the mid-1970s--to assist in raising tobacco, especially if their children are too young to assist or are enrolled in school. Initially, tobacco seedlings must be cared for in a seed bed for a period of about two months during which time daily watering is required. Further, intensive labor is required to transplant the seedlings and to harvest the crop. Then follow the tasks of sorting and curing the crop before its sale to the tobacco cooperative. Curing must take place in a specially constructed tobacco barn. By the mid-1970s, a grower might earn about 800 shillings on less than an acre of tobacco. Farmers emphasize that this income is insufficient to make up for shortfalls in food production which can result from insufficient labor or its improper allocation. Growers capable of hiring labor are at a decided advantage in raising tobacco. Such advantages enjoyed by the more prosperous Mbeere farmers in matters pertaining to cash crop production and to agricultural innovation more generally have been examined in Hunt's detailed survey (1975). Her study concludes that economic inequality will likely increase because wealthy farmers can muster the resources essential to innovation and can more readily bear the considerable uncertainties and threat of loss which innovation can augur.

Class formation has also been abetted by education, for schooling in the past promised the best means for securing steady off-farm income beyond that available to the unskilled. The value on gaining education remains firm, yet it is very doubtful if opportunities afforded by it will do anything but exacerbate the well-established tendencies toward class formation. An employed family member becomes a ready source of money for kin, to whom he is frequently obligated not only because of the bonds of kinship itself but also because kin often contribute to a young person's school fees. If someone gains a much coveted salaried position, he is thus expected to provide his supporters with money. In recent years, the onerous burden of school fees for primary education has been lifted with the granting of free public education through Standard VII. But whereas primary education was once sufficient to qualify one for employment as a minor clerk, its practical value is now little more than as a means to further education at the secondary level, which requires fees. Should one be able to complete Form IV, prospects for employment, or, more rarely, a place at the University, depend on distinguished performance on the Cambridge examinations. Despite an increasing number of youth in the educational system at all levels, there has not been a concomitant expansion of employment slots. Thus expenditure for secondary education may result in diminishing returns, creating the familiar hardship but without its likely alleviation in employment. Leys identifies similar tendencies and has summarized the relationship between education and class formation as follows:

> There was also the fact that . . . the rewards to education in terms of salaried or high-wage employment conferred huge potential advantages on families wealthy enough to pay the substantial school fees necessary to support several children through a full secondary education, so that the difference between a household income which made this possible, and one which did not, could prove critical for the long-run fortunes of the family. Hitherto, access to primary schooling . . . had probably tended to enhance the upward mobility of poor families. As the rewards to primary schooling declined and virtually vanished, a reverse process was liable to set in (1974:191).

Education continues to be a means for upward mobility, but it has become a considerably narrower channel for advance through which proportionately fewer individuals will pass.

Descent and Tradition

The Mbeere response to their incorporation into the modern state, replete with its energetic programs of development and land reform, raises theoretical questions of considerable importance for social anthropology. These questions center on the nature of lineage structure, its relationship to the territorial extension of kinship groups, and particularly, the impact of momentous historical change both on lineage organization and Mbeere conceptualizations about it.

Most discussions of lineage and territorial organization are set in a timeless ethnographic present without considering the effects of radical change on these social features. Even the most cursory review of the vast literature of African social anthropology and the theoretical discussions it has prompted reveals the pervasive concern among Africanists about the nature of unilineal descent in traditional society. Historically, the works of Evans-Pritichard on the Nuer and Fortes on the Tallensi provided the reference points for any examination of lineage structure and its relationship to territorial groups. Their influence has been so dominant that it is doubtless fair to say that, since the publication of their pioneering studies, each Africanist who has worked in a patrilineally-oriented acephalous society has pondered whether his data conform to the Nuer or Tallensi model of lineage and territorial relationships. I also suspect that various anthropologists have been tempted by the neatness of the received wisdom to stretch their data to fit a Procrustean bed of Nuer lineage and political-territorial segmentation or of interpenetrating Tallensi social fields, where lineage and territorial organization reveal a much closer fit than among the Nuer.

In earlier assessments of Mbeere descent and the several descent-based groups and coalitions they freely refer to by the term "clan" (Glazier 1972, Brokensha and Glazier 1973, Glazier 1976b), the corporate land-based aspect of these groups was emphasized not only because of the ethnographic reality of collective agnatic action centered on a landed estate but also because of the influence of the dominant paradigms of African lineages. The present study, by taking a diachronic perspective, goes well beyond the synchronic structuralism of classic British thinking regarding lineages; it demonstrates how the confluence of historical factors rewarding the activation of exclusionary descent groups defined in relationship to a landed estate marks the real source for the new association between lineage and locale. That association cannot be assumed *a priori*, but rather must be demonstrated through various sources of data, which in the present study include case records of land adjudication and also the transformation of Mbeere funerary custom discussed in Chapter 4.

In the recent history of Mbeere society, people refer to the new corporations as "clans." But these corporations are not entire clan units; rather they are segments of clans--either lineages or descent coalitions. These groups are organized in an attempt to maximize members' chances of gaining choice land to be registered to each individual and, if possible, to extend their claims beyond what would have been normal holdings prior to land reform. Costs of litigation and the necessity of proving at law the extensive use to which a group puts the land require a collective effort, and descent groups provide the social core of land-claiming units. Individuals acting only on their own would suffer a severe disadvantage against the challenges of social groups, but, more importantly, the perspective of customary law regarding land tenure (mandated by the government as the medium for dispute settlement prior to registration) is quintessentially social in nature. But despite the use of patrilineal ideology to justify these claims and to provide a descent charter for each group, the facts of common descent may be no guarantee of inclusion within the land-based corporation. One must also donate labor and money toward the various requirements of land demarcation and litigation if one hopes to gain land from the corporation. Moreover, included on the roster of many lineages and descent coalitions are the names of affines, matrilateral kin, and other non-agnates who have contributed money toward the group. These outsiders look to the corporation's favorable record in litigation in the hope that successful case outcomes will insure a division of freehold land among both agnatic and non-agnatic contributors. Thus one confronts in the Mbeere data a dual problem--explaining the relatively recent fixity in the relationship between descent groups and local areas and the participation in descent groups of numbers of people on the basis of criteria patently unconnected to descent.

The discrepancy between a demonstrable agnatic relationship to a descent group and specific non-descent criteria one can exploit to gain *de facto* membership in the group and entitlement to a share of land it is seeking clearly points to the necessity of

distinguishing between descent as an ideological or
symbolic marker of a social category and its activation
in specific behaviors centered on the organization of
social groups. In the latter instance, a group
crystalizes through the idiom of descent to organize
members' rights in land. The particular reasons for
the activation of descent are of course problematic in
each ethnographic case and should not be assumed merely
on the basis of an existent descent ideology or a
prevailing model better suited to other ethnographic
realities. The dominant paradigms of Africanist social
anthropology, particularly those positing descent as
the recruitment principle in the build-up of local
groups, are little-suited to the analysis of pre-
colonial Mbeere with its highly mobile domestic groups
and extended families forming multilineage parishes,
thus playing little on shared descent as a basis for
local group organization. The Mbeere case is
especially interesting, because it demonstrates how
pressures toward private land ownership, capital
improvements, and other modernizing trends have led, at
least in the short run and for the first time, to
unprecedented corporate activity by descent-based
groups and aggressive claims asserting long-term
linkages between these groups and specific local areas.
In this respect, perhaps ironically, modernizing trends
have led to the convergence of a new ethnographic
reality with the major descent paradigms constructed
out of studies of traditional societies. Through the
manifold effects of population pressure, land scarcity,
capitalist penetration, and official edict, descent
ideology has found new expression in the incorporation
of lineages, in the enhancement of their genealogical
depth, and in their new and continuing associations
with particular segments of land. All of this is
presented in the idiom of tradition, which the Mbeere
and the government have collaborated to construct. At
the same time, participation in the descent group by
affinal and matrilateral kin as well as by other
financial contributors obviates descent as a singular
recruitment principle. Rather, descent-based groups
can be constituted on non-descent criteria but, once
established, these groups enjoin their membership to
comport themselves like clanmates, despite the
transparency of that fiction.

The current significance of the clan moieties--
Thagana and Irumbi is now clear. They are
linguistically equated with the patriclans, yet they
prescribe no rule of exogamy despite assertions, albeit
vague, that everyone of a given moiety shares common
descent from a mythical ancestor said to antedate the
female founders of the patriclans. Moreover, kinship
usages, modeled on terms utilized within the domestic
circle and finding ready expression among clanmates,
are not characteristic of interactions among people of
the same moiety unless such usages have been
established on grounds other than common moiety
membership. Each moiety, without corporate rights or
obligations, manifests only the most tenuous unity, yet
that unity can be strengthened when activated by
specific issues, most notably those centering on land
conflicts. A large proportion of those who are
attached to agnatic lineages and descent coalitions
belong to the same moiety, and that common affiliation
is much emphasized as moiety unity becomes assimilated
to the ideology of descent in times of strife. The
symbolic and behavioral dimensions of descent,
especially when mutually discrepant, thus become fully
comprehensible only through a diachronic lens which
focuses on situational determinants of social action
and considers them against the backdrop of more stable
cultural constructions.

Other very critical issues concerning the nature
of descent ideology and the actual territorial
extension of descent groups arise from the Mbeere
material. Particularly apposite here is the use of
descent ideology to sanction corporate claims and to
talk about the relationship between local groups. But
affiliation to groups and participation in their land
claims by virtue of a financial contribution can rival
the facts of agnation itself in securing registered
title. Is descent, then, mere fiction? What is the
relationship between descent as an enduring symbol of
agnatic solidarity, on the one hand, and the actual
groups which form to claim land, on the other? Is the
reality of corporate claim and action to be found
instead in the actual territorial groups, composed to
be sure of agnatic kin but also including non-agnates

who together are motivated by self-interested strategies of land acquisition? Or is territory also a secondary factor which, like descent, is subordinated to the specific economic goals of coalitions and interest groups, whose members may be dispersed and whose kinship bonds are not structurally significant?

These questions have arisen in other ethnographic contexts and on their answers have turned theoretical issues of profound anthropological import extending well-beyond Africa. Leach, for example, in his study of Sinhalese land tenure, *Pul Eliya* (1961), raises similar concerns while challenging the fundamental value of descent theory itself, although in a different context from his earlier critiques of the dominant lineage model of British social anthropology. In opposition to Fortes and the jural perspective on descent derivative of Radcliffe-Brown, Leach takes a behavioral approach to the analysis of land tenure. That is, he objects to the derivation of actual behavior from the jural rules--the set of rights and obligations said by British structuralists to constrain the action of incumbents of each role within the lineage. Emphasizing unilineal descent systems as the action frameworks *par excellence* for the playing out of jural rules, orthodox descent theorists, best represented by Fortes writing on the Tallensi, argue that structure prefigures behavior as action follows from the rule. Leach, by contrast, criticizing the derivation of behavior from jural rules, prefers to chart the pattern of action (the statistical norm). Finding the structure of action divergent from the structure of rules and contingent on the constraints of the material environment rather than on an abstract system of moral rules, he argues for the necessity of distinguishing these two levels of reality (usually conflated by the descent theorists) and subordinating the rule to action. He says simply that he does not wish to follow what had been the prevailing approach to the study of kinship, namely, considering kinship as "a thing in itself," or attempting to isolate kinship behaviors as a distinct category explainable by jural rules without reference to context or economic self-interest (1961:305-306).

275

The discussion prompted by Barnes's now classic examination (1962) of African descent models in light of New Guinea ethnography has also been extremely illuminating in the process of "rethinking" descent theory. Barnes initially pointed up the highly mixed social affiliations of local group members in New Guinea societies, in part brought on by the great ease with which people change residence. He also noted the scant attention paid to genealogies, segmentation, and collective lineage activities including religious observances. Interested in the applicability of African descent models to the societies of highland New Guinea, Barnes found them seriously wanting. In the two decades since his pioneering article, we have been compelled to come full circle by asking not only about the relevance of African models to New Guinea but also about the explanatory value of these descent models (Nuer and Tallensi) to other African societies, where flexible social structures such as those found in highland New Guinea, are the rule. In these latter societies, attachments to locality rather than to descent group are often paramount, although descent often furnishes the idiom for talking about the organization of local groups made up of a variety of cognatic and affinal links. Appreciating the African departures from the Nuer and Tallensi orthodoxy, Karp has asked how developing New Guinea models can highlight the aberrant African cases, and he tries to salvage the African models by clarifying the ideological, jural, and behavioral dimensions of descent (1978). What we have come to appreciate from the various reexaminations of African descent theory in light of New Guinea studies is that the descent principle may serve to organize local groups, thus resembling the idealized Nuer system; or descent may simply provide the conceptual or symbolic framework for the playing out of relationships between local groups which are constituted on other grounds altogether. A more recent, broader review of lineage theory by Kuper (1982) makes no effort to refine existing lineage paradigms; on the contrary Kuper, in an extremely critical voice rivaling Leach's, argues that the entire theoretical enterprise is a sterile exercise in what he regards as a continual reordering of the same essential elements of a bankrupt model first presented by Maine and Morgan (1982:92,93).

These few examples illustrate the varied scholarly debate prompted by African lineage theory, but I do not propose to review this literature once again with an eye toward either modifying it or dismissing it for its various shortcomings, although I consider Kuper's extreme conclusions unwarranted. Rather, I wish to ask two fundamental questions, which in themselves are prompted by my view of the continuing value of descent theory, at least in its ideological and symbolic dimensions. My initial question is simply this: Why do the Mbeere find descent constructs the appropriate idiom for representing the social organization of land tenure prior to land reform when such constructs only partially image the actual group of claimants the ideology purports to explain? In addition to those claimants living on or near the disputed land, others reside in non-contiguous parishes, although they reside in the same sublocation where they seek land. A construct besides descent, it might be argued, would surely do as well, especially since the hard facts of economic improvement, capital investment through previous loans, or chiefly patronage are so pivotal in winning land cases. Secondly, why don't people simply organize themselves as an interest group without taking pains either to record official genealogies or to articulate to each other and to the government their land claims through the primordial symbol of descent?

It should be stressed at the outset in considering these questions that genealogies have assumed a wholly new place in Mbeere conceptualizations about social groups. Customarily, as I have argued throughout this study, shallow lineages and domestic groups under the pressures of environmental stress including drought and famine were highly mobile. Together with the threat of raiding, these factors tended to disperse kinsmen. The frequent movement of people in search of new sources of food, the ease by which people could be adopted into other clans where they settled, and the regularity of group fissioning occurred within a highly flexible framework adapted to the requirements of the natural habitat and social environment of Mbeere. Because land

277

was a free resource and the population did not press hard upon it, genealogical recall to legitimate claims to land or other property was at best nugatory. Livestock, the most significant moveable property, devolved across generations within the domestic group according to house-property complex principles. A genealogical matrix framing these processes of bequeathal and defining an order of inheritance over more than two generations could be expected to serve a more settled, stable population less subject to the vagaries of food shortage, but among the Mbeere genealogy customarily played little role in the organization of social groups and in the definition of rights at different levels of segmentation.

In addition to the imperatives of property inheritance, social anthropologists have identified political succession as frequently ordering the passage of office, thus representing yet another factor often instrumental in the structuring of agnatic groups into genealogical segments. But political succession was also not at issue in Mbeere society prior to colonial rule. Rather, the Mbeere polity was organized around *ad hoc* councils of elders whose situational positions and influence derived from a loosely structured age organization and from the elders' own personal abilities, not from the attributes of an office legitimated by agnation. Thus manifested, political leadership was highly diffuse, operating as it did without genealogical specification of chiefly position or other political roles at successive levels within a lineage organization. Noteworthy individuals gained reputations for their arbitration skills in council or from their warrior exploits in raiding or in arranging the *tubū* markets and controlling food distribution from them. After the colonial conquest, they were the first appointees to the new position of chief. Each appointee had been at best a *primus inter pares*, a "big man" (*mūnene*) in Mbeere parlance--a term which came to mean chief.

The structural similarities between such Mbeere figures and Melanesian "big men," who inform much of our thinking about Melanesian and New Guinea society in particular, ought not to be overplayed. Although the

278

Mbeere "big men" achieved their standing by personal exploits, they did not gather about them large followings of kin related through a variety of cognatic and affinal as well as agnatic links nor did they represent the center of continuing redistributive networks. Reciprocity rather than redistribution was the dominant principle of the Mbeere economy, and its highly variable and unpredictable yield from year to year did not enable men, however influential in council, to gain clients or followers who expected rewards in feasting or the like. "Big man" status in Mbeere was much more a matter of personal reputation gained in public oratory or in warrior service, where the material rewards were insufficient to enable these men to obligate others to them, except in the very short term. Moreover, the influential men in Mbeere did not enjoy their prestige at the expense of others or as the outcome of an aggressive competition for followers. The prestige and influence of the adept man in council did not inhibit the capacity of others to reach for similar recognition. The prototype of the New Guinea big man, the intensely competitive achiever seeking continuous validation of an always tenuous status, thus finds no analogue in Mbeere, or probably anywhere in Africa.

As an expressive counterpart of the political order, the Mbeere "ancestor complex" made little use of shrines or other ritual mnemonics dedicated to shades at different points in a genealogical hierarchy. On the contrary, Mbeere practice and belief regarding the ancestors imaged a socio-political order in which many critical social bonds were non-agnatic and transactional in their easy formation and dissolution. Emphasis was laid on the domestic group and shallow lineage. Moreover, when agnation structured social action, it did so independently of clearly defined genealogical charters, emphasizing instead the diffuse value on agnatic solidarity borne of common blood flowing from the eponymous ancestress of the patrilineal clan. But in recent years the alteration of funerary custom and the "domestication of death" have recast and hardened the once fluid relationship between lineage and locale in order to strengthen corporate claims to land.

Using the term "clan" to refer to any segment ranging from the minimal lineage to the descent coalition, the Mbeere invoke the primordial values surrounding all those claiming common descent. When people designate an individual as "ours" or "one of us," they unambiguously mean shared clanship. Here descent represents a cultural model setting out an exclusive category of people whose bonds are those of common patrilineal ancestry. Implicit in the descent dogma, moreover, is a complex of moral imperatives defining fraternal solidarity and common interest amidst diversity. The symbolism of descent thus models itself on the segmentation into house-complexes within the homestead, where fraternal bonds can be strained to the point of breaking when such matters as inheritance of always limited resources are at issue. Yet descent, as a diacritic or symbol of categorical exclusiveness, provides no absolute rule by which new land-holding groups are constituted, although these always contain a core of lineage mates to whom may be attached other members of the clan or affinal and matrilateral kin. The descent dogma, nonetheless, is utilized to conceptualize the group and to describe its common interests. This ideology constructs a symbolic relationship, thus creating a compelling medium through which to represent social attachments unconnected to descent.

Although a descent-based coalition can link clanmates unable to trace their exact genealogical connections to each other, it can also act to exclude other clan members who have not given money or labor to the corporate cause of gaining land. Individuals outside the clan, if they contribute money and labor, stand to gain land at the expense of kin not contributing to their agnates at the center of the coalition. Common descent thus does not absolutely insure entitlement to land claimed by these same groups, thereby obviating descent in and of itself as a recruitment principle guaranteeing membership in a group which will divide land. Social processes at times appear to contradict cultural constructions, as those with common material goals will utilize the dogma of descent to assert their collective interests which are defined on wholly other grounds. But once established, such interests are partly mystified through the symbolism of descent. That symbolism, despite the fluctuating fortunes of lineages and descent coalitions and their attached contributors, remains timeless and unchallenged as the primary reference point for group loyalty. Thus identification with the interests of a descent group does not imply incorporation into that group in the same way a true clanmate could customarily expect to gain land, that is, virtually for the asking. Rather, it means that once one has entered the rolls of the descent group through monetary or labor contributions (here membership is clearly not ascribed), expectations are framed within the symbolism of descent, however artificial it may be.

In this respect, the dissonance between the actual composition of various groups often referred to loosely as "clans" and the superstructure of the descent dogma begins to make sense. Historically accommodated to a mobile population responding to seasonal raiding, famine, and the stresses of environment, the descent ideology represented a constant value amidst the shifting fortunes and composition of local groups. Through the radical changes of the colonial and post-colonial eras, the dogma of descent has proven no less useful or adaptive as a charter for local groups defending land claims and seeking to expand them at the expense of other groups. The ideology has nonetheless taken a grotesque turn with the unprecedented exaggeration of genealogical depth and historical claim, thus responding to a new fixity in what had been a flexible relationship between shallow lineages and local areas. The solidarity and cooperation within groups designated "clans" is no less essential than in earlier days, although those values are now borne as much by contractual and monetary concerns as by the diffuse symbolism of the descent ideology. Emphasizing the bonds of brotherhood and the legitimating function of now lengthy genealogical pedigrees, descent ideology can also partially mask the blatant maneuvers of self-seekers scrambling for land, and attempting, although with limited success, to conceal their machinations from public scrutiny. Articulated tradition regarding

281

corporate control of land, abetted by government authority, paradoxically supports values which are systematically undercut by both the process and outcome of land reform itself. In this respect, the dynamics of change among the Mbeere resemble processes at work in other African societies where custom, or tradition, instead of upholding a particular social order, represents the very mechanism effecting social transformation. But given the often self-seeking strategies of particular people within Mbeere descent groups, the mystifying qualities of tradition represent only a thin veil. That is, the consequences of exploiting tradition for economic ends are often manifest, since they are frequently discussed by the actors, especially the unsuccessful ones, in the land reform drama. Compared to the Giriama (Parkin 1972), the Mbeere are experiencing a much less subtle transition into private land ownership and rural capitalism. Nonetheless, descent group leadership regularly claims to support tradition by acting solely on behalf of agnates in presenting corporate claims before official courts, committees, and boards.

Descent ideology has been essential in the complex, often recondite strategies for gaining land which have dominated Mbeere society for the past twenty years, and official policy has played a vital role in sustaining the ideology. Because both the colonial and post-colonial authorities mandated customary law as the vehicle for the adjudication of land disputes prior to tenurial alterations, the definition of custom became critically important; it evolved as an interplay of a naive but fundamentally self-interested understanding of custom by the government, actual belief and practice regarding land holding, and local perceptions and manipulations of official expectation. Convinced that customary tenure throughout Central Kenya was governed by "tribe," "clan," or other corporate bodies holding potentially self-seeking individuals in check, the colonial authority and its successor emphasized the restraints of custom and its support of the commonweal in the face of drives for private gain. The government paid hardly any attention to the precolonial bases of individual action preadapting Central Kenyan peoples to the eventual market economy. During most of the

282

colonial era, this highly conservative view of custom served the powerful interests of the European minority dependent on an abundance of cheap African labor blocked from landed entrepreneurship. Had the labor pool enjoyed easy access to cash crop production and other capital endeavors, African concern would have turned toward its own long-term economic interests at the expense of the settler economy built up on the alienation of African land and a plethora of African labor. By taking a conservative view of custom, the colonial government, up to the publication of the Swynnerton Plan, actively discouraged any departure by Africans from the perceived corporate quality of social life generally and land-holding in particular.

In the official view, then, such groups as age-sets (usually referred to mistakenly as "age grades"), "generations," and especially clans restrained African individualism and were supported; the clan became enshrined as the *sine qua non* of land-holding. The official view of customary land tenure, I wish to emphasize, was not so much "wrong" as incomplete. Although it recognized in limited fashion the corporate aspects of customary land holding, the official interpretation neglected the very real sources of individual rights regarding land. Even after the government did a complete about-face in regard to rural development by underwriting individual tenure among the African population, the prevailing view of traditional tenure persisted and became the medium through which local legal strategies were formulated and the adjudication of land disputes had to proceed prior to freehold deed registration. Individuals, even the most self-seeking in the land reform process, could advance themselves most successfully if they pressed a collective claim, drawing allies especially from agnatic kin but also from a range of other supporters. Then, within the context of the corporation, various individuals including chiefs, especially, could maneuver their way into the largest farmsteads among their kin. Tradition has thus come to represent a convergence between local and official interests.

In placing shifting patterns of land tenure, kinship and social organization in the broader context of changes altering Mbeere society since 1906, this study has considered two dimensions of the problem of social transformation. On the one hand, following from three periods of social anthropological fieldwork in Nguthi, I have set forth the continuities and changes in Mbeere social organization as they unfolded in the behavior of people and in their own depictions of the past within the highly circumscribed contexts of domestic groups, lineages, and elders' councils. This more "micro" perspective, informed by an interest in the fabric of small scale society and the social principles and values woven through it, is of course the conventional view of the social anthropologist. On the other hand, I have also considered matters of government policy in the colonial and post-colonial periods, for such policy, ranging from the cessation of raiding to the introduction of chiefs to the formalization of freehold tenure, has shaped local communities and constrained social organization in critical ways. At the same time, this dual perspective makes clear that local communities have been no mere passive registers of policy but have actively sought to use both official policy and "traditional custom," which exist in dynamic interrelationship. This dual perspective is vital for an understanding of former "tribal isolates" now embedded in the wider political order of the nation-state.

Appendix

The Contemporary Council of Elders

Ad hoc councils of elders do not enjoy official recognition from the government, although their continued existence enables people to settle certain of their disputes without appearing before a formally constituted judicial body, such as the Mbeere court at Siakago. The councils facilitate the local settlement of conflict and at the same time reduce the number of cases that otherwise might be heard at court. In some cases before councils, subchiefs may appear and even take an active role among elders in arbitration between the antagonists. Yet it should be emphasized that such participation is unofficial, for the position of subchief (and chief) does not subsume judicial duties. Subchiefs nonetheless can informally lend the authority of their offices to council proceedings in order to effect a settlement, but such action of course departs from the customary course of action in these *ad hoc* assemblies. But the assemblies remain informal in that no one keeps a written record of cases nor do participating elders receive a salary apart from the customary gratuities in meat and beer provided them by litigants.

The following case, which I present in its entirety, aptly illustrates the *ad hoc* constitution of elders' assemblies, the emphasis on arbitration, compromise, and reconciliation among antagonists, and finally the oath -- a procedural *sine qua non* of most council proceedings. The case occurred in Kathera Sublocation and was originally recorded on tape and subsequently translated by my research assistant and myself. Sarah, the widow of Jeremiah, was pitted against Jacob of Mūgwe clan. Sarah's late husband was in Jacob's shallow lineage, as both descended from the same grandfather. Figure 5 shows the relationship between antagonists and their kinsmen referred to in this case:

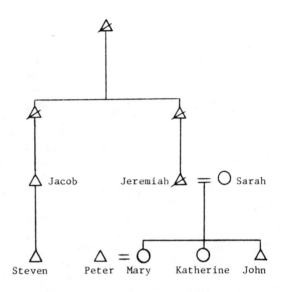

Kinsmen of Sarah and Jacob

Figure 5

Sarah accused Jacob of cursing her and of using sorcery against her. She had first sought the aid of some Mūgwe clansmen, but when that failed, she enlisted the aid of the Subchief, who helped arrange a council assembly before which Jacob would swear on oath that he would not harm Sarah. Sarah also used the case to air a variety of grievances against not only Jacob but also his son. A major issue was Sarah's belief that Jacob had tried to take the bridewealth for her elder daughter, Mary, which Sarah wanted to use as school fees for Katherine, her younger daughter. The assembly consisted of eight men, two of whom were chosen by both litigants; each litigant also chose three others. Of these eight men, three were Mūgwe clan members -- clanmates of Jacob and of Sarah's deceased husband. Two other assembly elders were of Ngugi and Cīīna

286

clans, both of which bear a phratry relationship (discussed in Chapter 4) to Mūgwe clan. The last three elders were selected by Sarah. They belonged to clans outside the phratry (that is, the group formed by Mūgwe, Ngugi and Cīīna clans), perhaps reflecting Sarah's desire that people within a wider circle gain awareness of her grievances. The case was also attended by an assortment of other local people who looked on but did not participate. The proceedings were held both inside and outside a small shelter built in a clearing in the bush near the home of the Subchief.

Sarah vs. Jacob

Subchief: Sarah has accused Jacob. Is Jacob here?

Jacob: I am here.

Subchief: Sarah, who will listen to your case?

Sarah: [names her councilors]

Subchief: Jacob, choose your people.

Jacob: [names his councilors]

Subchief: The members of the council should sit together here. Others should not sit with the council. Sarah, explain to the members of the council you have chosen and to those chosen by Jacob why you have accused him.

Sarah: Jacob's bull came to my home. I told my children to return it because it might kill our calves. Jacob came and asked why the bull was being beaten, and I told him about the calves. He asked me if I ruled the home. I asked him if he wanted the calves dead. He started insulting me. He said that I would die if I joked with him. We insulted each other, and the bull was taken back. Three days later we went to work in a neighbor's garden, and Jacob's son, Steven, was there. We started drinking beer. When the third gourd was brought, I saw that it was sugarcane beer, and I didn't want to drink it because that kind of beer makes me ill. When I was given my cup, I gave it to Steven jokingly saying, "You are my son, and I will 'marry' your daughter." He drank the beer, got drunk, then went to sleep in the bush.

Soon another person went to the place where he was sleeping and yelled, "Come and see Steven lying in excrement." Steven awoke and said, "It is Sarah who is saying I am lying in excrement. May she sleep with her father and have sexual relations. She is a clitoris."

Then I asked him, "Do you want to insult me as your father does, and you are my child? Are you abusing me, and your father did it too?" He said, "You will perish like that soil, together with your daughters of whom you are so proud." [The efficacy of such curses is very feared; retraction is believed essential if the curse is not to be realized.] When we returned home, I said to Steven, "You said that my children and I will perish like the soil; so pick up the soil and say I won't perish, and since I told you that

288

you will perish, I will also take it back." He bought snuff for me when he was told by some women that he had abused his [classificatory] mother, but he refused to pick up the soil and take back his curse. The next morning, I went to look for him and his father. I asked his mother if Steven had told her anything. She said she knew nothing because she had been drunk. I told her that Steven cursed me with soil, but she said she knew nothing about it. The next day I sent word to Jacob that his son had cursed me with soil the day before and if three days passed without picking up that soil [for retraction], then a goat would have to be slaughtered [meaning aid of medicine man would be required for the retraction, using the giītathira, or first stomach, of a goat]. I went home, but they didn't come to take back the curse. I went to the son of Njoka [clanmate of Jacob's] and told him the story. He called three men. When they came, we talked, and when Jacob was told about it, he said that the matter was simple and that I wanted him to kill a goat for nothing. When the men heard that, they went away. He said he would call me in the morning. He didn't call me; then I went to my garden, and then I saw a vehicle coming so I went for a vaccination.

Jacob: I am accused, yet I do good things for her. I told her that there is a curse left by our father [classificatory] not to insult people in the home, so don't insult me over the bull. Why didn't you report me to Nthiga of our clan? Why didn't you tell them? Isn't that sorcery you are accusing me of? I mean the curse. You are blaming me for sorcery, but I don't do it. Know that I am hated for doing good things. When Jeremiah died, you and I did the "washing" [ritual sexual relations to cleanse a home after death]. If I am committing sorcery, tell these people the good things I have done.

First
elder: She told you first about the bull, then you said you would use sorcery against her. You didn't tell us about that. After that your son . . .

Jacob: Don't tell me about my son. Talk about me. My son will speak for himself. He is here. I went for this woman four times -- this woman who called the clan which asked me to produce a goat.

First
elder: Did you speak with this woman after the clan departed?

Jacob: Yes, on the same day, and I said I would bring a goat. That was the day she was making beer for the clan; I went for her twice. I didn't come here for a case. All I want is to take the oath. I want people to direct me while I take the oath.

Second elder:	You should kill the goats now. Bring the beer. I know all about this case. Say what Jacob has done to you. I believe that he is your husband.
Jacob:	I am not the husband of this woman.
Sarah:	I am annoyed with him for telling Peter [pays bridewealth for her daughter] not to give me school fees for my child. One term concluded while she was unable to go to school. The next term he also prevented me from getting school fees.
Jacob:	Can you take the oath and say that?
Sarah:	May God see me [loosely, may I be killed by the oath if I lie]. I told Peter to sell one goat and buy clothes for the child. Why do you tell him not to give me the money? If that child becomes a teacher, won't she help you because she will get a salary?
Third elder:	He says when he went to Peter's the money was counted in the presence of others. Will you say anything if he swears that he didn't tell Peter not to give you the money?
Sarah:	When we take the oath, he should say that he won't steal anything from me, and he won't tell Peter not to give me what I ask. It will be all right if he takes the oath like that.

Third elder:	Do you think he can steal from you?
Sarah:	Why did he prevent my child from attending school. There are many widows here in Mbeere and are they treated in this way?
Subchief:	Sarah, I heard you saying that Jacob should swear that he will never steal from you. Didn't you also talk about a curse?
Sarah:	Yes.
Subchief:	How he had abused you?
Sarah:	Even if he abuses me I am not angry. I am his wife [through the levirate]. I only mentioned the curse from his son Steven. If Jacob abuses me in the worst way I wouldn't mind since he is my husband. I can abuse him in return.
Subchief:	You said that Steven won't take the oath.
Sarah:	Steven won't take the oath. I said that the curse with the soil should be taken back. I won't oppose what these elders say.
Third elder:	So you have a goat for the oath or for the retraction of the curse?
Sarah:	I have only one goat for the oath.

Subchief: The woman says she doesn't hate Jacob because he is her husband. She said that if Jacob abuses her, she too can abuse him. But she does fear that he might use sorcery against her or her children or else that he might steal something like the bridewealth paid for her daughter. [bridewealth for a girl should be used to pay the bridewealth for her full brother. Bridewealth is primarily the affair of a man, his wife, and her sons. Someone in Jacob's position has no rights in the bridewealth Peter pays for Sarah's daughter. At most Jacob can act as guardian.] She wants Jacob to swear that he won't use sorcery against her or her child nor will he steal anything from her.

Sarah: I want that.

Jacob: She insults me whenever she drinks beer brought for her daughter [as bridewealth]. Have I ever taken that beer? I received the money but have I spent even ten cents? Tell her what I have done. She has used sorcery against me; she insults me and says I have reproduced like a rat. [In this hearing Jacob has been equating curses and sorcery.] Have I insulted her about her children? I am subject to a curse in my home against such abuse. Do you think that I can cooperate with her when her husband could not? You drink beer all night, but I don't insult the man you are with. You also drink beer alone. But I am the father [classificatory] of your girl and I circumcised her [provided the celebration]. Have you ever heard of that in Mbeere? You only gave birth to that child, but I circumcised her. To shorten the case, I can't steal anything from your child and I can't poison you or your child. Beer is coming for the elders. I am glad the elders are here. This is not a case because we are not demanding anything from each other. I have nothing which can kill the woman or her children or anyone else in Mbeere. May the oath kill me if I have. Even if I see a snake or a bad thing, may the oath kill me if I let it reach her.

Sarah: I'll direct you in the taking of the oath.

Jacob: You won't direct me. I won't let you control me. You are foolish.

Sarah: My daughter is ill, and I think he is using sorcery against her.

Jacob: [Sarcastically] All right. I am the one who is poisoning her with sorcery.

Elder of the clan: Let me tell you before you take the oath that people of the clan are present and we heard what you have said. We will direct both of you.

Subchief: This is a case of Jacob and his wife. I want you to settle the question about the curse and the soil.

Elders: We shall take care of that.

> Subchief: We don't have a lot of goats in Mbeere to kill here and there.

At this point, the elders began drinking beer provided by the disputants. A short distance away, other elders, assisted by young men, slaughtered the two goats, provided by Jacob and Sarah. One elder killed the animals by puncturing their throats; blood from Jacob's goat was collected in a half-calabash and then set aside for the oath.

Just prior to roasting the goat meat, the government health inspector, who had accompanied the Subchief, examined the organs of the animals to insure that they were free of disease. A fire was built and portions of meat from each goat were roasted and eaten by the elders. Raw meat from Sarah's goat was distributed to the Subchief and council elders to take home. The Subchief refused to eat meat from the goat whose blood would be used for the oath; he said that as a Christian he was forbidden to eat meat from such an animal, and other Christians present agreed.

When the elders had finished eating, the oath-taking began. One of the elders took the half-calabash of blood, which had congealed, and placed a clot on each of four leaves; two of the leaves were then set before each disputant.

The elder preparing the blood for the oath also assumed the role of oath-leader. Responsibility for that role historically fell to an elder of the second council who was also a member of a generation-set empowered with ceremonial authority; in his absence, any elder could act as oath-leader. Nowadays, in each sublocation, two or three elders (regardless of council or generation-set affiliation) emerge time after time as primary oath-leaders because they stand out for their abilities to chant and to utter effective curses. These oath-leaders, it is said, know all the "proverbs of the oaths" (*nthimo cia kaurugo*) referring to the various formulae used in the chanting.

As other elders and the two disputants remained seated on the ground in a semicircle, the elder who had placed the blood on the leaves took his staff and began a rhythmic chant, cursing the blood placed before Jacob. Other elders clapped their hands slowly in rhythm with the oath leader's invocation:

> This is the oath for Jacob who is said to have used sorcery against the wife of Jeremiah and the children. The oath will seize your head and buttocks if you have eaten [taken] a bad [false] oath. If you use sorcery in your home against the wife of Jeremiah or use other sorcery so that you can have sexual relations with her, then the oath will enter your stomach and make it swell like a bag full of green grass. If you are using sorcery in order to get bridewealth in this home, then any medicine [antidote] you use after taking the oath will seize your kidneys, then your shoulders, then it will drop to your intestines. When you speak you will become sick. You will have an erection like a donkey's. The oath will make you sick. If you have not done these things, the oath will be like gruel from sorghum [nourishing and benign].

Accompanied by the clapping elders, the oath-leader brandished his staff as he cursed the blood designated for Sarah's oath:

> This is the oath for Sarah who says, "I am the victim of Jacob's sorcery because he wants the bridewealth from my daughter. He prevents my child from getting school fees." If you went to Tharaka [said to possess strong medicines] for sorcery against Jacob, then this oath will make you sick. The oath will begin in your head, making your brain boil. When you go to men, you will tell them to use your vagina. Your stomach will begin to swell and your back will swell. Your vagina will protrude. The oath will eat [destroy] you. If you are blaming Jacob for

296

something he has not done, you will be destroyed by the oath. When you meet children, you will tell them to use your vagina.

> An elder: Yours [your vagina] will be like a half-calabash.

> Oath-leader: If you have not done these things, the oath will be like gruel from sorghum.

Following this cursing (kūruma kaurugo), Jacob was instructed to take the oath first. At the conclusion of each phrase, "May this oath kill me," he ate a small portion of the blood.

> Jacob: We have killed goats for nothing in this oath. I have never used bad medicine, nor do I know where to get it in order to use sorcery against the child of a Mbeere. May the oath kill me if I know.

> Elders: It kills the one who lies.

> Jacob: May the oath kill me. Oh, it is slipping. [Blood began to fall off the leaf.]

> Elders: If it falls off, we shall say you threw the oath away. [You have refused the oath thus proving your guilt.]

> Jacob: May this oath eat [kill] me. In this home there are no bad things. I have a curse left by Jeremiah not to mistreat his son, John. I could do nothing to him. May this oath kill me if I do something bad to him.

Sarah:	Say you will not use the kind of sorcery against me which makes people forgetful [implying that he can make her forget about the bridewealth she seeks].
Jacob:	Although you hear her saying that I use sorcery against her, you should know that there is a curse in my home from long ago that I cannot abuse people. If I lie and if I abused her using any kind of harmful medicine, may the oath kill me. If I see something harmful approaching her home like fire, unless I lack strength, I will not let it reach the home. If it does, may this oath kill me. I do not know where I can get bad medicine to kill a Mbeere, or the people of Jeremiah, or the sons of my fathers [classificatory] or anyone else in Mbeere. May the oath kill me if I lie.
An elder:	Swear that "Sarah is mine and her young son is treated equally with my son. May the oath kill me if it is untrue."
Jacob:	If I hear Sarah crying because she is being beaten by someone . . .
An elder:	Maybe you will not be able to fight the man beating her.
Jacob:	If I use sorcery against Sarah or against any other person of Mbeere, may the oath kill me.
An elder:	Take the oath for the kind of sorcery she mentioned.

Jacob:	I do not know about that and I will not send someone to do that to her. May the oath kill me if I think of that.
Elders:	Take the oath slowly and do not consume all of the blood. This woman will direct you now. Tell him what you want him to swear.
Jacob:	I will not curse the children of Jeremiah, and if I hear someone curse them I will be very disturbed. May the oath kill me if I lie. Tell her to direct me now.
Sarah:	I want him to say that he is not using sorcery against me as a result of having a dispute; since this dispute began, I have become ill.
An elder:	No, he has already sworn about that.
Jacob:	I only told her that this case is costing me a goat, and she too is losing one. I will not try to give her any kind of bad medicine. I will not look for it. May the oath kill men if I attempt these things.
Elders:	He has finished swearing.
An elder:	This woman mentioned earlier that he told the man who married her daughter not to give her bridewealth.
Jacob:	That girl is not mine. I circumcised her. I complained because I paid for the beer. This child troubled me very much. Who

299

has ever taken that trouble in Mbeere? I do not steal anything paid for that girl. I have not stolen or hidden the bridewealth. I can only say that Sarah should be given something. May the oath kill me if I hid anything of hers.

An elder: Swear that you have taken the oath honestly.

Jacob: May this oath kill me if I have done anything to counteract this oath or if I will take anything to remove this oath. [It is believed that some medicine men have material to make an oath-taker "vomit" the oath, thus permitting him to swear falsely with impunity.]

An elder: Now throw that leaf backwards over your shoulder and step into the clot of blood on the other leaf. Give that woman her oath.

Sarah then held a clot of blood on the leaf just as Jacob had done; she then began to swear.

Second Oath-taking

Sarah: I know of no medicine which can kill the child of a Mbeere, my child, or my husband. May the oath kill me.

An elder: It kills the liar.

Sarah: May this oath kill me if I know of medicine which can kill a person. May this oath kill me if I lie. If I know anything which can kill a Mbeere, may this oath kill me.

An elder: Do not go quickly. Say that you will not curse Jacob or his children and that they are like your own.

Sarah: May this oath kill me if I do not use sorcery against a person who can use it against me. I will not curse him for nothing.

Elders: Swear about Jacob's children.

Sarah: May this oath kill me if someone trying to poison [with sorcery] me or my child does not follow me when I die. Unless the child of Jacob tries to poison me or mistreat me, I will not curse him. May the oath kill me.

An elder: There is a kind of poison which is available within a woman's body. [Refers to menstrual blood.]

Sarah: May the oath kill me if I try to use the sorcery of women against the child of a Mbeere or against my co-wife. If I know about sorcery against Jacob may this oath kill me.

Jacob: This woman will swear that she cursed me. She said that I have a lot of children like a rat; she should not say that again.

An elder: She will swear about that if she said it.

Sarah: May the oath kill me if I did not see that I was hated. If someone mistreats me, I will curse him.

An elder: No, do not threaten that. There is just speaking, and then there is cursing.

Jacob: Tell her to say that she will not curse again.

Sarah: May this oath kill me if I curse Jacob without his having tried to use sorcery against me or my children.

Here ensued a brief discussion by the council concerning curses and insults. It was agreed that simple insults are not as dangerous as curses. One elder equated a curse with sorcery (*kīrumi nī ūrogi*). Throughout the case, disputants and elders acted in terms of that equation, since it is believed that a curse invoking death can be as harmful as actual sorcery, which also aims to injure.

Sarah then finished her oath:

Sarah: May this oath kill me if I was not cursing Jacob when he was bothering me. May this oath kill me if I do that again.

An elder: Swear that you will not insult Jacob's children.

Sarah: I will do it if they do it to me. I have made Jacob's children equal to my children. They are one thing. May this oath kill me if I lie.

An elder: Throw that leaf backwards and then step on the other clot.

Typical of the legal activity of an *ad hoc* council, this case points up the absence of real power among the elders. Instead, moral influence -- not to curse, not to poison, not to misrepresent or steal -- is exerted under mystical threat through the oath,

which itself represents the political limitations of
the elders. Magical action thus firms up an
essentially weak role, distinguished by its moral
legitimacy rather than by any ostensible capacity to
coerce politically. The elders' council permits a
public airing of grievances and emphasizes pragmatic
solutions mutually agreeable to both disputants. There
is no equivalent effort to fix sanctions, which in any
case would be difficult to enforce apart from the
continuing opprobrium of public opinion, including the
threat of social ostracism. In no sense are the
activities of the elders' council adjudicative, for the
formal sanctions and coercive measures normally
supporting judicial decisions are absent. Of course,
the presence of the Subchief in this case lends a
coercive element to the proceedings, but his role
remained small, and he made no effort to use the
authority of his office in directing the course of the
hearing. It was the amorphousness of the *ad hoc*
councils and the absence of clearly delineated figures
of power which the colonial power transformed, while
paradoxically upholding the value of indirect rule and
traditional authority.

An elder questions Sarah

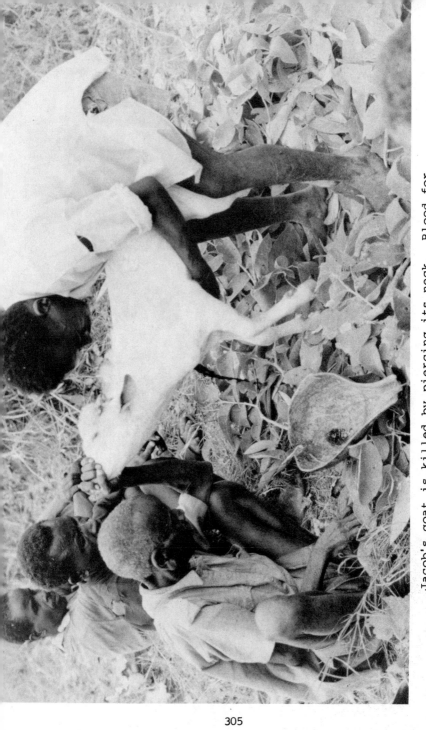

Jacob's goat is killed by piercing its neck. Blood for the oath is collected in a half-calabash.

Each goat is prepared either for immediate cooking or
for distribution in raw form to the elders for taking
home.

The health inspector examines the slaughtered animal and pronounces it fit for consumption.

The cooked meat is shared.

The oath leader chants curses over the blood.

Jacob swears the oath.

Sarah swears the oath.

Finishing her oath, Sarah tosses the leaf over her shoulder.

Sarah's final act is to step into a clot of blood.

Bibliography

Barnes, J. A.

  1962 African Models in the New Guinea Highlands.
        Man 62:5-9.

Barth, Fredrik, ed.

  1969 Ethnic Groups and Boundaries. Boston:
        Little, Brown and Co.

Baxter, P. T. W. and U. Almagor

  1978 Age, Generation, and Time: Some Features of
        East African Age Organizations. London:
        C. Hurst.

Beattie, John, and John Middleton, eds.

  1969 Spirit Mediumship and Society in Africa.
        New York: Africana Publishing Corporation.

Beech, M. W. H.

  1917 The Kikuyu System of Land Tenure. Journal
        of the African Society 17:46-59.

Benson, T. G.

  1964 Kikuyu-English Dictionary. Oxford: The
        Clarendon Press.

Bernard, Frank, and Derrick J. Thom

  1981 Population Pressure and Human Carrying
        Capacity in Selected Locations of Machakos
        and Kitui Districts. Journal of Developing
        Areas 15(3):381-406.

Bernardi, B.

    1959   The Mugwe, A Failing Prophet. London:
            Oxford University Press.

Bohannan, Laura

    1952   A Genealogical Charter. Africa 22:301-315.

Brain, James L.

    1973   Ancestors as Elders--Further Thoughts.
            Africa 43:122-133.

Brokensha, David and Jack Glazier

    1973   Land Reform Among the Mbeere of Central
            Kenya. Africa 43:182-206.

Chambers, Robert

    1969   Settlement Schemes in Tropical Africa. New
            York and Washington: Frederick A. Praeger.

Chanler, W. A.

    1896   Through Jungle and Desert. New York:
            Macmillan & Co.

Church Missionary Society

    1935   Annual Report. London: C.M.S. Archives.

Cohen, Abner

    1969   Custom and Politics in Urban Africa.
            Berkeley and Los Angeles: University of
            California Press.

    1981   The Politics of Elite Culture. Berkeley and
            Los Angeles: University of California
            Press.

Coldham, Simon

    1978   Land Control in Kenya. Journal of African Law 22:63-77.

Colson, Elizabeth

    1951   The Plateau Tonga. *In* Seven Tribes of British Central Africa. Elizabeth Colson and Max Gluckman, eds. London: Oxford University Press.

    1953   The Makah Indians. Minneapolis: University of Minnesota Press.

Comaroff, J. L.

    1980   Introduction. *In* The Meaning of Marriage Payments. J. L. Comaroff, ed. London: Academic Press.

Cotran, Eugene

    1971   Tribal Factors in the Establishment of the East African Legal Systems. *In* Tradition and Transition in East Africa. P. H. Gulliver, ed. Berkeley and Los Angeles: University of California Press.

Durand, Philip P.

    1970   Customary Oathing and the Legal Process in Kenya. Journal of African Law 14:17-33.

Dyson-Hudson, Neville

    1966   Karimojong Politics. London: Oxford University Press.

Eastern Province Planning Team

    1969   Mbere [sic] Special Rural Development Programme. Unpublished Report.

Eisenstadt, S. N.

　　1956　From Generation to Generation.　New York:
　　　　　Free Press.

Evans-Pritchard, E. E.

　　1931　An Alternative Term for "Bride-Price."　Man
　　　　　31:36-39.

　　1934　Social Character of Bridewealth With Special
　　　　　Reference to the Azande.　Man 34 (194):172-
　　　　　175.

　　1940　The Nuer.　Oxford:　Clarendon Press.

　　1951　Kinship and Marriage Among the Nuer.
　　　　　Oxford:　Clarendon Press.

　　1956　Nuer Religion.　Oxford:　Clarendon Press.

Fadiman, Jeffrey

　　1973　Early History of the Meru of Mt. Kenya.
　　　　　Journal of African History 14:9-27.

Fallers, Lloyd

　　1957　Some Determinants of Marriage Stability in
　　　　　Busoga.　Africa 27:106-124.

Fazan, Sidney

　　1956　Loyalist vs. Mau Mau.　Unpublished Ms.
　　　　　Oxford:　Rhodes House.

Fortes, Meyer

　　1945　The Dynamics of Clanship Among the Tallensi.
　　　　　London:　Oxford University Press.

　　1949　Time and Social Structure.　*In* Social
　　　　　Structure.　Meyer Fortes, ed.　Oxford:
　　　　　Oxford University Press.

1958   Introduction. *In* The Developmental Cycle of
Domestic Groups. Jack Goody, ed.
Cambridge: Cambridge University Press.

1965   Some Reflections on Ancestor Worship. *In*
African Systems of Thought. Meyer Fortes
and Germaine Dieterlin, eds. London:
Oxford University Press.

Fried, Morton

1975   The Notion of Tribe. Menlo Park: Cummings
Publishing Company.

Ghai, Y.P. and J.P.W.B. McAuslan

1970   Public Law and Political Change in Kenya.
Nairobi: Oxford University Press.

Glazier, Jack

1972   Conflict and Conciliation Among the Mbeere
of Kenya. Ph.D. Dissertation. Department
of Anthropology, University of California,
Berkeley.

1976a Generation Classes Among the Mbeere of
Central Kenya. Africa 46:313-326.

1976b Land Law and the Transformation of Customary
Tenure: The Mbeere Case. Journal of
African Law 20:39-50.

1984   Mbeere Ancestors and the Domestication of
Death. Man 19:133-147.

Gluckman, Max

1950   Kinship and Marriage Among the Lozi of
Northern Rhodesia and the Zulu of Natal. *In*
African Systems of Kinship and Marriage.
A. R. Radcliffe-Brown and C. Daryll Forde, eds.
London: Oxford University Press.

Goody, Jack

 1958 The Developmental Cycle in Domestic Groups.
     Cambridge: Cambridge University Press.

 1971 Technology, Tradition, and the State in
     Africa. London: Oxford University Press.

 1973 Bridewealth and Dowry in Africa and Eurasia.
     In Bridewealth and Dowry. Jack Goody and
     S.J. Tambiah, eds. Cambridge: Cambridge
     University Press.

 1976 Production and Reproduction. Cambridge:
     Cambridge University Press.

Goody, Jack and Ian Watt

 1971 The Consequences of Literacy. *In* Literacy
     and Traditional Societies. Jack Goody, ed.
     Cambridge: Cambridge University Press.

Gorfain, Phyllis and Jack Glazier

 1978 Sexual Symbolism, Origins, and the Ogre in
     Mbeere, Kenya. Journal of American Folklore
     91:925-946.

Government of Kenya

 1907 Embu District Record Book.

 1911 Embu Political Records.

 1915 Emberre [sic] Record Book.

 1916 Embu Annual Report.

 1925 Embu Local Native Council Minutes.

 1930 Embu Local Native Council Minutes.

 1930 Embu Annual Report.

 1932 Embu Local Native Council Minutes.

1932   Embu Annual Report.

1933   Embu Annual Report.

1939   Embu Handing Over Report.

1940   Embu Local Native Council Minutes.

1941   Embu Local Native Council Minutes.

1941   Embu Annual Report.

1945   Embu Local Native Council Minutes.

1945   Embu Annual Report.

1946   Embu Annual Report.

1947   Embu Local Native Council Minutes.

1953   Embu Annual Report.

1954   Embu Annual Report.

1955   Embu Annual Report.

1956   Embu African District Council Minutes.

1958   Embu Annual Report.

1969   Development Plan, (1970-74).

1971   Kenya Population Census, 1969. Volume III.
       Ministry of Finance and Economic Planning.

1973   Embu District Agricultural Report for June.

1979   Development Plan, (1979-83).

Gray, Robert F.

1960   Sonjo Bride-Price and the Question of
       African "Wife Purchase." American
       Anthropologist 62:34-57.

Gray, Robert F., and Philip H. Gulliver, eds.

    1964   The Family Estate in Africa. Boston:
           Boston University Press.

Gulliver, Philip H.

    1955   The Family Herds. London: Routledge and
           Kegan Paul Ltd.

    1961   Land Shortage, Social Change, and Social
           Conflict in East Africa. Journal of
           Conflict Resolution 5:16-26.

    1963   Social Control in an African Society.
           Boston: Boston University Press.

    1971   Introduction. *In* Tradition and Transition
           in East Africa. Philip H. Gulliver, ed.
           Berkeley and Los Angeles: University of
           California Press.

Hailey, Lord

    1957   An African Survey. London: Oxford
           University Press.

Helm, June, ed.

    1968   Essays on the Problem of Tribe. Proceedings
           of the 1967 Meeting of the American
           Ethnological Society. Seattle: University
           of Washington Press.

Heyer, Judith, Dunstan Ireri and Jon Moris

    1969   Rural Development in Kenya. A Report by the
           University College, Nairobi for the Special
           Rural Development Program of the Goverment of
           Kenya.

Hunt, D. M.

1975   An Examination of the Distribution of
       Economic Status and Opportunity in Mbeere,
       Eastern Kenya. Institute for Development
       Studies, Occasional Paper No. 11. Nairobi.

Huntingford, G. W. B.

1953   The Nandi of Kenya. London: Routledge and
       Kegan Paul.

Ingle, Clyde R.

1972   From Village to State in Tanzania.   Ithaca:
       Cornell University Press.

Jackson, Tudor

1970   The Law of Kenya. Nairobi: East African
       Literature Bureau.

Jacobs, Alan

1965   The Traditional Political Organization of
       the Pastoral Maasai. Unpublished Ph.D.
       Dissertation, Oxford University.

Karp, Ivan

1978   New Guinea Models in the African Savannah.
       Africa 48:1-16

Kenyatta, Jomo

1938   Facing Mt. Kenya. London: Secker and
       Warburg.

Kopytoff, Igor

1971   Ancestors as Elders in Africa.   Africa
       41:129-142.

Kopytoff, Igor and Suzanne Miers, eds.

    1977   Slavery in Africa. Madison: University of
             Wisconsin Press.

Krapf, J. L.

    1860   Travels and Researches in Eastern Africa.
             Boston: Ticknor and Fields.

Kuper, Adam

    1982   Lineage Theory: A Critical Retrospect.
             Annual Review of Anthropology 11:71-95.

Lambert, H. E.

    1945   Unpublished Papers. University of Nairobi.

    1950   The Systems of Land Tenure in the Kikuyu
             Land Unit. Communications from the School
             of African Studies. University of Cape
             Town, New Series No. 22.

    1956   Kikuyu Social and Political Institutions.
             London: Oxford University Press.

Leakey, L. S. B.

    1952   Mau Mau and the Kikuyu. London: Methuen.

    1977   The Southern Kikuyu Before 1903. New York:
             Academic Press.

Leach, Edmund

    1961   Pul Eliya, A Village in Ceylon. Cambridge:
             Cambridge University Press.

Lewis, I. M.

    1962   Marriage and the Family in Northern
             Somaliland. Kampala: East African
             Institute of Social Research.

Leys, Colin

    1974   Underdevelopment in Kenya. Berkeley and Los
            Angeles: University of California Press.

Lienhardt, Godfrey

    1961   Divinity and Experience. Oxford: The
            Clarendon Press.

Livingstone, Ian

    1979   The Socio-Economics of Ranching in Kenya.
            In Research in Economic Anthropology,
            Volume 1. George Dalton, ed. Greenwich:
            JAI Press Inc.

Lloyd, Peter C.

    1968   Divorce Among the Yoruba. American
            Anthropologist 70:67-81.

Low, D. A.

    1965   British East Africa: The Establishment of
            Colonial Rule, 1895-1912. *In* History of
            East Africa, Volume II. Vincent Harlow, et
            al, eds. London: Oxford University Press.

Maher, Colin

    1938   Soil Erosion and Land Utilization in Embu.
            Mimeographed Report. Nairobi: Ministry of
            Agriculture.

Maine, Henry Sumner

    1861   Ancient Law. London: Murray.

Mair, Lucy

    1962   Primitive Government. Baltimore: Penguin
            Books.

Michuki, D. N.

    1962 Būrūri wa Embu [The Country of Embu].
           Nairobi: East African Literature Bureau.

Middleton, John

    1965 The Lugbara of Uganda. New York: Holt,
           Rinehart and Winston.

Middleton, John and Greet Kershaw

    1965 The Kikuyu and Kamba of Kenya. London:
           International African Institute.

Migot-Adholla, S. E.

    1979 Rural Development Policy and Equality. *In*
           Politics and Public Policy in Kenya and
           Tanzania. Joel D. Barkan and John J. Okumu,
           eds. New York: Praeger.

Mitchell, J. Clyde

    1961 Social Change and the Stability of Marriage
           in Northern Rhodesia. *In* Social Change in
           Modern Africa. Aidan Southall, ed. London:
           Oxford University Press.

    1963 Marriage Stability and Social Structure in
           Bantu Africa. *In* Proceedings of the
           International Population Conference. New
           York.

Morgan, Lewis Henry

    1877 Ancient Society. Chicago: Charles H. Kerr
           and Co.

Mungeam, G. H.

    1966 British Rule in Kenya, 1895-1912. Oxford:
           Clarendon Press.

Munro, J. Forbes

1967   Migrations of the Bantu-Speaking Peoples of
        the Eastern Kenya Highlands: A Reappraisal.
        Journal of African History 8:25-28.

Mwanīki, H. S. K.

1973   The Living History of the Embu and Mbeere.
        Nairobi: East African Literature Bureau.

Nyerere, Julius K.

1967   Freedom and Unity. London: Oxford
        University Press.

O'Connor, A. M.

1967   An Economic Geography of East Africa.
        London: G. Bell and Sons, Ltd.

Orde-Brown, G. St. J.

1925   The Vanishing Tribes of Kenya. London:
        Seeley Service and Co.

Parkin, David J.

1972   Palms, Wine, and Witnesses. San Francisco:
        Chandler Publishing Co.

Phillips, Arthur

1944   Report on Native Tribunals. Nairobi:
        Government Printer.

Porter, Philip W.

1965   Environmental Potentials and Economic
        Opportunities--A Background for Cultural
        Adaptation. American Anthropologist 67:409-
        420.

Public Record Office of Britain.

    1906   Colonial Registry. London.

Read, James B.

    1972   Customary Law Under Colonial Rule. *In*
           Indirect Rule and the Search for Justice.
           H. F. Morris and James S. Read, eds.
           Oxford: The Clarendon Press.

Richards, Audrey I.

    1960   Some Mechanisms for the Transfer of
           Political Rights in Some African Societies.
           Journal of the Royal Anthropological
           Institute 90:175-190.

Rigby, Peter

    1969   Cattle and Kinship Among the Gogo. Ithaca
           and London: Cornell University Press.

Roberts, John

    1965   Oaths, Autonomic Ordeals, and Power.
           American Anthropologist 67:186-212.

Saberwal, Satish

    1967   Historical Notes on the Embu of Central
           Kenya. Journal of African History 8:29-38.

    1970   The Traditional Political System of the
           Embu. Nairobi: East African Literature
           Bureau.

Schneider, Harold K.

    1979   Livestock and Equality in East Africa.
           Bloomington and London: Indiana University
           Press.

Sorrenson, M. P. K.

    1967   Land Reform in Kikuyu Country. Nairobi:
             Oxford University Press.

Southall, Aidan

    1970a   The Illusion of Tribe. Journal of Asian and
             African Studies 5:28-50.

    1970b   Rank and Stratification Among the Alur and
             Other Nilotic Peoples. *In* Social
             Stratification in Africa. Arthur Tuden and
             Leonard Plotnicov, eds. New York: Free
             Press.

Spencer, Paul

    1965   The Samburu. Berkeley and Los Angeles:
             University of California Press.

Stenning, Derrick J.

    1958   Household Viability Among the Pastoral
             Fulani. *In* The Developmental Cycle in
             Domestic Groups. Jack Goody, ed. Cambridge:
             Cambridge University Press.

Swynnerton, R. J. M.

    1954   A Plan to Intensify the Development of
             African Agriculture in Kenya. Nairobi:
             Government Printer.

Tait, David

    1961   The Konkomba of Northern Ghana. New York:
             Oxford University Press.

Tignor, Robert L.

    1976   The Colonial Transformation of Kenya.
             Princeton: Princeton University Press.

Tuma, Elias

    1965   Twenty-Six Centuries of Agrarian Reform.
           Berkeley and Los Angeles: University of
           California Press.

Vogt, Evon

    1960   On the Concepts of Structure and Process in
           Cultural Anthropology. American
           Anthropologist 62:18-33.

Watson, James L. ed.

    1980   Asian and African Systems of Slavery.
           Oxford: Basil Blackwell.

Watts, E. R.

    1969   Agricultural Extension in Embu District of
           Kenya. East African Journal of Rural
           Development 2 (1).

Wilson, Godfrey and Monica Wilson

    1945   The Analysis of Social Change. Cambridge:
           Cambridge University Press.

Wilson, Monica

    1951   Good Company. London: Oxford University
           Press.

    1957   Rituals of Kinship Among the Nyakyusa.
           London: Oxford University Press.

achievement: indigenous
sources of, 71
administration, 12ff,
31n
age organization, 72ff,
82
age-sets, 67, 68, 69,
72, 76-78
alliances: in raids,
58-59
Almagor, U., 76
ancestral shades:
social basis of, 172,
173, 178, 180, 181,
279; beliefs about,
173-176, 179, 180; and
misfortune, 174, 175,
178, 179, 180; and
mortuary practice,
176, 177, 178

Barnes, John, 276
Barth, Fredrik, 22
Baxter, P. T. W., 76
Beech, M. W. H.,
199, 205
Benson, T. G., ix
"big men," 62, 65, 79,
128, 171, 278, 279
Bohannan, Laura, 166,
168
Brain, James L., 179
Brokensha, David, 195,
220

capitalism, 4, 14, 27
change: local view of,
21; types of, 106-107
Chanler, W. A., 44
chiefs: conflict with
elders, 78f, 86f,
89, 229; and Local
Native Council, 86,
88; and factionalism,
91; and land 184
Christianity, 21, 22
clans: identified with
land issue, 9, 10;
joining, 62, 160;
history of, 41,
151ff, 161ff (see
descent)
Cohen, Abner, 26
collectivism, 4
colonial rule, 79ff
Colson, Elizabeth, 22
Comely, J. 91
co-wives, 113-114
crops, 17, 18 (see
(domestic economy)
curses, 108, 143ff,
175, 296, 302,
(see oaths)
custom: and civil
administration, 204,
206, 207, 231, 232,
264
customary law, 228,
230, 231, 236

descent: coalitions,
181, 184, 185, 186,
188, 189, 280;
scale of groups, 184,
190, 191; ideology,
272, 273, 281, 282
development, 2, 3, 4
218
domestic economy: crops
and animals in, 117,
118, 119, 120;
wild foods in, 121
domestic groups: and
politico-jural domain,
105; change in, 106,
107; in relation to
homestead, 107; and
matricentric houses,
111, 112, 114, 115;
and woman marriage,
116, 117; types of
136ff
Durand, Philip, 237

East African age
organizations, 71ff
ecology: upper and
lower areas, 17, 18,
19; zones, 43ff
education, 15, 21, 269-
270
Eisenstadt, S. N., 76
elders' councils, 66,
68f, 70, 84ff, 232,
285ff
Embu District, 11, 13,
15, 16, 20, 39, 43, 52,
54, 79, 80, 81, 83, 85,
86, 88, 91, 92, 200,
201, 202, 203, 204,
206, 207, 208, 210,
211, 229, 231, 253, 256
ethnic relations:
and famine, 55ff; and
land, 212, 213, 214

ethnography, 10, 12
Evans-Pritchard, E. E.,
124, 125, 154, 271

Fallers, L., 130, 131
famine, 43, 50, 52, 53
54, 55ff, 61, 62
Fazan, Sidney, 213
female circumcision,
21, 91-93
fictive marriage,
115-117
fieldwork, 8ff, 14
flexibility in Mbeere
culture, 67, 70, 71,
75
food production, 46ff
Fortes, Meyer, 105f,
137, 138, 271, 275
Fried, Morton, 22

GEMA, 25, 237
genealogies, 27, 166ff
generation-sets, 41,
42, 43, 55, 66, 72
Gillespie, I. R., 88
Girouard, Percy, 84
Glazier, Jack, 195,
220
Gluckman, Max, 111,
130, 131
Goody, Jack, 106, 124,
128, 170, 172
Gray, R. F., 106, 124
Gulliver, P. H., 17,
22, 106, 119, 133,
148

Hailey, Lord, 205
Helm, June, 22
Heyer, Judith, 195
history: and Mbeere
origins, 40ff;
legitimating function
of, 162ff

homestead: physical
aspects of, 108ff
Horne, E. B., 88
house-property
complex, 111, 112
(see domestic groups)
Hunt, D. M., 269

inheritance, 111,
115ff, 139ff
Ireri, Dunstan, 195

KANU, 25
Karp, Ivan, 276
Kenyatta, Jomo, x, 25
Kimbeere language, ix-x
kinship terminology,
112, 117
Kopytoff, Igor, 128,
179, 180
Krapf, J. L., 44
Kuper, Adam, 276

Lambert, H. E., 40, 55,
78, 170, 205, 210, 233
land: reform and its
consequences, 1ff,
218ff, 266-268;
adjudication, 6, 252,
252ff; use, 47-49;
disputes, 183, 186;
tenure, 193, 194ff;
sale, 199, 200, 205,
233; colonial policy,
200ff, 215; loans,
216, 217; and statute
law, 219ff; and legal
evidence, 227, 228,
245, 246, 257, 258;
and agnatic conflict,
259ff
law: institutions of,
228ff; trends regarding
land, 263, 264
Lawrance, J. C. D., 219

Leach, Edmund, 275,
276
Leakey, L. S. B., 205
Lewis, I. M., 130
Leys, Colin, 270
Lindsay, K. D., 85
lineages, 7, 28, 29,
70, 71, 72, 180ff,
188, 190, 271
literacy, 168ff
livestock: relative
importance of, 117ff
Livingstone, Ian, 220
Lloyd, P. C., 130, 131
Local Native Council
(LNC), 86ff, 200ff

Maher, Colin, 46, 212
Maine, Henry Sumner, 277
Mair, Lucy, 207
markets: modern, 15,
20; precolonial
(tubu), 55, 59ff,
127
marriage, 61, 121,
116, 117, 121ff
Mau Mau, 4, 5, 17, 22,
24, 209, 211, 213,
214, 215, 237
Mauss, Marcel, 11
medicine men
(magico-medical
practitioners), 58,
60, 62, 64, 158, 159
methodology, 3
Michuki, D. N., 171
Miers, Suzanne, 128
Migot-Adholla, S. E., 4
migration, 16, 17, 20,
45, 61, 62, 212, 202,
203
Mitchell, J. Clyde,
130, 134
modernization: and
descent groups, 273

moieties, 154, 155, 157, 159, 234, 274
Morgan, Lewis H., 277
Moris, John, 195
mortuary practice (see ancestral shades)
Mungeam, G. H., 80
Munro, J. Forbes, 40, 41

Northeastern Bantu, 39
Nyerere, Julius, 4

oaths, 22, 25, 61, 161, 207, 236ff, 251, 296ff
Orde-Brown, G. St. J., 84

Parkin, David, 27, 28
parish, 17, 58, 66
paternal authority, 141ff
Phillips, Arthur, 84, 85, 228, 229
phratries, 154, 157, 287
political organization: precolonial, 66ff; and colonial rule, 79ff
Porter, Philip W., 51n
production (see domestic groups)

Radcliffe-Brown, A. R., 275
rainfall, 44ff,
res judicata principle, 235, 236, 255
Richards, Audrey I., 162 166
Rigby, Peter, 106, 118
Roberts, John, 69
rural stratification, 89, 90, 265ff

Saberwal, Satish, 40

sacred groves, 177
Schneider, Harold K., 64, 79
Shungwaya myth, 40, 41
sorcery, 21, 108, 113, 114, 115, 290, 293, 294, 298, 300, 301
Sorrenson, M. P. K., 5, 209, 213
Southall, Aidan, 22, 73, 76
Stenning, Derrick K., 106
Stone, R. G., 44, 158, 199, 205
subchiefs (see chiefs)

Tait, David, 137
tenants, 197
Thom, Derrick J., 267
tobacco, 48, 49, 268, 269
tradition, 21, 27, 28, 180, 193, 281-283
tribe: concept of, 22ff

Vogt, Evon, 107

wage labor, 14, 15, 79, 142
warfare, 57ff
Watson, James L., 172
Watt, Ian, 170
Wilson, Godfrey, 106, 107
Wilson, Monica, 106, 107, 173, 179
women: and descent group loyalty, 132, 133; changing status of, 135, 136 (see domestic groups)

334